BIRMINGHAM'S
FRONT LINE

BIRMINGHAM'S FRONT LINE

TRUE POLICE STORIES

MICHAEL LAYTON

AMBERLEY

First published 2016

Amberley Publishing
The Hill, Stroud
Gloucestershire, GL5 4EP

www.amberley-books.com

Copyright © Michael Layton, 2016

The right of Michael Layton to be identified as
the Author of this work has been asserted in
accordance with the Copyrights, Designs and
Patents Act 1988.

ISBN 978 1 4456 5787 5 (print)
ISBN 978 1 4456 5788 2 (ebook)

British Library Cataloguing in Publication Data.
A catalogue record for this book is available
from the British Library.

Typesetting and Origination by Amberley Publishing
Printed in the UK.

CONTENTS

INTRODUCTION

During the early morning BBC News on an extremely cold day in November 2013, the words of a very successful crime fiction writer caught my ear. He had just completed his twentieth novel about a fictional career detective, based on a real-life character in Scotland, and he had many contacts within the police service who had provided him with invaluable background knowledge. During an interview with the presenter, he said that many 'cops' were keen to write about their experiences but that they didn't know when to 'take the boring bits out'.

The reality is that much about policing is routine, and it can be mundane and boring; at the same time, it can also be unpredictable, exciting and occasionally explosive.

This book, in part, recounts my journey over a twelve-year period, from being a young officer attached to the Criminal Investigation Department in the West Midlands Police in 1976 through to becoming an experienced detective sergeant on a very busy city-centre division, before being promoted to the rank of inspector in 1988.

If you see a police officer on patrol, you rarely look at the age of the officer behind the uniform that gives them immediate authority. Working in plain clothes, or as a CID officer, presents different challenges, and your authority comes more from the way in which you conduct yourself as an individual, and how you use your own personality to achieve success.

During those years I was proud to work with many accomplished police officers who regarded their job as a profession, and their duty to protect the communities we served. I learned from them and, in due course, others learnt from me.

On occasions, I was involved in the investigation of robberies, rapes, and murders, and saw at first-hand the effects that such crimes have on both the victims and their loved ones. As 'guardians of the law', our job was to confront those who sought to inflict such misery on ordinary people and that's what we did 'day in, day out' relentlessly. We were not fanatics but, for the most part, we were very determined.

Relatively few people in life are lucky enough to experience the many positive things that come from becoming a police officer, or the sadness of being exposed to so many tragic situations. I decided to put myself to the test to see if I could 'miss some of the boring bits out', and tell just a small part of the inside story about my life as a police officer in Birmingham.

A number of retired officers, who also worked during this period, have added their own first-hand recollections of working the streets of Birmingham. They provide a unique insight into policing in Britain's 'second city', set against a backcloth of some of the major national and international events of that time.

Sometimes funny, sometimes sad, and often extremely serious – but all true.

Michael Layton QPM (2015)

I

INTRODUCTION TO THE CID, AND 'CHIP' KEEPS IT UP

On 23 October 1975, I attended a force board at Lloyd House police headquarters in Birmingham to be considered for an attachment to the CID. The interview board consisted of Chief Superintendent John Bagnall and Superintendent Lenehan, who afterwards wrote,

> PC 9364 M. W. J. LAYTON, C Division, was a young officer of smart appearance with a most pleasant personality. Expresses himself in a convincing manner and has a good practical and theoretical knowledge. He is qualified for promotion and was considered by the board to be an outstanding prospect. Graded 'A'.

I hated interviews but they were a necessary evil in the police service, and you had to learn how to play the game to get through them. It was as important for you to research the members of the board and to know what 'made them tick' as it was to know your subject matter. Speak too slowly and you ran the risk of being considered boring, speak too quickly and you might look as if you were stressed. I had a Birmingham accent and was proud of it, but it didn't suit all of my senior colleagues, who hailed from various parts of the UK and were loyal to their origins. I didn't belong to any groupings, and didn't want to, but diplomacy was a must if you were to survive – 'barrack-room lawyers', with an opinion on everything, rarely did.

I had passed this particular test, and now all I had to do was to wait for a vacancy to start my CID attachment. I was excited about the future.

I had thoroughly enjoyed my time in uniform, and was extremely proud to wear it, but I wanted to specialise in criminal-investigation work.

And so it was that, at 9.00 a.m. on Monday 23 February 1976, I presented myself at King's Heath police station for an interview with a detective superintendent, whom I had never met before, but who would ultimately have a lot of influence as to whether I would become a detective constable within the West Midlands Police. He turned out to be a Welshman, with a very direct approach, and he made it clear that I was there to listen, learn and do as I was told. I was most definitely the 'new boy' on the block and at the bottom of the pecking order of things.

Interviews with senior officers rarely lasted long in those days and I was soon on my way. Many of the officers were highly skilled investigators in their own right, but had learnt their trade in a strictly hierarchical regime, which was not about to change quickly; the road to earning respect would be a long one. For the most part, they were autocrats and proud of it.

I had just spent the previous twelve months working on the Theft From Vehicles Squad at Ladywood police station on the 'C' Division and, although I was still only twenty-three years old, I had a reputation for being a 'thief taker'. I desperately wanted to transfer to the CID and, working within a small team, predominantly in and around the busy nightlife of Broad Street, and the Hagley Road, I had developed a taste for dealing with lifestyle criminals, who stole vehicles continuously and then used them to commit other crimes.

Prior to that I had worked on C Unit at Ladywood with a group of officers who had an intense sense of loyalty towards each other and a routinely high arrest rate. Where one went, the rest followed, and they were fearless. There was also a great social atmosphere among the team, many of whom were given questionable nicknames. We had two 'Bunnies', one of whom was PC Tony 'Bunny' Everett, who joined the job in 1969 and retired with thirty years' service. He recounts some of his memories later in the book.

In those days you could not get onto the CID unless you had completed an official six-month attachment, and there were no vacancies on my division, so I opted for the risky strategy of going to another neighbouring division where no one knew me. I swapped jeans and t-shirts for suits and ties, which is what 'proper detectives' wore.

As I later walked into the front enquiry office of Bradford Street police station in Highgate, Birmingham, on that chilly Monday morning, I was excited but also had a sense of trepidation. This was to be my new home for six months, and I was a stranger here and didn't even know what the door codes were to get in. It was a cold, unwelcoming building, which fitted in well with the factories and office buildings in the grey streets that surrounded it. Just on the edge of Birmingham city centre, it serviced an inner-city area, with high levels of social deprivation. The CID office was at the rear of the building and I was immediately struck by the starkness and lack of warmth about the place. The detective inspector had his own office, but the main office had rows of metal desks facing the same way, as in a classroom.

There was no 'royal welcome' and within an hour of arriving I was on my way to Deritend with a colleague called Bob to arrest someone for theft from his employer. Bob was of a very thin build, almost frail, but was a very experienced officer whom I came to respect greatly. His strengths came from being able to communicate with people rather than to wrestle with them. I couldn't tell his exact age, but he looked to be in his forties.

We duly made the arrest of a twenty-two-year-old from his place of work and took him back to the station. I was allowed to sign for him as the arresting officer, which also meant I got all the paperwork to do. A quick interview, and a full admission to the offence, and he was in and out within two hours to appear in court the next day.

The following day I worked a split shift, which was common then. This entailed working between 9.00 a.m. and 1.00 p.m. and then dashing home for something to eat, before being back in the office for 6.00 p.m. Although you were supposed to finish by 10.00 p.m., you never did because this was the time for meeting informants and generally being seen around in the local pubs.

On this day I was teamed up with another detective constable, another Welshman who took something of an instant dislike to me and didn't try too hard to conceal it. Underneath it all, he wasn't a bad guy, but he seemed to be permanently under pressure and worried about everything. His desk was piled high with boxes and files, which made it look as if he was swamped with work. Clearly, having a young newcomer upsetting the balance of the office was not welcome and we maintained a fragile peace from the very start.

I was introduced to the joys of contacting scrap-metal dealers in the morning to try and trace some stolen property, and the pleasure of a couple of beers in the pubs around the Stratford Road area in the evening.

There was a large number of Irish pubs; these could quite quickly become 'rough and tumble' places, with people being propelled through doors with a boot up their backsides if they played up, but which were also generally fun places to be, with loud Irish music playing on the juke boxes.

Everyone in the pubs would know who we were, and we didn't try to hide it but, for the most part, they were safe zones where police, criminals, and those who just liked a pint mixed freely and respected each other's space. Most licensees welcomed our presence, although in some cases we were also seen as a 'necessary evil' to be tolerated.

I was never a big drinker, but there was no such thing as a 'tee-total' detective in those days, and so I learnt to drink halves, and drank them slowly. I can't say I ever really liked the taste of beer, but you couldn't talk to people with an empty glass in your hand. Eating nuts or pork scratchings might also be okay, but packets of crisps weren't seen as quite so cool!

On Thursday 26 February 1976, I went with a colleague to make my second arrest of the week, one of a twenty-three-year-old from St Martin's Flats in Leopold Street, Highgate, for criminal deception. We had a local Department of Health and Social Security office near to the station, and routinely got quite a few fraud jobs from them. While it wasn't the most exciting work, it served to help to get to know the local criminals, who rarely restricted their activities to one type of offence. Another interview, another admission, and a £35 fine at court next day.

I was there to see how things went and to cultivate the prisoner a bit. Most informants start life as prisoners, and it was part of your 'trade' to develop relationships with people who might be useful at a later stage. It was all about finding out as much detail about the person's life as you could, and pressing the right levers that would motivate them to 'grass' on their friends and sometimes even their family. Financial gain was rarely the primary thing that motivated them.

The following week I was back out with Bob and, although we started the week by investigating the theft of clothing from a washing line, it got better when we made an arrest for burglary at an address on the Pershore Road. We got lucky that day because the prisoner, a twenty-year-old West Indian lad, was well-known and could be quite a handful to manage. We had not expected him to be at the address we visited and initially he made it clear that he intended on going nowhere with us.

Finally, Bob talked him round and, after a few anxious moments, we were on the way to the station, talking all the way in the car about anything in an effort to keep him calm. The grounds for arrest came from a fingerprint identification at the point of entry of the scene of the crime, so we knew we were on safe ground. He was interviewed and charged for court the next day.

Those first few minutes at the time of an arrest were always crucial, and I learned all the tricks as to how to keep things calm, which often included sending the prisoner's 'other half' off to make a cup of tea while we explained the consequences of playing up. While you might be nervous, you had to appear calm and relaxed and in control of the situation.

I went to court with the burglar on the next day; he pleaded guilty and was given a six-month suspended prison sentence. Cultivation, however, was out of the question; his becoming a 'grass' was simply a non-starter.

On Tuesday 9 March 1976, I went to Her Majesty's Prison Winson Green in Birmingham to interview someone for deception – yet another DHSS fraud. Built in October 1849, I was always fascinated to visit this place, which, it seemed, was full to the brim with hard men, as well as the more vulnerable in life. The interview rooms were a relatively safe environment to be in but, on the odd occasions where I needed to go onto the wings, I quickly learnt to stay under the walkways to avoid all the spit dropping on my head from the landing above.

I recall on one future occasion having to visit the kitchens, which were in the very bowels of the prison, following the sudden death of an inmate. He had been serving a short sentence for motoring offences and was working in the kitchen, cutting up frozen meat, when he suffered a classic butcher's injury. As he was drawing the knife through the carcass towards him, it went through a piece that wasn't frozen and, with the pressure being exerted, he finished up stabbing himself in the top of his leg. The knife hit his artery and proved fatal.

There was fear and tension in these places, combined with the smell of urine and stale air. Men with nothing to do but stare at any stranger did just that and knew when the 'pigs' were around. I had great admiration for the prison officers who, while small in numbers, somehow kept some kind of order in this strained environment, where tobacco had currency and being fed was the highlight of the day. Giving someone a cigarette while you were interviewing them was okay, but giving them the packet could land them, and you, in trouble with the prison authorities.

Bob and I made another arrest for theft the following day at St Anne's Hostel in Moseley Street, Highgate, from where many homeless men drifted in and out. Some of these individuals were real characters with great stories of life to tell. The fact that many of them had fallen on hard times did not mean that they had nothing to say for themselves, but personal hygiene could be an issue and, if you went home with an itch, it was worth having a good long bath! Custody officers hated it when we brought someone in who needed delousing, as it took one of the cells out for the day and created an unpleasant smell in a confined space that was already not the most fragrant. You also had to fumigate the car with which you had brought in the prisoner.

On Saturday 13 March 1976, Bob and I did some observations in Watery Lane regarding thefts from motor vehicles during football matches at Birmingham City Football Club at St Andrew's stadium. What this actually meant was that, having had a look around, Bob duly took me to the match, where I proceeded to be bored silly for two hours as I hated football. I was, however, fascinated by the crowd dynamics and the behaviour of individuals, many of whom were very drunk. Little did I know then that, some eleven years later, this fascination would be rekindled when I set up Operation Red Card to combat the activities of Birmingham City's organised hooligan faction, the 'Zulu Warriors', who were to become one of the most violent and feared groups of hooligans in the UK.

On Thursday 18 March 1976, Bob took me on my first rounds of the scrap-metal dealers to check and sign their registers. We would look for suspicious vehicles, suspicious names, or suspicious quantities of metal, but the reality was that stolen metal was hardly likely to be registered under the right details, if it actually went into the register at all.

Many dealers had regular contacts in the police in those days so, if they were going to put a decent job in, it certainly wasn't going to be to Bob or me, but nevertheless we went through the motions and, where appropriate, 'rattled a few cages' to keep them on their toes. We were not the big boys from any of the force squads but, as local CID, they knew that we could still be a nuisance to trade if we sat outside their yards all day.

I was carrying my own workload now and doing my best to do well, but it was not easy to find quality jobs and yet more fraud interviews followed. By that time, I was convinced that everyone was fiddling the DHSS in some form or another. The favourite modus operandi was to report falsely the non-receipt of a benefits giro in order to claim a replacement and then to cash both. What most failed to understand was that, eventually, both giros would be married up and either the signatures tallied or fingerprints found on the paper would be sufficient to prove a case.

My detective chief inspector was a tall man by the name of Roy, who had a West Country accent and wore glasses. He was an inherently polite person and I only ever saw him get angry over something on one occasion, when he started swearing and went bright red to the point where I thought that he was going to burst a blood vessel. Most of the time he was office-bound and happy for things to proceed without too much fuss around him.

On the evening of Wednesday 31 March 1976, we had a breakthrough in relation to a burglary dwelling house; Bob and I, together with Sid, the detective inspector, dashed out to an address in Grantham Road, Sparkbrook, where we arrested three men in their twenties. We were rather outnumbered at the address but, thankfully, they didn't play up. By the time I got home after dealing with the prisoners, it was 2.00 a.m., and the lights were off, and the house and occupants very silent. The evening meal was in the bin but it wasn't the first time and wouldn't be the last.

I was back at work for 8.00 a.m. to do the remand file for their court appearance and duly went to Birmingham Magistrates' Court, situated at Victoria Law Courts in Corporation Street, to object to bail for one of the three persons we had arrested.

The foundation stone for Victoria Law Courts was laid by Queen Victoria on 23 March 1887 and the courts were opened in 1891. In those days, it was the only 'assize' court in the rapidly growing town of Birmingham. A statue of Queen Victoria sits proudly over the main entrance and the whole of the front of the building, which is now a Grade I listed building, is faced with deep-red terracotta from the clay of Ruabon in North Wales.

If ever you want to feel real fear, you need to stand in a witness box and feel numerous pairs of eyes staring at you intently, waiting for you to make a mistake. However, it was also a huge adrenalin rush, especially if you managed to keep someone in custody despite the protestations of a defence solicitor. In the courts, we all knew that it was 'no-holds barred', as police and solicitors sparred with each other. Outside, it was a different story and, over the years, I got to know some on first-name terms and even socialised in the same pubs. For most it was not personal and, apart from the odd solicitor who would be anti-police, we respected each other's professional positions.

The key people were the magistrates and judges and, if you failed to show due deference and gave out the wrong signals in terms of body language, they simply might not believe your evidence. Magistrates were referred to as 'Your Worship', and judges as 'Your Honour', and the two were not to be mixed up. The oath had to be read with feeling, your right hand raised, and not simply read in some automated manner from the card in your left hand. Your name, rank and station needed to be clear and confident, not mumbled, and, while questions would come at you from different directions, you always addressed your responses to the bench and tried not to upset the court clerks, who were very influential.

A few small steps up into a square box with wooden railings around it and you were standing on the 'X-Factor' spot of the courts. The only question was whether you were going to stay in the contest or not – and, in this case, singing would not help!

The following week, I went out for the first time with Doug, another detective constable, who I would best describe as a 'bit of a character'. He was short, but made up for this with personality and had an effortless approach to cultivating informants and interviewing people under caution.

In April 1980 Doug was one of four West Midlands Police detectives who received commendations for their work with other forces on Operation Ohio, which led to the end of a six-year run of armed robberies by organised criminals known as the 'Thursday Gang'. They were London-based, but committed fourteen armed robberies, and conspiracies to rob, in the West Midlands area, mainly on a Thursday. They stole nearly £325,000 in the West Midlands offences alone and, ultimately, forty-eight people were charged, with the ringleader subsequently receiving a prison sentence of twenty-one years.

With a legal system that actually told people from the outset that 'they were not obliged to say anything unless they wished to do so ...', there was not always an inducement to tell the truth if they were guilty. Everyone had a different approach to interviews and, over a period of time, mine was to try to 'bore them to death' to the point where they got fed up of hearing the sound of my voice. It was surprisingly successful and, on one occasion, I vividly remember one individual actually bringing the interview to a halt by owning up and begging me to stop talking.

On Thursday 8 April 1976, we started looking for a suspect of a burglary, committed at some shop premises in Hickman Road, Sparkbrook. He proved to be elusive but, the next morning, Doug and I tracked him down in Colonial Road, and he was duly arrested and charged.

Two days later, I was out with Doug again and we arrested two individuals from the Sparkbrook area for unauthorised taking of a motor vehicle, which we later recovered in Sydenham Road nearby. Both of the individuals were quite well-known and one subsequently went to prison for twelve months. This was more like it, and the type of street crime that I was well used to dealing with.

It was fun to work with Doug and I got the chance to visit places with exotic names, such as the Zambezi Cafe in Stratford Road, during the course of 'routine enquiries'. We were dealing with a constant round of burglaries at houses in the area, and many of the stolen goods finished up in the second-hand shops, which were a feature of the main Stratford Road.

At 6.40 a.m. on Saturday 8 May 1976, I attended Sparkhill police station for a briefing regarding a search warrant that was going to be executed at an address in Ladypool Road, following information from an informant.

We were expecting to find firearms used in an offence of aggravated burglary, so we would be 'mob-handed', and there was a sense of anticipation as officers lounged around the office and scavenged for tea and coffee. There was always banter, even at that time of the day, and despite the fact that some of us had not met before, but we shared a common bond and the messing about would stop when the serious business started.

We sorted out who was going to cover the back and the front of the house, but risk assessments were not a sign of those times and we would just aim to get in as fast as we could, and to dominate and control the situation as quickly as possible. No shouts of 'police, police' as shown on the television today; physical presence, and an angry police Alsatian dog with bared teeth, was usually enough.

Doors would be smashed in, but we also resorted to subterfuge. The 'postman' often called with a large package on these occasions, as officers hid behind walls and bushes, ready to dash in as the door opened.

At 7.45 a.m., the warrant was executed and stolen property was recovered, together with an air rifle and a sawn-off .22 rifle. A twenty-three-year-old was arrested at the address by other officers, and he was later sentenced to four years' imprisonment. By 9.00 a.m., I was on my way to Birmingham Magistrates' Court again to apply for a remand in custody for another burglar.

Back on my old policing area, officers faced a major challenge on Saturday 15 May 1976 when a demonstration took place outside Winson Green Prison in support of Robert Relf, who was a political activist from the far-right. Relf was serving a sentence for contempt of court, following an incident where he advertised his home for sale to an English family only. National Front supporters clashed with anti-fascist demonstrators, resulting in sixty-nine police officers and two police horses being injured. A total of twenty-eight arrests were made throughout the day.

On Thursday 20 May, my first experience of paying an informant came when I paid the princely sum of £2 to an informant, supervised by an experienced detective sergeant called Jim, who had a broad Scottish accent. While it was only a small amount of money, the process for recording it was the same as it would have been for hundreds of pounds.

We met on the Warwick Road and I was given information about drugs dealers and burglaries in the Handsworth area, and given promises to the future about other crimes. The same day I dealt with a burglar arrested by the Special Patrol Group, who operated in teams headed by a sergeant, and were extremely effective in public-order situations.

Around the same time, I recall writing an open letter in the *Police Review* magazine about the CID, and the fact that, just because you had years of service, it did not mean that you had years of experience. My Welsh colleague took it personally, and virtually 'sent me to Coventry' for a few days, refusing to speak to or acknowledge me.

On Friday 21 May 1976, I started looking for a suspect for a burglary at Grantham Road day nursery from another fingerprint identification. I realised quite early on during my attachment that the Midlands Criminal Records Office at force headquarters contained a wealth of information about suspects, associates and last known addresses, as well as tattoos, *modi operandi* and known vehicles. I used to spend hours going through all the box files and poring over the antecedent history of offenders. It was all rather tedious, but it often paid dividends and, years later, this process helped me to identify a murderer.

Around this time, I also started looking at another suspect for burglary and, although it was to be a few more weeks before we came face to face, he eventually became a first-class informant. He had connections in the Highgate and Ladywood area, where I had previously worked, and hoped to return, so I had a vested interest in developing this particular target. I started to study his lifestyle in detail and, on 28 May 1976, another informant gave me his whereabouts and the nature of crimes he was committing. This was the way it worked; you played one off against another, without ever divulging that either was giving information. I will refer to him as 'Chip'.

Chip was in his early twenties and was unemployed, with convictions dating back as far as seven years for burglary and stealing cars. He had learned his decorating skills while doing a period of borstal training, after progressing through the traditional route of probation and conditional discharges. He once showed me how to paint stripes on a wall using a plank of wood. His next conviction would result in a prison sentence, and he knew this. He had a girlfriend, but couldn't shake off his lifestyle and the common friends that went with his past history.

Life continued apace, and I got involved in the investigation of a sudden unexplained death, fingerprinting and photographing someone for attempted murder. Meanwhile, at the other end of the spectrum, I continued with the grind of DHSS frauds.

On Thursday 3 June 1976, I booked on at Ladywood police station, and teamed up with a detective constable called Rick, who was actually my neighbour in the row of police houses we lived in. We were looking for Chip, and found him at the employment exchange in Selly Oak, where he was signing on. He was interviewed at Ladywood and then bailed for further enquiries. My fish was on the hook.

Back at Bradford Street, Doug started looking at a series of thefts of blank excise licences, which were being sold on the cheap in pubs. He had a good informant who put the name of the thief in and, on Sunday 6 June 1976, Doug and I got the culprit out of bed at an address in Anderton Road, Sparkhill, and interviewed him. He was police-bailed, but promptly 'did a runner' and failed to answer his bail.

The following day, another informant pointed Doug in the right direction of a suspect for a serious offence of wounding with intent. We went to White Road and arrested a thirty-nine-year-old man, who was later charged and bailed.

On 16 June, Bob and I dealt with a fourteen-year-old juvenile offender for a dwelling house burglary and he was charged and bailed. We interviewed him again on the 21 June, and he admitted a further five burglaries. He eventually got sent to a detention centre for three months.

On Wednesday 23 June, Chip answered his bail at Ladywood police station and I took no further action at that stage in relation to any of his offences. He didn't know that in any event I did not have all the evidence I needed but, on balance, he decided to accept my offer to sign up as an informant. He immediately gave me the names of three active criminals with the promise of more names. In return, he got paid the sum of £2.

Informants were curious individuals who engaged in this type of activity for a variety of reasons. Many did it out of revenge, to pay back someone for perhaps even doing the same thing to them or running off with their wife or girlfriend. Others did it through fear of being sent down and doing a prison sentence. A few did it for the money, but no informants ever got rich unless they were able to put big jobs in involving top-class criminals. Apart from expenses, we paid on results only, besides which senior officers who supervised handing money over would often look to minimise payments if they could, in an effort to stay within allocated budgets.

Some informants did it because they actually enjoyed the thrill and excitement of 'sailing close to the wind', and the danger of knowing what would happen to them if they were ever discovered. A small number did it because they genuinely developed a relationship based on trust with the officer, like that of an employer and employee, and they wanted to do a good job and feel valued.

Chip embraced all of these elements and, although I actually liked him, I never lost sight of the fact that managing informants was a dangerous business, and you broke the rules at peril of losing your job, or worse if an informant participated in a crime themselves. Playing a minor role in a job that had already been planned might be okay, but playing the role of *agent provocateur* and setting up jobs that would never have happened but for them encouraging the crime to be committed was not allowed.

On Tuesday 29 June, our fourteen-year-old juvenile reared his head again and Bob and I arrested him at his home in Main Street, Sparkbrook, for burglary at shop premises. We already had another member of his team in custody and had recovered some of the stolen property from an area at the rear of the Tasty Chic. takeaway on the Stratford Road. His other partner in this crime was another fourteen-year-old lad from Stratford Road, who was also well-known to us.

We arrested him later that day, and further stolen property was found at his house. Even at such a young age, he was already a lifestyle criminal. His mother was Irish and his father, who was absent, West Indian. His mother was extremely protective, disliked the police intensively, and was a formidable opponent both in terms of size and temperament. Fortunately, Bob had a good way with her and we managed the arrest without any violence. He was later placed in care and, by the time we had finished our investigations, we had charged a group of six juveniles, who were all dealt with at the Birmingham Juvenile Courts.

That same day, Sid the detective inspector completed my three-month staff appraisal at the half-way stage of my attachment and said, 'PC Layton is of quiet disposition and unassuming nature, but this doesn't prevent him from asserting his opinion whenever he considers it necessary ...'.

On Thursday 1 July 1976, I met Chip in Selly Oak and he gave me some information on a robbery that had occurred on the Belgrave Road area. The following day, I went with Doug in the morning to Winson Green Prison to interview a prisoner, did a split duty, and at 7.00 p.m. I found myself at Cannock police station in Staffordshire with Sid the detective inspector. We liaised with the local CID and arrested a twenty-one-year-old woman from Norton Caines for theft. She was the company secretary for a firm in Highgate, and had been fiddling the books for some time. We recovered paperwork and cash from her address and then escorted her back to Bradford Street. By the time we had interviewed and charged her, it was 2.00 a.m.

On Thursday 8 July, I met Chip again in Weoley Castle. We always had to take great care as to where meets would take place, as there was always a chance of accidentally bumping into someone, and his stylish hair and 'cool look' contrasted greatly with my short hair and suit. I paid him £5 for information regarding a robbery, which had proved to be accurate, and he also told me about a burglary in Selly Oak, and some people involved in giro deceptions.

On Monday 12 July, I worked with Doug on a case of burglary involving the theft of metal from a local company that did die-casting. We went to Saltley and arrested a twenty-seven-year-old, lodging him in the cells at Bradford Street police station. Meanwhile we visited a scrap-metal dealers over in Park Road, Hockley, where we checked some receipts for metal weighed-in that linked him to the offence. He was later charged and bailed, following which we traced a second person involved in Highgate, and dealt with him in the same manner. Doug was a prolific informant handler and, by the following day, we were looking for a borstal absconder following yet another tip off.

On Friday 16 July, I was on my way to Birmingham Crown Court with Sid the DI, when we literally fell across a twenty-five-year-old from Castle Vale stealing a carton of shoes that were part of a delivery to some premises in New Canal Street. We arrested him and dropped him off at Digbeth police station to be dealt with by a local officer.

The following day, Doug and I had a productive evening meeting an informant about a post office job, and finished the night with a visit to the Daddy Long Legs Club regarding an assault, which detained us until midnight. The club, on the corner of Stratford Road and Coventry Road, had a reputation for being a bit of a rough place in the seventies, where serious drinking was routine, but the management kept a tight rein on clients – who ranged from car dealers to those who enjoyed the strippers on offer – and stood no nonsense.

On Wednesday 21 July, Bob and I went to Wellingborough Borstal to interview someone who was serving a custodial sentence for stealing cars. We interviewed him under caution and he admitted a number of other similar offences, which would be 'written off' to him while he was inside.

This was a common practice in those days, and criminals often asked to see you once they had been sentenced so that they could 'clear their slate', which would not normally attract an additional sentence, as it was not in the public interest. They nearly always refused to have offences taken into consideration at court, because they ran the real risk of additional sentencing. However, equally, they didn't want a 'gate arrest' when they were released so they opted for 'write offs'. Unfortunately, as the years passed, the system fell into disrepute and the Home Office eventually discouraged the process.

Bryan Davis retired from the West Midlands Police as a sergeant in 2005. During the summer of 1976, he was a probationer constable on B Unit at Digbeth police station and recalls some early memories about life in the police service:

> I lived in single-men's quarters at Digbeth police station for more than five years. The room was basic and consisted of a single bed, a wardrobe, and a set of drawers. There were about fifteen of us living there and, although the facilities were sparse, there was a great atmosphere. We survived on beer and curry, and had some great parties at Christmas when we used to invite nurses from the Accident and General hospitals.
>
> We used to go clubbing in the city centre off-duty and, one night, I remember we had finished a late turn and, at about midnight, turned up

at Barbarella's nightclub. As we tried to enter, we suddenly realised that it was an Afro-Caribbean night and, as two white men with short hair, we looked somewhat out of place!

Some of the things you do in the police service stick in your mind; for example, the first sudden death I went to was at the Albany Hotel. I was on a late-turn duty and I was sent after one of the chambermaids, who had knocked on one of the room doors, got no reply, I went in and found a man lying dead on the bed. There were no obvious suspicious circumstances and, for a while, I sat on the end of the bed watching the tennis at Wimbledon on television while waiting for the undertakers to arrive. On one of the side-tables was a half empty bottle of whisky and a half-eaten sandwich.

Shortly afterwards another very experienced officer attended as well. He could tell that I was really nervous and jokingly said words to the effect of 'Do you fancy a drink', pointing towards the bottle. I politely declined. When the undertakers arrived, they lifted the body and, underneath, we saw lots of powder and capsules on the bed. It suddenly became clear that he had in fact committed suicide and, when we checked the whisky bottle more closely, we could see lots of bits of tablet floating in it. We searched the room and found letters addressed to the coroner, his children, and his wife – a very sad case.

By contrast, on another occasion during this period, I went with one of my inspectors to deliver my first death message. We discussed it all beforehand and we went through things like checking that neighbours were available to give support. It was at a block of flats and, when we got there, we delivered the message to the family in a sensitive way, at which point they all started cheering and celebrating the fact that this person had died!

On the morning of Friday 13 August, I went to Ladywood police station to see the detective chief inspector in charge of the CID on C2 subdivision to discuss my transfer to the CID there. He was a short but vocal Scotsman called Jim, who had a good heart and always joked that he did his best interviews with prisoners after he'd had a drink. I was pleased at the thought of working for him again, even though I foolishly tried to keep up with him on one night out drinking, and found myself vomiting in the toilets of a back-street pub. A one-off that was not to be repeated!

I went back to Bradford Street, said my goodbyes to Bob and whoever else was there, and that was it. I had made twenty-nine arrests, done countless interviews and lots of paperwork, and was now drinking pints, albeit slowly.

I was appointed as a detective constable at Ladywood police station with effect from 23 August 1976. I started off by covering the area around Broad Street, with which I was already very familiar, and was soon investigating a spate of thefts of purses occurring in Barbarella's nightclub in Cumberland Street.

The name of the club was taken from the French sci-fi film, *Barbarella*, starring Jane Fonda, and was one of Eddie Fewtrell's clubs where he promoted known rock bands at the time, such as AC/DC, Dire Straits, Queen, The Sex Pistols, and The Clash. Duran Duran's drummer played with punk bands there in the seventies and I once witnessed a DJ, who went on to become a famous television personality, eat a whole Spanish onion as part of his act!

As an eighteen-year-old, before becoming a police officer, Steve Burrows remembers the club as being the only place he could get into wearing bike leather and jeans. Most visits were followed by a customary curry in Broad Street after 2.00 a.m., when the club closed.

The city centre was full of restaurants, which catered for all tastes. Unfortunately, many of the customers using these establishments during the early hours were heavily under the influence of alcohol, and problems with so-called 'bilking', wherein customers ate their meal and then ran off without paying, were common. Bill Rogerson was a PC with the BTP in the seventies and recalls one such incident:

> We were just coming back from Digbeth police station after depositing a prisoner and, as we were passing the old bus station, we suddenly became aware of two men running out of an Indian restaurant. They were closely followed by an Indian guy, who was carrying a huge sword that was so big that he was holding it with both hands! He was shouting at them, and it was obvious that they had not paid for their meal. We joined in the chase, although I told the Indian to leave it to us, as I didn't want two headless corpses on our hands. We caught up with them after a hundred yards and then handed them over to some local officers.

Barbarella's was a popular venue, which got very crowded and, while women were on the dance floor, someone was dipping into handbags that had been left unattended at tables. The darkened room and flashing lights were ideal for opportunist thieves, and whoever was doing it was emptying the contents of purses in the nearby male toilets before the victims had even noticed, then hiding the empty purses in the cisterns.

On one Saturday morning, I was in Hockley on the Brookfields Estate and managed to track down a thirteen-year-old absconder from Tennal Grange assessment centre who was returned to care. He was well known to us and was suspected of committing crimes on the estate, but admitted nothing. Having already grown beyond his years, he was a tough nut to crack.

On the weekend of 30 August 1976, hundreds of police officers and carnival-goers required medical treatment after disturbances took place at the Notting Hill Carnival in West London. More than sixty arrests took place as police officers armed themselves with dustbin lids and milk crates to fend off missiles in a sign of further disturbances to come, with officers ill-equipped or not properly trained to deal with large-scale civil disorder.

On Wednesday 8 September, I met Chip in Lodge Road, Hockley, and he gave me some information on street drug dealers and a burglary in the Stechford area. We did not have the luxury of mobile phones then so, in the main, I relied on him getting in touch with me, unless I could pick him up by chance off the street near to his home. It could be a frustrating process, but his safety was paramount.

On the next day, I went to see the absconder again at Tennal Grange and this time he and another resident admitted a specific burglary at a house in Crabtree Road, Hockley. Juveniles had to be interviewed in the presence of a parent, or a responsible adult if they were in care, as well as being entitled to legal representation if they asked for it. Interview rooms could get quite crowded in such situations, sometimes making it harder to establish a rapport. They had to have their rights, however, as otherwise any admissions would actually be inadmissible in court.

I went home for lunch and was then back in the office for 9.00 p.m. I had arranged to go to Barbarella's and, together with another DC, and a female officer, we set up in the club from 10.15 p.m. We were all young in service, but enthusiastic, and the plan was to mingle with the customers, including on the dance floor. The female officer had a police radio in her handbag, a big blue object with a red transmit button and a stubby black plastic-covered aerial on the top.

As the night wore on, we lost concentration on the objective.

At 1.45 a.m. I went to check the gents' toilets to see if anything had been dumped already – nothing. When I came back the other two officers were having a dance. My sixth sense told me that something was wrong and I immediately checked our table. The female officer's handbag was gone and I instantly had grim visions of being kicked off the CID after just one month. I grabbed my colleagues' attention and we ran to the toilets and, inside, we found a twenty-five-year-old Arab male standing outside one of the cubicles, which was locked. I rapped on the door, got no response, and forced it open. Inside another thirty-year-old Arab male was in the process of emptying the female officer's bag, and looking somewhat mystified as to what the police radio was for.

Both were arrested and were swept out of the nightclub within minutes. The first man maintained his innocence, but the second was 'bang to rights', and was later charged with theft.

We didn't finish until 5.30 a.m. and I was exhausted. There was no sense of elation at all, as it had been a really close shave. Losing a police radio in such circumstances would have caused all sorts of problems, the least of which would have required us to 'stun' the frequency, so that it could not be used again either to make or receive calls. In the worst-case scenario, we would have been facing a discipline enquiry for neglect of duty and loss of police equipment. We were never able to prove it against the first man, but the second later pleaded guilty and went to prison for three months.

On Friday 17 September, I visited the Masonic Temple in Stirling Road, just off the Hagley Road, following a burglary. It was an impressive building, although I wasn't shown around it all, and I was quite intrigued by the place. Many of my colleagues were Freemasons, although very few of them openly admitted it. I didn't play golf, or belong to any clubs, and I had no plans to become a Mason. I did not like the secrecy, although people always stressed the charitable side of the organisation. I always made my views known and, not surprisingly, I was not asked to join. It was great fun to receive a 'secret handshake', though, and to register the look of disappointment when I did not reciprocate.

Years later, I was engaged on an 'outside force' complaints investigation in Wales, which was supervised by the then Police Complaints Authority. One of the agreed lines of enquiry when interviewing local officers and other witnesses was to ask them whether they were or ever had been Freemasons. The responses were sometimes interesting, and occasionally akin to 'touching someone with an electric cattle prod', but I have to say that, when these enquiries led to a visit to the Grand Lodge in London, I received nothing but positive help and was even given some books to read, which I used to leave on a shelf in my office for inquisitive visitors to find.

On Monday 27 September 1976, I started to focus on thefts from motor vehicles in the car parks at the Tower Ballroom at Edgbaston Reservoir, famous for Bobby Johnson and his Bandwagon, and a revolving stage – and, in police circles, for their so-called 'Grab a Granny Nights'.

Built in 1827 by Thomas Telford, the Tower Ballroom began life as a roller-skating rink, until it became a ballroom in the 1920s. It flourished for many years as one of Birmingham's top night spots until 2005, when it closed for three years, with the last night line-up including Dave Berry and the Cruisers, Marmalade, The Fortunes and The Searchers.

I recovered some stolen property from an address in Leslie Road and, on the next day, interviewed a juvenile offender in the presence of his father, who was later charged and bailed in connection with that offence.

On Saturday 2 October, I went out for the first time with an Irish detective constable called John to visit premises in the Jewellery Quarter. He was a brilliant detective, from whom I would learn a lot. He walked with a slight limp, was going bald, and had a strong Irish accent, but could twist people round his fingers with his sense of humanity and honesty. Equally, he was tough and not to be messed with.

On Monday 4 October, I started my first week as the night duty CID officer for the whole of the C Division, which included Ladywood, Winson Green, Hockley, Edgbaston, and Handsworth. Only one officer worked nights and you were responsible for all crime-related matters that happened between 10.00 p.m. and 7.00 a.m., and had to complete a night-crime summary at the end of each tour. It was all quite disconcerting, because the fact that I was young in service was irrelevant. I was the detective and, no matter what the ages, rank, or service experience of my uniform colleagues, I would be expected to have the answers. As I arrived on duty for the first shift, some of the late-turn CID were still around, and a few came in later from the pub next door. By 11.30 p.m., however, everyone had gone home and I was on my own in the CID office on the first floor. I felt very lonely and vulnerable!

I took a few deep breaths and took myself out and about around the division. During the next seven nights, I completed bail checks, arrested another suspect for theft from Barbarella's, and dealt with: a wounding, thefts from the person, and eleven prisoners, some of whom were arrested for burglary. Just before I finished on the Monday morning, I went over to Golden Hillock Road in Sparkhill and recovered a stolen vehicle used in one of those offences. I felt a sense of achievement, and slept well during the following day.

It had been a busy weekend elsewhere in Birmingham, following a so-called 'friendly' football match on Saturday 9 October 1976 between Aston Villa and Glasgow Rangers at Villa Park.

Scores of Rangers fans arrived on a night sleeper train from Glasgow before the game. The train itself was delayed due to trouble en route, and some fans were thrown off at Wigan. Others arrived at Villa Park in fifty coaches, some as early as 3.00 a.m., and many of them engaged in wholesale drinking, including a fifteen-year-old who collapsed after drinking too much.

The game was abandoned after fifty-three minutes due to crowd violence, which came to a climax when Frank Carrodus put Villa 2-0 up the minute before. Missiles were thrown and 200 Rangers fans invaded the pitch to engage with Villa fans.

More than seventy people were injured at the game, including two with stab wounds, and thirty police officers were hurt, one of whom suffered a suspected fractured skull. The violence continued in Birmingham city centre afterwards, as eight buses were vandalised and innocent shoppers terrorised. One woman and her daughter were sprayed with milk and assaulted in the Bull Ring.

The day became known as 'Sick Saturday', but retired DC Ian Mabbett from the British Transport Police recalls officers being busy from the Friday through to the following Monday, as drunken Scottish fans gathered in large numbers on New Street station, with drink cans and bottles scattered everywhere. The home secretary of the day ordered an enquiry, as one newspaper headline read, 'Birmingham's day of Tartan terror'.

On Tuesday 12 October 1976, I went to Tennal Grange assessment centre again with a DC called Dave to interview my absconder yet again. It was laborious work, but he eventually admitted another three offences of burglary at dwelling houses near his family address on the Brookfields Estate.

The following day, Eric the detective inspector wrote on my annual appraisal: 'DC Layton has completed two months' transfer to the CID. During this short period he has acquitted himself well, I am well satisfied with his progress to date ...'

On Thursday 21 October, I had my first outing with a detective constable called Neil. He was a real smoothie with the ladies and prided himself on his appearance. I never once saw a hair out of place, and he dressed like a Burton's model, but he had an easy way with him and we eventually became personal friends.

On Thursday 28 October, I met Chip in the evening in Hockley. He had been quiet for a while, but he came up with the name of a suspect for a burglary in Kidderminster, as well as two people involved in the theft of jewellery valued at £4,000, one of whom was wanted on a Crown Court bench warrant for failing to appear in respect of another case. It was good-quality information, and the next day I liaised with a detective sergeant called George from Number 4 Regional Crime Squad. We identified where the theft had taken place at premises in King's Norton, as well as the full details of the other suspect, who was a female, and lived in Rubery.

On Saturday 30 October, John and I dealt with our elusive juvenile burglar together with one of his brothers, who had been detained with the help of uniform officers. Both were interviewed in the presence of their parents, and subsequently charged with a house burglary and then bailed. In the evening, I paid a visit to the Saints and Sinners Café in Broad Street, a very aptly named establishment, apart from the fact that saints were in short supply. It was a gathering place for local criminals, especially car thieves who used to pop in for something to eat or to collect drugs after frequenting the club areas and taking vehicles for a joy-ride.

The trick for us was to find out where they had hidden the stolen car and then to sit up nearby waiting for the thieves to return. They had to be given a chance to get back into the vehicle, so that we could connect them to it evidentially, but we also had to make sure that we could block them in quickly with a plain police car to avoid dangerous chases.

The same situation applied to the Tow Rope Café at the other end of Broad Street, where the clientèle included all-night clubbers who used to go in there for a full English breakfast during the early hours.

On Monday 1 November, I met Chip again, and he pinpointed where we could find our jewellery suspect and also put me onto a team who were planning to do post office and petrol station robberies in the Moseley area. Shortly after 10.00 p.m., I made my way with the officers from the Regional Crime Squad to a tower block in Small Heath, where, in one of the flats several floors up, we found our man. It was too high up for him to go anywhere, so that was it. We also arrested the flat owner for non-payment of fine warrants.

What we were most interested in, however, was the fact that he was also one of the two people named as potential robbers, and this gave us a great chance to gather strong intelligence on him. We took them both to Digbeth police station and, by the time we had finished documenting and charging them, it was 2.30 a.m. I drove home and was back again for court by 9.45 a.m., tired but elated at a great result. The jewellery thief eventually got sent down for three-and-a-half years.

On Saturday 13 November 1976, PC Mel Harris from the British Transport Police, and PC David Wardle from the West Midlands Police, provided a vivid illustration of how acts of courage were routinely carried out by police officers involved in potentially violent and life-threatening incidents.

During the course of that day, a female climbed over a wall onto a 2-foot-wide parapet directly above platforms 10 and 11 at Birmingham New Street station, and threatened to jump. PC Wardle was the first officer on the scene and climbed over the wall onto the parapet to try to engage her in conversation, while two of his colleagues maintained a grip on the officer's right arm through a hole in the wall.

PC Harris was directed, with other BTP officers, to the platform and, on arrival, he found the fire service in attendance. Mel saw the female standing approximately 35 feet above him on the parapet, shouting and screaming. After confirming that all electrical power had been switched off on the overhead lines, and that trains had been brought to a standstill, an extendable ladder was placed against the parapet and PC Harris immediately ascended the ladder, followed by the fireman.

As the officer arrived at the top, PC Wardle made to catch hold of the female, and both of them, with the female kicking and struggling, fell forward towards PC Harris. With only his feet to hold him onto the ladder, Mel pushed his right shoulder into the female and attempted to push her back towards the wall. At this point he almost fell.

The female became even more hysterical and, in an effort to bring her under control, he punched her in the jaw, which dazed her for a moment while the officers tried to tie a rope around her to secure her. After a few moments she started to struggle again but, finally, the officers managed to subdue her and succeeded in dragging her back over the retaining wall. Throughout this whole experience, PC Harris was balancing on the rungs of the ladder with no other means of holding on.

The officers undoubtedly saved the life of this individual.

For his efforts, PC Harris was bitten through the sleeve of his tunic on his right arm by the female, and he ended up having to attend hospital for a tetanus injection. He recalls the incident well and commented, 'I was twenty-nine years of age and physically fit. I never gave it a thought when I looked up. Someone had to go up there and help, so I just did it. There was no time to think about the danger.'

During the course of this month, I returned a knife, which had been an exhibit, to a woman who had used it to stab her violent partner, who had been attacking her. She was clearly a victim of sustained domestic violence and, during one such attack, she had just snapped while she was in the kitchen and stabbed him once in the stomach with a knife that she used for peeling vegetables. He sustained a serious injury but refused to assist the police and the prosecution solicitors eventually took the view that it was not in the public interest to prosecute her, and so the exhibit was duly returned.

It still had blood on it when I took it back, but she insisted that it was a good knife and that she wanted to put it back into use in the kitchen. He disappeared off the scene after realising that she would tolerate him no more. It was said that, on average, a victim of domestic violence would be assaulted thirty-two times before they got to the point of making an official complaint. Many of the victims stayed in the relationships for the sake of children, and we the police and other agencies were just not very good at recognising and dealing with such types of crime. Without a statement of complaint, there was a reluctance to proceed to court and, on occasions, reports were either 'no crimed' or cleared – 'guilt of the offender is clear but complainant declined to prosecute' – which did little to discourage the perpetrators from re-offending.

On Sunday 28 November, a burglary occurred at Tricketts, a butcher's shop in Monument Road, where a safe had been stolen. Two days later, I met an informant in the evening, and was given the identity of one of the burglars, who was a very-good-class villain. I did some research as usual at the Midlands Criminal Records Office the following day and positively identified him. At 5.45 p.m., we gathered in the CID office together with officers from Number 4 Regional Crime Squad for a briefing. At 7.30 p.m., a DS called John led us to York Road, Edgbaston, where we smashed the door in at an address, arrested a thirty-two-year-old, and recovered some of the property from the safe.

On Wednesday 8 December, I started looking for yet another borstal absconder whose family lived in Coxwell Gardens, Ladywood. He was suspected of breaking into houses in the area. We stuck with it and widened our area of interest to include a road near to Monument Road, where another well-known family lived, and with whom he was associated. This family was headed by a very formidable lady. She would think nothing of verbally abusing any police officer and was usually obstructive, protecting her children at any cost. I came to know the family well and, even though I later dealt with some of her sons for criminal matters, I eventually had an open invite to a cup of tea there.

On Wednesday 22 December, while I was out with a detective sergeant called Stan, we finally captured the absconder just after he had carried out a burglary in Abbey Street. We recovered stolen property and he was lodged at Winson Green Prison for the night prior to being sent back to borstal.

Christmas Eve came and I met Chip. He provided me with further information on the robbery suspects and a very prolific criminal, who came from another very well-known family in Ladywood. John, the Irish DC, and I went down to the Jewellery Quarter for a drink and mingled with Christmas revellers, and that was it for three days.

There was always something about Christmas that I enjoyed but, in terms of work, there was no let-up and, if anything, it was busier. Uniform colleagues were constantly dealing with either comatose drunks, who needed to go to hospital, or aggressive drunks who needed to go to a cell. For the CID, it was a constant stream of assaults and woundings, mixed in with a sprinkling of burglary dwellings, including those where burglars with no conscience had stolen the family's Christmas presents from under the tree. Scrooge had nothing on some of these people!

During 1976, a total of 125,148 crimes was recorded across the whole of the West Midlands police force area, a third of which related to thefts of and from motor vehicles. Somewhat worryingly, offences of robbery and wounding showed sharp increases, and the force was directly affected by seventy-three cases of criminal damage as police vehicles were deliberately targeted.

In 1976, an officer, who I will refer to as Dave 'J', joined the force and was posted to D Unit at Digbeth police station. He went on to serve thirty years in the police and retired as a detective sergeant. He initially recalls that,

> I was either the second or third Asian officer to join the force. I can say in all honesty that it was the best time of my life and I never experienced any form of racism from my colleagues. In those days, the police were a family and, if someone had a problem, everyone rallied around to help. Some of the senior officers could be very strict but when you needed them they were there for you.

On Monday 24 January 1977, we started the week looking at a spate of metal thefts in the Hockley area. Plenty of the local factories used various types of metal in their production processes, and the area also serviced quite a number of registered scrap-metal dealers, not all of whom were straight.

The following day, Chip gave me a job relating to the theft of a pad of sixty rings from a jeweller's in Dale End, Birmingham, some twelve months previously. He identified the shop premises and the offender; once again, after some enquiries at MIDCRO (Midlands Criminal Records Office) and checking with a local beat officer in the Sutton Coldfield area, I managed to identify a further two suspects. This job was off my area and we were extremely busy at that time, so I decided to pass it on to my contacts in the Regional Crime Squad.

The metal thefts continued, and I spent a lot of time with John working around the Hockley and Brookfields Estate. There had been another substantial theft from a factory in Carver Street of tin anodes, but John was confident that we would get to the bottom of it. On 15 February 1977, we met one of his informants in the Roseville Tavern in Vyse Street, Hockley, and were given some good leads.

Our breakthrough came three days later, when a further burglary occurred at a factory in Western Road, and copper tubing was stolen. After a round of visits to scrap-metal dealers, I assisted John that evening with the interview of a thirty-one-year-old small-time scrap dealer. He was later charged with receiving the copper tubing, knowing it to have been stolen. Once we had finished with him, we went out again, as we had the names of the two burglars.

We arrested the first one on the next day in the afternoon. He was upset because, although he admitted to breaking into the factory and stealing the copper tubing, he claimed that someone else had then gone on to steal it from his hiding place. Therefore, he was going to get done for something from which he had gained nothing. He was charged and bailed, and the next time I was to see him was in the A&E department of a local hospital.

He was a real hard case, regularly getting drunk and into fights. He had gone looking for an associate with whom he had fallen out; the culprit had evened things up by arming himself with a crook-lock, which fitted under the clutch and over the steering wheel of a car.

One blow struck him directly under the nose and separated the bone between his lip and his nose. It wasn't a pretty sight, but he refused to tell me who had done it. It would just add one more scar to his already damaged face. He was a violent individual, who was prepared to attack the police but, for some reason, the code between the CID and these people was different and I never felt personally threatened in his company.

We interviewed the second suspect the next day at Harborne police station, after he had been arrested by local officers for other matters. The building was originally built as the first free school in Harborne and was eventually demolished in 1995.

I have very fond memories of this very old station, which stood at one end of the high street and was home to a small number of officers, many of whom had worked there for years.

One of them was even called the 'Sherriff of Harborne', but they knew everyone and fiercely protected their positions. There were only a couple of cells at the station, and the front-office PC doubled up as the custody officer. It was all quite a relaxed affair and our prisoner admitted offences that were put to him.

On 24 February, we made a third arrest for theft of more copper piping from the company in Western Road and then got our scrap-metal dealer back, who had been on bail, and he was further charged, this time with burglary.

On the next day, John and I went to yet another scrap dealer in Howe Street, and recovered the stolen copper piping. We had stirred up a figurative hornet's nest, and got a really nice result from it.

John and I had a good partnership, and trusted each other implicitly. The experience that John gave me and the links I was creating with the scrap dealers were invaluable and, while they were not all engaged in criminal activity, they knew what was going on in their area. One of them was a very short guy with a pot belly, who wore gold chains on his neck and wrists. He would always insist that, if ever I visited the yard to sign the books and he had customers present, I was to give him a hard time and read him the so-called 'riot act'. We would go through the same charade each time, and then sit down and put the world to rights in his office with a coffee, or something stronger at Christmas.

Between 21 March and 25 May 1977, I attended my initial CID course, number 53, at Tally Ho police training centre in Edgbaston. Syndicate 53A consisted of thirty-four officers from nineteen forces, with just three female officers. Syndicate 53B, of which I was a member, consisted of thirty-three officers from eighteen forces, and only two female officers.

During the course, although I lived only half an hour away, I was required to stay in accommodation at the training centre, as there were officers from other UK forces and the Royal Ulster Constabulary on it. As the host force, we were expected to look after our visitors. The RUC officers in particular were on a hard-earned rest from the 'troubles' in Northern Ireland. They were in a safe environment and made the most of the chance to socialise, and to try and relax. I recall one of them actually sleeping full length on some seats in the lecture theatre throughout an entire lesson, and then suddenly sitting upright at the end of the visiting lecturer's presentation!

Every day was the same routine: lessons on criminal law, evidence and procedure, and general and scientific issues, followed by an early evening visit to the bar and regular trips to Indian and Chinese restaurants.

On one evening, I took a group of seven from my class to the Tower Ballroom in Edgbaston. We used our warrant cards to gain entrance, which was normal in those days, and started to progress towards the bar at the very end of the venue. Bobby Johnson was busy blasting away with his band, and the stage was revolving as usual. The dance floor was packed with women and, by the time I reached the bar, six of my colleagues had disappeared and were not seen for the rest of the evening. One of them actually met someone and moved in with them during weekends for the duration of the course.

I finished the course with 85 per cent in my examinations, achieving second place overall. My final report said, among other things, that 'my conduct while at the centre could not be faulted', which probably did not appear on everyone's! I had a week off, and my first day back on 6 June was spent on standby in the vicinity of Handsworth Park, where a black power march was supposed to be taking place. Finally, nothing of any consequence happened.

I tried to rekindle my relationship with Chip, and found him next day when he gave me some information about a number of people receiving stolen property. By now, he was on bail for burglary himself and keen to put as much information my way as possible, seeing as he was looking at getting 'sent down'. With the knowledge of prosecuting solicitors, we were allowed to present sealed 'text' letters to either the magistrates or judges sentencing such individuals, which outlined how useful an informant had been and could sometimes lead to a reduced sentence. They were, however, very strictly controlled and some informants did not even want the judiciary to know what they had been up to.

At the beginning of July, Chip went to prison after being convicted of burglary and I visited him in Winson Green Prison a couple of days after he was sentenced. He wasn't in a good place mentally. Life was going to be tough for a while, but he only had himself to blame. He had been stupid and I told him so. Although I was a police officer and he was essentially a partially reformed criminal, there was a bond of humanity between us. As I had relied on him for information, he had relied on me to keep him on the straight and narrow with a good talking to every now and then, when necessary. I felt a sense of responsibility for him, even though it was not required or called for. We were still on good terms, but I was not sure what the future held for him.

On 1 August 1977, John and I went to a report of an internal theft of thousands of nickel rounds from a factory in Great Hampton Street, just off Birmingham city centre. It was the start of a complex enquiry, which was to last ten months before we totally cracked it. A substantial amount of the metal was missing from the secure storeroom. Interviewing the member of staff in charge of the storeroom got us nowhere. It was a complete mystery as to how such a large quantity of metal could leave the factory without anyone knowing, and all the paperwork showed that all deliveries had been accounted for.

During the same month, my uniform colleagues were again facing challenges in relation to National Front activities. Major confrontations had taken place in Lewisham in London, where police riot shields were deployed for the first time in the UK outside Northern Ireland, and disturbances took place in Ladywood, where twelve police officers were injured. Some criminals took advantage of the trouble to start looting, and there was an attack on Thornhill Road police station after left-wing demonstrators were unable to break into a National Front meeting being held in a local school. At the time, the National Front were contesting the Ladywood by-election.

My annual appraisal was completed in October 1977, and later the divisional chief superintendent, whom I barely knew, commented in blue ink and carefully crafted writing: 'I am satisfied he has the makings of a competent detective. He is a sensible young man who is obviously intent on proving himself as a detective before applying for promotion. He should do well in the service'.

On the morning of Friday 28 October, I was directed to one of the tower blocks in Hockley, where I liaised with a uniform sergeant who had been called to the sudden death of a male child under the age of one year. The circumstances surrounding the death were suspicious and scenes-of-crime officers and a police photographer attended, together with other CID officers, and items of clothing were removed as evidence. I remained there for some time, until the body was taken to the central mortuary in Newton Street, Birmingham.

Together with a detective sergeant by the name of Hugh, I went to the mortuary and was present when the post-mortem examination took place. It revealed multiple internal injuries. A very difficult situation, made even worse as it was a baby involved, but you had to learn to put personal feelings totally to one side, and to focus on the job – otherwise you risked doing an injustice to the victims of crime.

Post-mortems always had the potential to present personal challenges and, at that time, we stood alongside pathologists as they conducted their work, wearing our suits but no protective clothing or masks at all. You had to cope with the visual impact of what you were seeing, so close to a dead body, as well as the combination of smells in the room, which would stick to your clothing for hours afterwards – particularly the formaldehyde, a chemical preservative and disinfectant. After we had finished, we went back to Ladywood police station, bagged up our exhibits, and completed the laboratory forms, before taking them to the forensic science laboratories in Gooch Street in the afternoon.

Other officers carried on with the enquiry, and I got on with other things, finishing the day with a couple of pints and some reflection as to how complicated and tenuous life was. A few years earlier, I had attended my first sudden death as a nineteen-year-old PC in the British Transport Police, when a man had committed suicide by placing his head on a railway line in Smethwick. On my arrival, I was met with the sight of a decapitated body on the tracks and a piece of clothing covering his head, which was about 50 yards further up the track. They say that you never forget your first one, but that didn't mean dealing with the next one would be any easier.

Delivering of 'death messages' to the families of victims was even more of a challenge. Arriving outside an address would lead to the same ritual. Even the most law-abiding members of the community get concerned at the sight of a police officer on the doorstep. The trick was to make sure that you were at the right address and then to try to get inside and to get people seated before saying anything.

Getting the first name of the deceased right was critical, and the choice of words really important. The outcome was the same and you needed to be direct but not blunt. Remembering that it was not your job to take on other people's grief was also very important, so as to make sure that you got all the facts needed. Compulsory cups of tea and making arrangements for people not to be left alone were all part of the process. Someone would need to identify the body formally in due course – establishing who that was going to be was another job to navigate.

When people lose a loved one, they go through many emotions, one of which is a thirst for information. The sensitive way in which that information was disseminated was crucial to the picture left in people's minds. In this case, I would not have shared the decapitation.

On Wednesday 9 November, we were back at the factory in Great Hampton Street, looking at the theft of nickel rounds, which were valued at £4,000. On this occasion, we had a specific line of enquiry at some premises in Cateswell Road, Hall Green, and took the delivery driver from the factory with us. It was quite simple; the driver was insisting that he had made a delivery and the staff at the premises in Cateswell Road were insisting that they had no such stock on their premises.

The driver was a thirty-seven-year-old from Woodgate Valley and a very cool customer. He stuck to his story. We made a decision, and he was duly arrested and taken to Ladywood police station, where he was later charged and bailed. We took him back home afterwards and recovered some stolen property from his garden shed and garage, but it was small stuff compared to the thefts we were investigating. He continued to deny everything completely. It was an intriguing case, which I was determined to get to the bottom of, and part of the process was extensive visits to scrap-metal dealers to try and track down the stolen metal.

We had a case against the driver, but he knew it was up to us to prove he had stolen the nickel rounds – we would struggle at court if we couldn't find out where they had been disposed of. On Wednesday 23 November, we went back to the company in Hall Green and saw the production manager regarding the thefts of nickel rounds. A very important fact came to light. As well as the factory in Great Hampton Street, they had two other suppliers of nickel rounds and the deliveries from all three frequently overlapped. The important thing for the production staff was that, when they needed nickel rounds, there was available stock in their storeroom, and they didn't distinguish between the three suppliers and where the stock came from. This gave us some food for thought.

On Friday 25 November, I was at the factory in Great Hampton Street for the whole day, spending time with one of the directors, and taking statements from the metal-compound supervisor and loading supervisor. I went through a lot of documentation, looking for some answers, because I now knew that every delivery to the company in Hall Green had to be signed for. On the face of it, every delivery had been.

On Monday 28 November, three of us went back to the company in Hall Green and spent some hours interviewing and taking witness statements from members of staff at the premises. We also took handwriting specimens so that we could compare some of the signatures on delivery notes. By now, we were investigating the theft of nickel rounds that had risen to over £15,000. A significant amount of money in those days! No one was admitting anything, but we believed that we were getting closer to the truth. What I didn't know was that someone was already panicking, and went home later that day and burned several hundred pounds in his kitchen sink, fearing an imminent search of his home.

The following day, Neil and I interviewed the delivery driver again under caution in relation to further offences, but he continued to deny all knowledge. He was difficult to develop any sort of rapport with.

On Wednesday 30 November, an urgent job came in, and Neil and I went down to the Hockley Centre, in the Jewellery Quarter, and liaised with two company directors from a company specialising in making diamond rings. We teamed up with Hugh and a couple of female constables and, within the hour, went to premises in Caroline Street to arrest a twenty-year-old female employee and recover some stolen property. She was taken to Ladywood police station and interviewed. Following this, we went straight back to the firm and arrested another eighteen year-old female and a twenty year-old male employee for theft, with yet more stolen property found in lockers. No sooner had we put these two into custody than we arrested a further two females, who were in fact twins. It was a classic case of internal theft, whereby, one by one, all five of them had been drawn into a criminal enterprise. Five arrests and it was a late finish by the time they were all charged and bailed.

On Monday 5 December, I was back at Great Hampton Street seeing the staff again, and I wanted to make sure that the word went around that the police were still on the case. Two days later, the delivery driver made a court appearance at Birmingham Magistrates' Court and was remanded on bail, while further enquiries continued. By now I was focused on the staff at Hall Green and, in particular, a twenty-five-year-old storeman. I went back to Cateswell Road in Hall Green with Neil in the afternoon, and spoke to him and other staff again to arrange further forensic analysis. They were all still being treated as witnesses, but we wanted them to realise that we were not going to go away and that our investigation wouldn't stop.

I did a week of night-duty cover just before Christmas, and it was a chaotic seven days where I was involved in dealing with more than twenty-four persons for various offences. People were very much into the 'Christmas spirit', in more ways than one.

During the course of 1977, recorded crime increased significantly across the force, with 154,141 offences being recorded. In an effort to stem offences of robbery, which rose by 30 per cent, a Force Robbery Squad was formed. Once again, a third of all crime related to vehicle crime, and nearly a third of all crimes detected were committed by juveniles.

The force faced major challenges in policing public order events, with seven demonstrations involving National Front supporters and anti-National Front demonstrators. One in particular, held on the occasion of the Ladywood by-election, led to serious disturbances, many arrests, and the deployment of protective shields.

West Midlands Police officers were required to police 232 football matches in the region, which boasted five First Division teams in the force area. This year also saw the first national strike called by the National Union of Firemen, which, while an orderly affair, required additional police engagement.

The new year came, and I got some information regarding a burglary suspect breaking into factories in the Jewellery Quarter during the night. The suspect was a close friend of a relative and, although this was all a bit 'close to home', I was determined to follow it through. Neil and I did some enquiries, as a result of which we identified two provable fingerprints at burglaries in Hockley and Edgbaston and, on 4 January 1978, we arrested a man. He fully admitted his part in the offences and identified his partner in crime too, whom I knew. The circle was completed and I left it to Neil to make the second arrest.

On Monday 9 January, I paid another visit to the factory in Great Hampton Street to take yet more statements from staff. The next morning, I went back to the company in Hall Green with Neil, for yet another round of interviews with staff.

We had been there for a while and, as I was talking to my suspect, the storeman, intuition told me that something had changed. I leant across the table and said quietly to him, 'Is there something that you want to tell me?' He didn't answer straight away but, eventually, he replied in a very tired voice, 'Yes, there is.'

I wanted him to trust me and not to make him feel cornered, so I took a chance. I knew that he rode a motorbike, and I told him not to say any more at that point, but to leave work without making a fuss and to follow us to the police station. It was a gamble, because he could have regained his composure or just ridden off, but thankfully he did the right thing. When he finally arrived at the station, he was arrested and made a full and frank admission to his part in the thefts of the nickel rounds. It was a weight off his mind, and he wouldn't be burning any more money in the sink. He wasn't a career criminal, just someone who had been sucked into the temptation of easy money by a stronger character and, once he was in, had no way out.

The thefts had been carried out in a very simple way and had gone on for some time. The nickel rounds from the factory in Great Hampton Street would be loaded up, but would never actually be delivered to the premises in Hall Green, instead going straight to a metal dealer. The delivery driver would then meet the storeman in a local transport café and he would sign the delivery note to confirm delivery, knowing that the delivery of nickel rounds from the other two suppliers would ensure that stock would be available for production purposes. It all went wrong when they got greedy and took the load in November, not knowing that one of the other suppliers was going to cancel a projected delivery, which would leave the storeroom empty.

It was clear that he couldn't have committed the crimes all on his own and, after charging and bailing him, we went to Chelmsley Wood and arrested a second storeman, aged twenty-six, who we had previously interviewed as a witness. In light of what we had, he folded very quickly and also elected to make a written statement of admission before being charged. We had the thieves, but now we wanted the receivers of the nickel.

On Monday 16 January, we dealt with a general hand from the premises in Great Hampton Street, who had been stealing chemicals and nickel from the firm. We couldn't connect him to the activities of the first driver, and he was an obnoxious individual who was obstructive and disliked the police intensely. There was to be no rapport-building with this man, and we had to bail him for a time while we looked for further evidence. We then charged him a week later.

The following day, Neil and I re-arrested the first delivery driver at his home in Woodgate Valley and took him back to Ladywood police station. This time, he admitted everything and it took two hours to record his statement under caution. The next day he stood in the dock at Birmingham Magistrates' Court, together with the two storemen, his co-accused, and they were remanded on bail. Now we turned our attention towards finding one of the receivers.

Initially, we had just a first name to go on but, on 25 January, I met an informant in the Gothic pub in Great Hampton Row, Hockley, and was given the full name. This particular pub had a lot of history to it, and was made a Grade II listed building in 1982. At the start of the Second World War, they used to hold Saturday night functions, with a band playing in the ballroom on the second floor, while the ground-floor bars did a good trade with workers from the Jewellery Quarter.

On Friday 27 January I was again at the premises in Great Hampton Street, and started looking at a second delivery driver, who was believed to be involved in unrelated thefts. In the afternoon, I saw Chip, who was now a free man, and looking to renew our relationship.

On Wednesday 1 February, I went with Neil to Great Hampton Street again and arrested the second driver. We lodged him in the cells and went down to some jewellery premises in Spencer Street, where we recovered some stolen property. A second man was arrested for receiving stolen property, and we later found some more in a garage and the kitchen of an address in Streetly – both were charged.

On Thursday 2 February, we made an early start and executed search warrants at a house in Newtown and the scrap yard of our known suspect. The outcome was the arrest of two men, who were related to each other and ran the yard. We found some stolen property and an unlicensed shotgun, and we seized the metal registers. One of them was charged with receiving nickel rounds, and we regrouped to consider the next step of getting access to their bank records through obtaining a Bankers' Evidence Act order from the stipendiary magistrate. The purpose of this was to marry up the dates of payments made by the receivers to the thieves and to compare them with the dates of the thefts. It also went some way to proving that the receivers knew that they were dealing with stolen property, because the price paid would be far less than the worth of the metal.

On Monday 13 February, we arrested a third driver from the factory in Great Hampton Street for the theft of chemicals that were recovered from his home address. It seemed that there would be no end to this enquiry; the more people we spoke to, the more they had something to tell us.

On Saturday 18 February 1978, West Midlands Police braced itself for a major demonstration in Birmingham city centre, after it was discovered that 200 young National Front members intended to hold a meeting at Digbeth Civic Hall. It became known as the 'Battle of Digbeth', as 2,210 police officers faced more than 5,000 demonstrators from opposing factions, with other officers drafted in from Warwickshire, West Mercia and Staffordshire. For the first time, a helicopter was used by police, and numerous police officers were injured.

Andy 'B' was a PC at the time and remembers the event well:

It was a bitterly cold day; I know that because I was stood outside Digbeth Civic Hall, right in front of the main doors, for five hours with 2,000 other officers. 200 National Front were being allowed to exercise their right to hold a meeting inside, while several thousand people outside, who vehemently opposed their views, were hell-bent on getting inside to stop the meeting. The crowd began to get frustrated, because they couldn't get through, and a couple of hundred of them decided to start throwing bricks and other bits of street furniture in our direction. This was in the days before officers were supplied with full protective riot gear. We didn't draw our 'pegs' (truncheons) – we just had to stand there and take it.

The day was saved when other officers were deployed from inside the building, who ran out with shields and tackled the rioters head-on. They were a pretty scary bunch of officers and very effective. They just piled into the troublemakers and dragged some away. I had only been on the streets for eighteen months and, although I had been in a few scuffles on the beat, this was something a bit different. It was a sign of things to come when Birmingham was hit by riots a few years later.

Dave Cross retired as a constable in West Midlands Police in 1995 and since then has been the keeper of West Midlands Police museum. He was on duty that day and recalls,

I was the local beat officer for High Street Deritend and was posted to traffic duties, as some of the roads were cordoned off. It was a particularly cold day, and one of the car showrooms opened up the canteen so that we could keep warm with cups of tea.

At one point, the rioters broke away from the demonstration at Digbeth Civic Hall and started making their way towards the city centre. A radio message came over the air, telling all available officers to make their way towards Digbeth. He sounded in a bit of a panic. Another officer was on traffic duty directly opposite the Civic Hall, and she was wearing a yellow fluorescent jacket. As she responded to the call, she came across some rioters and was forced to take refuge temporarily in a pub nearby. She told me afterwards that she stood out like a 'bloody walking daffodil'. It was a really violent day.

Bryan Davis recalls, 'We were on the shift at Digbeth that day. We were told not to get involved in the demonstration, and to respond to normal calls. However, as it turned out, the violence spread everywhere and it was difficult to avoid it. One of the shift had a house brick thrown at him, which knocked his front teeth out.'

John Swain was the police officer referred to and recounts the story in his own words:

I was on a twelve-hour shift that day, and I was out at about 2.45 p.m. when I saw a couple of hundred of people walking from Moat Lane in the direction of the Civic Hall. There were no police officers with them, so I just followed behind. There was some chanting but no trouble.

I went with them as far as Rea Street, where I saw lines of police cordons. Next thing, a coach appeared behind me and, as it turned a corner, about twenty people started banging on the sides of the coach and bricks were being thrown.

I ran to the coach and, as I got to it, a young lad threw a brick, which hit me full on in the mouth. I grabbed him, despite being in great pain and hung onto him until other officers arrived and took him away to a van. I was covered in blood, and realised that I had lost several front teeth. I was taken to the Accident Hospital, where I was treated and discharged, although I was then off work for a month.

I lost six front teeth and had to have two dentures inserted. I have a daily reminder of this incident, because they sit in a jar of water every night in the bathroom!

I remember that I got told off by my sergeant for getting involved and, for a while, I was working without any front teeth. The person responsible eventually went to Crown Court and tried to say it was a case of mistaken identity. From two yards away, there was no doubt in my mind, or the jury's, and he went to borstal for eighteen months.

In his annual report for 1978, Chief Constable Philip Knights noted,

Quite serious public disorder took place on this occasion when police officers forming part of the cordon outside the Civic Hall were subjected to a barrage of missiles, which not only caused quite severe injuries to several police officers but also necessitated the use of shields and visors ... The majority of demonstrators on this occasion proceeded peacefully but a group of about 300 not only attacked the police but also caused considerable damage to buildings and vehicles.

On Thursday 23 February, we searched a pub in Lawley Street and recovered some chemicals from the same source again. The licensee was initially arrested and bailed, and we then arrested a labourer from the company, who worked on the delivery decks; he was later charged with theft. The licensee was released from his bail on the grounds that there was insufficient evidence to prove the offence of receiving stolen property.

On Wednesday 1 March, we searched yet another address in Sparkbrook, the home address of another deck-man. We recovered stolen property, including from another jewellers in Hockley. Another one was charged, and there was no let up, with several more staff members interviewed in the coming weeks. I seemed to spend half my life in Great Hampton Street and the other half in scrap-metal yards. It was apparent that stolen nickel had been circulating around a number of metal dealers, and we seized some more registers from a yard in Watery Lane on 21 March.

On Thursday 23 March 1978, we arrested a fifty-seven-year-old security officer from the factory for handling stolen nickel rounds, and then went to Sparkbrook and arrested the owner of some premises who had received chemicals and stolen metal. Both of them were charged and bailed. Five days later, in a follow-up enquiry, we arrested a driver from his home in Maypole and charged him with the theft of scrap metal valued at £2,000. I was fast becoming an expert on scrap-metal registers and, while many of the entries contained false details, if you did enough research you could generally come up with a positive lead. All this time, and we were still looking for the main receivers for the stolen nickel rounds.

2

DEALING WITH STREET CRIME IN BIRMINGHAM CITY CENTRE

Our breakthrough came on Wednesday 26 April, after visiting yet more scrap dealers in the Smethwick area, when we found lines of enquiry in relation to two missing loads of nickel rounds from the factory in Great Hampton Street. Later that day, I went with Neil to a substantial scrap-metal dealer in the Hockley area, where we saw the owner, who was a jovial individual, and also a leading Freemason. We were pleasant but formal and, after finding evidence relating to the missing load of nickel rounds stolen on 9 November 1977, we seized the scrap-metal registers and left. There were no smiles on the way out, just a few serious looks exchanged between the yard foreman and the owner.

We then went straight to another scrap yard in Aston and seized yet more registers relating to another load on 6 July 1977, which had been sold to them by the younger brother of the dealer in Hockley. It was all looking very interesting and the timeframes were right. We started following the upwards chain of sale of the metal, which involved enquiries in Rotherham as we continued to build our case.

On Wednesday 3 May, we went to a scrap yard in Great Hampton Row and arrested the younger brother. He wasn't exactly cooperative, and we police-bailed him later that day, pending further enquiries.

On Tuesday 9 May, Neil and I went back to the scrap yard in Hockley and arrested the yard-foreman on suspicion of receiving the stolen property. He was police-bailed. The next day, we went back for the fifty-four-year-old elder brother, the owner of the yard. Despite his denials, we charged him later that day with receiving stolen nickel rounds, knowing them to be stolen, and bailed him. His arrest attracted interest from a number of police colleagues, and I speculated at the time that Freemasonry was the common link, although of course I could not confirm that. We were all polite with each other, but I was under no obligation to discuss the case with officers who had no connection to it.

On Friday 19 May, we took no further action against the yard foreman we had on bail but re-arrested the younger brother, fifty years of age, and charged him with receiving 900 kg of stolen nickel rounds. He denied everything.

On 31 May, I spent the day supporting the CID at Dudley Road police station, dealing with four men for the rape of a fifteen year-old girl.

On Tuesday 6 June at 10.00 a.m., I attended my central promotion board at Lloyd House police headquarters, with an assistant chief constable and two chief superintendents. I hated interview boards, but it had to be done and I came away feeling okay about things. My board report subsequently stated that I was now ready for promotion.

On Thursday 8 June, seven of those arrested in relation to the original thefts at the factory in Great Hampton Street were committed to Birmingham Crown Court for trial. We were not quite done yet, however; on Saturday 10 June, Neil and I went to Northfield and arrested yet another employee, who was a general hand. Then we were off to Nechells to arrest another employee, a storeman, and, in the afternoon, we completed the 'hat trick' with the arrest of a machine-operator from Small Heath, who had stolen property valued at £500.

All three were charged and bailed. These arrests brought an end to what had been a long and often frustrating enquiry, but it was also a very satisfying result. We just had all the paperwork to do and many more witness statements to take.

On Tuesday 13 June 1978, I presented myself before the deputy chief constable and was told that I was to be promoted to uniform sergeant and posted to the F Division, which covered Birmingham city centre. Two weeks later, on a Monday, I turned up for my first official parade at Digbeth police station. Officers were always required to stand up when the inspector entered the parade room, and appointments, in the form of pocket books and truncheons were produced, and hats worn. The officers were deployed individually to fixed beats on foot, or in cars on areas that were normally double-manned.

I stood there, acutely aware of some very new and shiny stripes on my arms, and watched it all with interest. The other two sergeants were both long in service. One of them, who normally stayed inside and did the radio, could barely hide his contempt at seeing someone so young bearing the same rank as him. He had a military bearing and a very polished pair of shoes. The second was more pleasant, but initially kept his distance.

Shortly after starting, I did a week of nights and was appointed as the custody sergeant. I sat there at a big desk in the front office at 10.00 p.m. and waited. Within fifteen minutes, the outside door crashed open and in came two officers struggling violently with a drunk. More crashing and banging ensued as they progressed through the office and into the cell block. Fifteen minutes later, the door crashed open again and another prisoner, with accompanying officers, came hurtling through, shouting and screaming. This was normality and I loved it.

The trick was to stay calm, or at least to look calm, and to give officers time to sort themselves out. With more than a dozen cells, there was plenty of room and the more the merrier as far as I was concerned. During the early hours, when things had quietened down, and people had stopped banging on their cell doors, there would be a row of shoes lined up outside in the cell passageway to signify occupancy. Meanwhile, my desk would be covered in large white paper custody records, on which I had to laboriously monitor each prisoner's movements.

Richard Bryant retired from the West Midlands Police as a superintendent in 1994. In 1978 he was the detective inspector at Digbeth police station and has provided a summary of what it was like to serve in the CID at that time:

Stories often circulated among officers, some totally true, and others not quite so. I remember one story in particular wherein a CID team went to an address in Lee Bank, just outside the city centre. They were certain that stolen property was being stored at the address.

They knocked the door, and were confronted by a woman with a cigarette dangling from her mouth, who said words to the effect of, 'You can't come into my house without a search warrant.' Even from the doorway, the officers were able to observe that the house was filthy, with old bikes propped up against walls, rubbish scattered everywhere, and dog mess on the floors. An experienced CID officer retorted, 'Madam. You are under arrest. This is not a house – it is a hovel. Now step aside!' They went on to recover a large amount of stolen property.

The CID officer was renowned for his skills in the witness box and probationer constables were often sent to sit in court to watch the 'master' at work. He knew exactly who to look at, and when, and used his spectacles like a prop to gain emphasis on particular evidential points.

Violence in pubs and clubs was pretty routine in the city centre, although the police had a good relationship with door staff at these establishments, and were often able to sort things out quite quickly. You never knew when it was going to happen, and much of it was drink-fuelled.

On one occasion, I recall dealing with a fight at a small restaurant at the back of Deritend. Members of a very well-known criminal family were in there eating and, for no reason at all other than an unwanted glance, or an innocent word exchanged, they started attacking another group who were also having a meal. The place was wrecked and chairs were broken up, with the legs used as weapons. All of the victims were hospitalised and we managed to arrest four or five of the main instigators, who were really nasty pieces of work.

On one occasion in the late seventies, I dealt with a nasty murder, which occurred in the Sherlock Street area of Highgate. Once again, it was alcohol-fuelled and involved a dispute between two men who knew each other. After having a disagreement on the telephone over family issues, they arranged to meet up. As one arrived in his car, the other attacked him with a sword and murdered him.

The suspect was arrested that evening, and I was called out to oversee the investigation. I did the interview and the file for the director of public prosecutions, and the case was subsequently heard at Stafford Crown Court. I remember at one stage that there was a disturbance in the court, as the evidence was being presented to the judge and jury. One of the barristers had the photographs of the murder victim open on the desk in front of him, and people in the public balcony above could see the horrific injuries that he had suffered and were really upset. The defendant was convicted of murder.

During the same period, street robberies were a real problem for us. One day I was sitting in my office, and an officer who was attached to the CID came in. He was well known for his somewhat eccentric behaviour and said words to the effect of, 'We have had an old lady robbed in the markets but the good news is that some of the market traders managed to detain the robber and recover the purse. The bad news is that he is dead!'

It seems that a number of market traders had chased and restrained the robber and, in so doing, one of them had held him around the neck until the arrival of the police. We subsequently held two post-mortems at Newton Street to try to establish the cause of death, one by a Home Office pathologist, and another by an independent pathologist to ensure transparency and openness. We didn't wear much in the way of protective clothing in those days, and stood next to the pathologists while they did their work. I seem to recall that it was my wedding anniversary but I didn't make it home to celebrate.

It transpired that a small bone in his neck had been broken while being restrained. I completed a file for the director of public prosecutions after interviewing the market traders concerned, but it was subsequently decided that no one would face prosecution over the death and that their actions had been justifiable in the circumstances.

Football violence was another regular feature as both home and away fans followed a well-worn route from Birmingham city centre on their way to matches with Birmingham City FC at St Andrew's football ground. On one occasion, I dealt with the death of a Chelsea fan who had been assaulted in Digbeth High Street before a game. After being punched by a Birmingham fan, he had fallen back against a bus and then fallen under it, receiving fatal head injuries. I considered trying to get the match called off but, in any event, we managed to arrest the person responsible within a few hours.

This tragic death was reported in the media as having happened on 25 September 1978, about thirty minutes before the kick-off. The dead man, aged about twenty years, was on his way to the match with a fellow Chelsea supporter. Both men were described as being black. They became involved in a scuffle with about eight Birmingham City fans, who grabbed the scarf belonging to the dead man's friend. There was pushing and punching and the man who died was pushed into the road, where he fell under the rear wheels of the bus.

Dave Cross has his own memories of public order incidents in and around Birmingham City Centre at about the same time.

The first time I ever got assaulted was when I tried to break up a fight outside the Grand Hotel in Colmore Row among a group of lads. Somebody's fist connected with my nose, and I finished up covered in blood, but you learnt to just get on with it, as such incidents were routine.

Ask any police officer whether they would rather deal with a drunk male or a drunk female, and most will say give me a male any time. One night I was on duty near the city centre, when a call came in of a disturbance. I walked around the corner and came face to face with a crowd of up to forty people, gathered around two rather large drunken women who were having a fight. Both of them were stripped off to the waist and the crowd were really enjoying the spectacle, which I have to say was a sight to see! I called up for assistance and two vans turned up; we put one in each.

On another occasion I remember coming across a man beating a bus driver up at the side of the road. He was holding the driver against a wall and I swear that his feet were not touching the ground. I called for assistance, got my truncheon out and hit the attacker twice, two hard whacks to the back of each leg, and he went down.

At this stage, I was joined by a bus inspector and we sat on the prisoner until other officers arrived. When we searched him at the police station, he was found to have £680 on him. He was charged with assault and appeared at court next morning.

I was in court when he pleaded guilty, and it was pointed out that he had an outstanding default maintenance order for the sum of £600 against him. The magistrates' clerk had a copy of the large blue charge sheet in front of him, and I pointed out the amount of money he was in possession of. After some discussions, the magistrates fined him £80 for the assault, and ordered him to pay this fine and the DMO forthwith.

Ada Howles, a former police constable in the West Midlands Police who was also stationed at Digbeth, recalls some of his public order experiences in the city centre during the seventies:

It was often complete mayhem. I can remember on one occasion attending a huge fight at a club opposite the Locarno in Hurst Street, where someone was stabbed. It was so bad that as I was about to go in, my partner dragged me back and told me to wait for backup.

On another occasion, I was on night duty when, at about 11.30 p.m., we got called to another stabbing in Hill Street. Arsenal had been playing Villa that day and, when we got to the scene, we found a Villa fan lying on the pavement, with his legs stretched out in the roadway. He was bleeding heavily from a stab wound to his right leg and I had to remove the leather belt on my trousers to use as a tourniquet until the ambulance arrived. We put a call out for observations for Arsenal fans and, lo and behold, at about 2.00 a.m. an officer found a coach in Masshouse car park with fifty Arsenal fans on board but no coach driver. We arrested them all and

I drove the coach to Digbeth where they were lodged all over the station for the CID to deal with.

Another incident that sticks in my mind was when a PC on the shift, who was fairly new in service and had the nickname 'OJO', was beaten up in Hurst Street after he stopped four men who had been drinking in an Irish pub. He shouted for assistance and, when we got to him, we found him barely conscious lying in the middle of the road. We managed to bring him round a bit before the ambulance arrived and got a brief description of his attackers; in particular we knew that one of them had been bleeding from a mouth wound. We did a search of the area and, while we were checking vehicles in a car park in Pershore Street, near to the markets, we found a guy hiding under a lorry. The tell-tale blood on his mouth was enough for us and he was arrested.

Richard Bryant recalls an event on 18 November 1978:

Demonstrations and public order events were also a regular feature of policing in Birmingham city centre and I remember one lighter moment when we were required to provide protection for the visit of the Indian prime minister, Indira Gandhi, to the Albany Hotel. An officer called Bill Thomas was posted to the service lift to make sure it was kept secure from rival factions, who were demonstrating outside. While in the lift, the catering manager for the hotel asked him if he was okay for food. Bill presented his packed lunch and the catering manager promptly arranged for a table to be put into the lift and for Bill to be served with a full-course meal, including wine!

At the end of the year, the force and community in the West Midlands were reminded of the threat of terrorism when, on 17 December 1978, a bomb exploded in the centre of Coventry. A significant amount of explosives caused damage to shops, although no persons were injured, and the incident was linked to similar attacks in other major cities.

John Swain was a member of the Special Patrol Group from late 1978 for three years and recalls his own public-order experiences:

I was on C Serial at Bradford Street and always sat next to the sliding side door when we were in the van. It was my seat, and I wanted to be first out when there was a prisoner to be had. During my time on the SPG, I literally arrested scores of people for football-related violence. I wouldn't tolerate any misbehaviour and had my fair share of knocks. I once got hit by a flying bottle and had my nose broken. One tactic that we often used in the grounds was to form an empty 'box' in the crowd with four lines of officers, into which we would take prisoners if we made arrests.

On one occasion, I remember arresting a lad from Liverpool for picking up road cones and throwing them at the opposition. Next season I was involved in policing Liverpool fans again when, lo and behold, I saw a youth kicking someone. It turned out to be the same offender.

At Birmingham City games at St Andrew's, we routinely came out of the ground covered in spit. On one occasion I was trying to clear a gangway with another officer in the Tilton end when a lad pushed another guy on top of me. Thinking that I was being attacked, my colleague grabbed the first person, I grabbed the second, and then all hell broke loose with a massive fight, as supporters tried to attack us. Loads of officers piled in and we finished up making about twenty-five arrests.

During another game at St Andrew's, I was again standing in a line of officers in the Tilton end, when one officer was struck with a dart. Next thing, a coke can came flying through the air and I put my hand up to stop it, hitting the officer next to me. Unfortunately, I just succeeded in knocking his helmet off instead, at which point he was struck on the head by part of a brick. Needless to say, I didn't get any thanks for my efforts!

In 1978, the force dealt with a total of forty-five violent deaths, thirty-nine of which were recorded as murder cases, and six as manslaughter. Three of those cases remained unsolved, including that of father-of-three, Bill Norman Cowie Simpson, a forty-five-year-old man shot dead at point-blank range in his workshop in Small Heath. A .38 revolver was established as being the murder weapon, delivering a single bullet to the head, and the killer set fire to the victim's body afterwards. Across the area, a total of 151,838 crimes were recorded during the year, of which more than 5,000 were of offences of wounding.

On a lighter note, at 2.00 p.m. on Saturday 24 March 1979, we organised a sponsored bed-push and completed six laps of Cannon Hill Park in a converted bed frame with wheels on it, borrowed from the ambulance repair depot in Sparkbrook, and purpose-built for the occasion. The press photographs taken beforehand were taken with us in uniform, but on the day we turned up in fancy dress. I was the comedy character Frank Spencer from *Some Mothers Do 'Ave 'Em*, wearing a red beret and a raincoat. The idea was to raise £700 for equipment that we wanted to buy for the ICU at Birmingham Accident Hospital. We started off from the boat house by the lake to the sound of bagpipes played by the West Midlands Police pipe band. Miss ATV 1979, Debbie Shore, newscaster Helen Piddock, and actor Gerald Harper were present, together with the Deputy Chief Constable Maurice Buck and Assistant Chief Constable Coles.

The May issue of the *Beacon Force* newspaper showed a photograph of all the celebrities and the deputy chief constable seated on the bed frame, being pushed along by several male officers in nurse's uniforms, who had rather hairy legs. It was great fun, got great press and a lot of smiles from the public – B Unit had done well.

The first ever Force Election Control room was set up in April to monitor security arrangements for the whole of the general election campaign in the West Midlands. While open until the end of district election counts on 4 May 1979, the team dealt with over 1,000 phone calls, and monitored 143 general election candidates, 616 local council candidates, and 1,508 polling stations.

The general election was held on 3 May 1979 to elect 635 members to the House of Commons. The Conservative party, led by Margaret Thatcher, ousted the Labour government, led by James Callaghan, with a parliamentary majority of forty-four seats. There is no doubt that the Conservative campaign had been helped by a number of industrial disputes during the winter of 1978/79, which became known as the 'Winter of Discontent'.

Margaret Thatcher was to become something of an iconic figure on the world stage and nationally – and, more specifically, in police circles, where the majority of officers at that time saw the 'Iron Lady' as being a huge supporter of the police.

Also during April, Princess Margaret officially opened the new force control room at Bournville police station. During a tour of the police station, she met WPC Mandy Elcock, who had been awarded the Queen's Commendation for Brave Conduct the previous year for scaling 40 feet of scaffolding around a building in Edmund Street, Birmingham city centre, and stopping a man throwing himself off.

At the beginning of 1979, the sub-divisional superintendent at Digbeth had set up a unit consisting of a uniform sergeant and four police constables. It was a sort of halfway house between uniform and CID work, and its terms of reference were 'to pay attention to special crime problems such as persistent robberies, burglaries, thefts of and from motor vehicles, shoplifting and purse snatching. Also special public order situations at licensed premises, shopping centres and other premises'. It was called the Digbeth Special Unit – the DSU for short.

On Monday 4 June, having done just under a year of shifts in uniform, I was appointed as the sergeant in charge of the Digbeth Special Unit. I was sorry to say goodbye to B Unit, but that was the way of the police service. I can only describe the next sixteen months as manic but memorable. It was also the only time I was deliberately assaulted while on duty during the whole of my forty-two years of policing.

During the course of the first week, I spent two days at Birmingham Crown Court with the younger of the two brothers arrested for receiving stolen nickel. He pleaded not guilty but was found guilty and sentenced to twelve months' imprisonment, suspended for two years. He wasn't happy about it and expressed his feelings, but the reality was that the evidence against him was strong and he just didn't like the fact that he had been caught.

The following week, I went with Neil to Henley-in-Arden Crown Court for the trial of the elder brother. It was a strange place to have a crown court, and was very different to Birmingham. He also pleaded not guilty and, after a trial lasting four days, the jury agreed with him. The trial judge, in his summing up, likened the offence of receiving stolen property to a horse race over fences; you first of all had to establish that the property was stolen. If you could prove that, you were up and over the first fence and onto the next fence. Then you had to prove that the person had taken the property into his possession; up and over the next fence. Then you had to prove that at the time the person knew or believed that the property was stolen. This analogy clearly appealed to the jury, who came from the local rural community. I don't know which fence we fell at, but I never took these things personally. It was my job to put the case before the courts and from there it was out of my hands.

Neil and I had an ice cream on the high street in the warm afternoon sunshine and then went home. None of the evidence Neil and I had given had been disputed but, as soon as any judge directs a jury that they need to reach a verdict based 'beyond reasonable doubt', the pendulum of justice almost always tips in favour of the defendant.

Back in Birmingham city centre, the Bull Ring shopping centre, the Indoor Market, and the Tennant Street areas all became my regular haunts. The Bull Ring attracted gangs who intimidated shoppers and were involved in thefts and robberies. The Indoor Market was a haven for purse thieves and men who liked to get too physically close to female customers, and Tennant Street and the side-streets were a magnet for car thieves. We were spoilt for choice and not short of work by any means.

Towards the end of the month, I was out with an officer called Keith when we arrested a thirty-seven-year-old man employed as a jewellery-setter in Hockley, in relation to the theft of nearly £3,000 worth of jewellery. The following week, we arrested a couple of traders from the Rag Market on suspicion of receiving stolen property from the proceeds of this theft. Keith had a quirky sense of humour and needed to be held on a tight leash, so to speak, but he was an exceptional investigator and could virtually smell a thief from 100 yards.

On Tuesday 26 June, I met Chip again. I had not seen him for a while but he promised information in relation to drugs offences and city-centre crime. Every informant had a 'shelf life' and eventually that rich thread of information would be broken, so I wasn't overly optimistic.

In June 1979, thirteen letter bombs either exploded, or were defused, at post offices in the Birmingham area. Fortunately, only minor injuries were caused by those that exploded. The incidents necessitated protracted searches being undertaken at postal sorting offices, including one in Birmingham city centre.

On the evening of Friday 29 June, we received information on the two good-class burglars, whom we had been looking for since I started on the DSU. I liaised with the detective inspector and sent a teleprinter message off to the police in Lincolnshire. The two suspects were having a holiday in a caravan at Skegness, and we had a good idea which caravan they were in, even though the area boasted thousands of them all lined up in neat rows.

They were arrested on the next day and, on Sunday 1 July, I came in on my day off and went with three other officers to Skegness police station to pick them up. They were annoyed to see us, probably more so when we left their girlfriends to finish their holiday. By the time we got back, it was late, so we lodged the suspected burglars in the cells overnight to interview them the following morning. The twenty-year-old admitted serious woundings at Romeo & Juliet's nightclub, and we went on to investigate a stream of dwelling house burglaries in the Bournville, Alvechurch and Warwick areas, as well as a number of outstanding warrants. They were both charged and kept in custody.

The chief superintendent from Redditch police station later summed up the result:

> On 1 July 1979 two persons were arrested for serious offences of assault. Their arrest eventually resulted in the detection of fourteen offences of burglary at good-class dwelling houses. The value of property stolen was in the region of £19,000 and a number of persons were arrested in the West Midlands area for handling some of the stolen property. As a result, property to the value of £4,000 was recovered. Both defendants appeared at Birmingham Crown Court. One went to prison for three years and one for thirty-one months. One of them also later went on to admit twenty thefts of motor vehicles. They were in effect a 'mini crime wave'.

Around this time I started to take more of an interest in the various sub-cultures and groups frequenting Birmingham city centre. Skinheads were the first group that we started to engage with, and I spent time particularly in the areas around the Crown pub in Hill Street, the Jester pub in Bristol Street, the Viking pub in Smallbrook Queensway, and Manzoni Gardens.

The Jester became one of the first openly 'gay' pubs in Birmingham City Centre, as did the Viking. The regulars all knew that we were police officers if we paid a visit, but we were generally left to our own devices and these places were good sources of information. The Crown pub had a lot of connections to the music industry, particularly in the sixties and seventies, and was regarded by many as key to the birth of 'heavy metal'. Groups like Black Sabbath started life there; the premises were also frequented by members of Led Zeppelin, Punk Band GBH, The Who, Duran Duran, Thin Lizzy, The Move, and even UB40. In 1962, Ian Campbell recorded the country's first live folk album at the Crown, and it was the place where Ozzy Osbourne faced a crowd for the first time.

History has it that, during the First World War, corpses were stored in the pub's cellars before being removed to a nearby church, and that visiting judges used to stay in the upper rooms when sitting at the Law Courts.

During my time, the place had seen much better days but I became a regular visitor to the Crown pub, and Keith and I got to know the regulars and even arrested a borstal absconder in there on one occasion. In later years, it was to become the haunt of Birmingham City's 'Zulu Warrior' football hooligans.

On 10 August, we arrested another really good-class burglar, whose family originated from my old area in Ladywood. A couple of days after that, the whole team was engaged in the arrest of an offender, who admitted more than 100 offences of theft from motor vehicles. This led us to a suspected receiver and, on Wednesday 15 August, we executed a search warrant at a second-hand dealer's premises in Smethwick and arrested the thirty-year-old proprietor.

We emptied his shop and started the laborious task of checking property against stolen lists and reported crimes. A chore but it paid off a month later, when we made another arrest for burglary. A lot of this work involved liaising with senior CID managers and my old friends at No. 4 RCS. The car thief eventually got sent to prison for three years.

At the beginning of October 1979, I travelled with Clive, another member of the DSU, to pick up a burglar we had been after, who had been arrested in Abergele in North Wales. After a fifteen-hour day, we charged him and kept him in custody. Clive was a young but very shrewd officer, who later went on to become a senior CID investigator. Our burglar eventually admitted eighty-three offences, and was sentenced to two years and three months in prison.

As autumn was upon us, different problems started to emerge in the city centre and we needed to respond to them. On Monday 19 November 1979, while out with another officer from the team, who I will call 'John', we received a report of a street robbery at the Midland Red bus station, in Edgbaston Street next to the Bull Ring. It was one of the country's first fully enclosed bus stations and, on the *Birmingham History Forum* years later, 'sistersue61' described the atmosphere there: 'Oh yes, the Midland Red Bus Station. I recall that well, complete with the resident tramp in the corner who was frequently moved on!! It was a bit scary at night though, if you were by yourself, and health and safety would have a field day with the fumes today ... '

John was a tall, muscular guy, who was very handy to have around when you were wrestling with people, but he needed firm supervision. He eventually parted company with the police service and, in later years, served a prison sentence after being convicted of serious offences.

We managed to find and arrest the offender, a fifteen-year-old absconder, who was from an approved school in Hereford. He was interviewed in the presence of a social worker and he was kept in custody overnight to appear at the Juvenile Court in Newton Street, a place I had become very familiar with over the years. He pleaded guilty next day and was remitted to Hereford to be sentenced on other matters.

Three days later, we acted on some information we had received regarding stolen vehicles being altered in a garage in Alum Rock. The norm was for false plates to be put on, and for chassis plates and engine numbers to be changed, with a paint respray for good measure. We recovered some property from one stolen car and then found another stolen car, which had plates on it relating to a JCB.

Initially we arrested a male and a female. Another two arrests from the same family, who had Irish connections, were then made and eventually three out of the four were charged. This was organised crime and we brought the Force Stolen Vehicle Squad in to assist. At one point, we also discovered some stolen property from the factory in Great Hampton Street – there was no getting away from the place!

One of the complainants in this case was an Irishman, who was extremely pleased to get his property back. Two of the team, including John, went out one day to get a witness statement from him. He showed his gratitude by plying them with whisky and, in due course, I had a phone call to go and rescue them. I took another member of the team, who lived in single-quarters at Digbeth, with me and we found the two officers very drunk. I was livid and, while my priority was to sort the immediate problem out, they knew that there would be consequences.

We took them both back to Digbeth and locked them in the officers' single-quarters at Digbeth for several hours to sober up. Just as we were guiding them through the station and up the stairs to the accommodation, we narrowly missed the superintendent, who was not known for his sense of humour. In a few moments of madness they could have destroyed all of our efforts and reputation.

Their behaviour was inexcusable and, about four weeks later, John returned to uniform duties 'due to the near completion of his attachment and a shortage of drivers on his unit'.

3

SKINHEADS, MODS, BIKERS, PUNKS AND PUBLIC ORDER

I had done my research: 'Skinheads' were the youngest age group, but adopted intimidation tactics by virtue of the size of numbers that they could put out. Numbers fluctuated weekly, depending on which football team was playing at home. They were responsible for the majority of disturbances, offences of assault and minor robberies in the city centre. They rarely gathered for long in one place and, at the first sign of police action, ran away, which made it more difficult to make arrests. They frequented the Crown in Hill Street and the Rail Bar on New Street station, as well as the Bull Ring Open Market and Edgbaston Street.

The 'Punks' were much smaller in numbers, and did not cause a great deal of trouble. However, due to their exhibitionist tendencies, they tended to attract attention to themselves anyway. At times they aligned themselves with the skinheads and frequented the same areas of the city centre.

The 'Mods' were still emerging as a group identity, and initially caused no major problems. In December 1979, they initially aligned themselves with skinheads but subsequently distanced themselves from them.

The 'Teddy Boys' were a group of about twenty-five seen every Saturday, together with a small number of females under sixteen years of age. On their own, their numbers were not sufficient to cause serious trouble; however, when grouped together with 'Bikers', they became much more aggressive.

Between 2.00 p.m. and 5.00 p.m. on Saturdays, they could be found at either The Hole in the Wall in Dale End, The Golden Eagle in Hill Street, or Bogart's in New Street. They also congregated around Reddington's Rare Records shop in Moor Street Subway.

Reddington's was a veritable institution for lovers of vinyl records, who would spend hours browsing through box upon box of second-hand records looking for long lost classics. The business was owned by Dan Reddington, who, more than three decades later, sold his entire remaining stock of 75,000 albums and singles for just £1 each.

The same group of bikers, twenty-five strong, were seen every Saturday. Numbers were sometimes swelled by groups from outside the city. While they did not class themselves as Hell's Angels, they sometimes operated on a similar 'chapter' system and were potentially capable of causing serious problems. Drink could play a contributory part in their behaviour.

Steve Burrows, who retired as a chief superintendent, has first-hand knowledge of biker activity in Birmingham during this period and recalls,

The Hell's Angels of USA wore what were known as top and bottom 'rockers', which included the words 'Hell's Angels MC', a death's head symbol and the name of their chapter at the bottom. You had to be officially sanctioned by the Hell's Angels to wear these symbols and were liable to a 'stomping' if found to be wearing them without approval.

More locally, there were 'Bikers' and 'Greasers', who generally wore sleeveless denim jackets and leather jackets, with perhaps one or two pairs of trousers, one of which would probably be pretty dirty. They formed biker clubs centred around clubs and pubs, so, for instance, there was the 'Horse & Jockey Motorcycle Club', which was twenty strong and met at the Horse & Jockey pub in Sparkhill. It was usual to have nicknames. The culture of Bikers is to shock people without much thought. They do not want to be 'Norman Normal'. There were even 'posh' Bikers, who wore good-quality leathers.

In the seventies, there was already a very strong group of Hell's Angels based in Wolverhampton. They regularly came into conflict with a group known as the 'Cycle Tramps', who originally had some connections in Hay Mills and at the Speedwell pub in Tyseley. At some point, they became one of the biggest groups in Birmingham. Another group known as the '69 Club' used the Royal Oak pub in Hockley Heath as a meeting place, and also came into conflict with the Cycle Tramps. Yet another group emerged, which became known as the 'United Bikers of Great Britain'.

Violence was endemic among these groups, as inter-group rivalry erupted into street battles on occasion.

During this period, the Motorcycle Action Group was also formed, which sometimes attracted thousands of bikers to rallies and demonstrations. On one occasion hundreds of bikers rode through Birmingham city centre, protesting about new laws on the wearing of crash helmets.

The biker culture was not new to Birmingham city centre and, even in the early seventies, retired BTP Detective Constable Ian Mabbett recalls a robbery he dealt with, involving a group of six that he arrested single-handedly:

> I was on patrol in uniform on New Street station at the top of the steps leading up from Station Street, when I saw a youth covered in blood, who had been kicked and punched in the face. We looked over the balcony and he pointed out the attackers, all wearing leather jackets and jeans, who had robbed him of just fifty pence. I went after them and stopped them outside the Crown pub, where I drew my truncheon and ordered them to stand facing the wall with their hands against it. Fortunately, they did as they were told and other officers arrived after I radioed for assistance. We recovered three lengths of motorcycle chains nearby, which they had threatened the victim with.

The public-order problem on Saturdays in particular revolved around an average of some 200 youths in total from these groupings, and it was our job to sort them out. Normally public-order problems were dealt with by officers in uniform, but I decided that we needed to get up close to them, so we would stay in plain clothes. It was a risky strategy, but I had confidence in the team and our ability to control situations, even if outnumbered. Any arrests were to result in immediate handcuffing for safety reasons, and we would frog-march them down to Digbeth police station as fast as we could, which would be quicker than waiting for a police car to pick us up, and also helped to avoid crowds gathering. Speed and surprise were essential. I was also keen to maximise on media opportunities, and my plan was to bail those arrested to specific court dates so that we could highlight the problems, as well as, importantly, what we were doing to address them.

On Saturday 15 December 1979, I booked on duty at 9.15 a.m. and went to court with a prisoner we had arrested the day before. I came back and briefed the team and we went out at 1.00 p.m. to cover the areas where our troublemakers met. Just over an hour later, we made two arrests for threatening behaviour in the Rag Market, lodged them, and went straight back out.

At 2.35 p.m., I was with three of the team in the Outdoor Market area and observed a group making their way towards the glass doors leading into the Indoor Market. As they were about to enter, some of the group pounced on a young mod, and started punching and kicking him. Everyone surged through the doors, as he tried to escape from his attackers, and down some steps into the market, which was crammed with stalls and shoppers.

We ran after them and, as we did so, I ran through one set of doors and straight into the screaming melee. My team went through the adjacent set of doors and, in that instant, we became separated among the crowds of ordinary shoppers. I jumped on one of the attackers, shouting 'Police' as loud as I could. He lashed out, punching me. We fell to the floor in the struggle, and I hung on with him on top of me. I was now the centre of attention, with various boots flying in my direction. Fortunately, my prisoner, a twenty-two-year-old from Quinton, took most of the kicks. A Markets police officer ran forward and was also assaulted.

After what seemed an age, the crowd parted and my team seemed to fly over the heads of the attackers; four more arrests were made. The rest scattered, as uniform officers arrived. We had our five prisoners and, after a quick check-up with Doctor Wilson at the General Hospital for bruising to my back, we spent the next few hours documenting them.

Secretly, I think the team felt a bit guilty that I had got a kicking, but it was not their fault and, apart from some initial banter, I chose not to give them a hard time over it. My attacker, who later got sent to prison for a month, kept apologising profusely and showed real regret for his actions. I had been involved in many scrapes when struggling to arrest people but this was the first, and the last time, that I was actually deliberately assaulted during my police career.

We had made a start, and this was reflected in media coverage over the next couple of days. One headline read, 'Policeman hurt, 18 arrests in battle – Gangs fight it out among shoppers', and a reporter described events of the day as follows:

A security man and a police sergeant were injured and eighteen youths were arrested as gang violence plagued Christmas shoppers in one of Birmingham's Indoor Markets. Mothers with children, pensioners and families out buying presents became embroiled in the disturbance at the Bull Ring Indoor Market. At its height it involved as many as 150 youths, 20 West Midlands policemen, 20 security men and five corporation markets department security men. It was the second week that gangs of youths – many dressed in the jeans and jackets of Hell's Angels – caused trouble in the area. Last week stalls were overturned and produce scattered as fighting spread. Yesterday's trouble flared when a gang of 50 youths began assaulting a 'mod' in the Indoor Market. Police Sergeant Michael Layton and a member of the market's police security force were knocked to the ground and kicked in the back. Other policemen moved in and made further arrests. A senior police officer said later, 'The two men who were kicked were not seriously injured and have remained on duty. Unfortunately it is a fact that we do get this kind of violence in the city centre particularly between rival gangs.'

On Saturday 29 December, we were back out again in the Edgbaston Street area, looking for troublesome skinheads and punks. We were in the right place at the right time and made five arrests for burglary at a restaurant. After lodging them in the cells, we went out and made an arrest for threatening behaviour in Corporation Street, followed by yet another one an hour later in Station Street.

On New Year's Eve, we were out again in the afternoon and dispersed a group of fifty skinheads, who had gathered in the Bull Ring shopping centre. Our tactic was to maintain relentless pressure on them until they got fed up of the attention and went away.

Bryan Davis recalls one of his public-order experiences in 1979:

We turned up at a huge fight in John Bright Street and jumped out of the panda car to start separating people. These were not occasions for taking prisoners, as we didn't have the numbers, so people were told in no uncertain terms to 'move on'. We made a mistake in that we left the windows of the police car open. When we got back to it, a number of people had urinated through the windows all over the seats. We didn't repeat that mistake.

In 1979, the force recorded 147,350 crimes, which appeared to show an improving picture, but analysis of the figures seemed to indicate that most of the reductions had taken place during a three-month spell of severe weather conditions at the beginning of the year. The weather was often referred to as the 'policeman's friend'. A total of forty-three crimes of violence involving death were investigated across the force area, with thirty-nine of them classified as murder, and four as manslaughter.

Thirty-seven of the murder cases were detected set against a backdrop of nearly 6,000 recorded offences of wounding. But for the skills of surgeons in hospitals across the county, the fatality figure would no doubt have been much higher.

Between 1 February 1979 and 3 January 1980, the DSU had made a total of 160 arrests, cleared over 300 crimes, and assisted with two major enquiries, one being the wounding, and the other in relation to the offences of sending of letter bombs to Royal Mail offices, where we assisted the search teams.

On Saturday 5 January 1980, the full team went out on plain-clothes patrol again and, within an hour and a half, we made our first arrest for threatening behaviour in the Bull Ring. Within ten minutes, two further arrests in Moat Lane followed for threatening behaviour, or so-called Section 5 Public Order offences, and possession of offensive weapons. We finished the day with two further public-order arrests in Allison Street.

The plain clothes worked a treat, as we were able to stand close by them in some instances as they carried out acts of wanton aggression between opposing groups. The sight of a helmet in the distance always sent them running, but we were able to surprise them and restrain them very quickly before they realised what was really happening. We tolerated no discussions or debate; they were simply handcuffed and removed quickly from the area.

Dave Faulkner recalls his own experiences of dealing with skinheads and punks in 1980:

> The licensee of the Crown pub decided that he wanted to bring skinheads and punks together, so he started organising functions on a Thursday night with skinhead music upstairs and punk music downstairs. We were obliged to start putting a public-order van out to deal with the incidents that inevitably started to happen. We were always outside the pub at 10.30 p.m. to try and shepherd people towards the bus station to get them out of the city centre.
>
> On one particular occasion, I was present when a confrontation started between a punk with a blond Mohican haircut, who was with his girlfriend, and some skinheads. I asked them to move on and the punk told me to 'fuck off'. I told him that he was under arrest and took

his arm, at which point he took a swing at me, trying to punch me, so I punched him first. He was, however, shorter than me and, when he ducked, I broke the little finger of my right hand when I struck the top of his head. I grabbed him and he gave up. The hospital later described it as an 'impact injury'.

I booked the prisoner in and, because he was of 'no fixed abode', he was kept in custody to appear in court, where he pleaded guilty to threatening behaviour and was sent to prison for seven days. Twelve months later I got a cheque from the Criminal Injuries Compensation Board for £100!

On Tuesday 22 January, I made arrangements for my team to work with the Divisional Plain Clothes Unit, who were responsible for vice and licensing issues on the division. They were having problems with males importuning for sexual purposes in the toilets opposite the Crown in Hill Street, and I said we would lend a hand, just to make a change.

Joe Tildesley, the Plain Clothes Unit sergeant, who eventually retired as an inspector, recalls his role at the time:

During this period of time, homosexual men were routinely victims of crime, and were often assaulted and robbed. By virtue of the nature of their activities, they made themselves very vulnerable and we knew that if we didn't do something the problem would only get worse. The toilets in Station Street became known nationally as a meeting point and we kept a very basic card index for people we dealt with, which was often accessed by other forces dealing with attacks on gay people. We dealt with a lot of ostensibly happily married men during our operations, who were usually absolutely beside themselves when they were arrested.

Joe briefed us and we paired off to start the operation. I knew nothing about this type of work, but he made it quite clear that, while we were expected to stand at the urinals and watch what was going on, we should just pretend to urinate and under no circumstances should we remove 'our own person' from the front of our trousers!

Joe recalls:

We learnt from experience and prepared detailed maps of the toilets to use in court. There was always at least four of us, with two inside the toilets at any one time, and we would give it at least fifteen minutes to observe someone to prove an offence of importuning for immoral purposes. It was important to avoid eye contact, and we didn't want the police officer carrying out the observations to be the person importuned, if we could avoid it. This was sometimes difficult, and we had one officer who I will call 'Eddie', who was good looking and seemed to mesmerise some of the punters, so we had to be very careful.

This was my first introduction to 'cottaging', as it was known, and I quickly realised it wasn't going to be my line of work! We all went down the steps to the toilets in pairs. When it was our turn, we walked down and I stood at a urinal. I was faced with a row of men, all of whom were paying particular attention to each other's private parts, masturbating, smiling and nodding. The cubicles behind me were all occupied, and I was already aware that holes had been made both in the doors and the partitions between them, which were big enough for an eye to see through or something else to protrude through. I couldn't control myself; I began laughing and hurried back upstairs into the street.

As time wore on, the teams made arrests and whisked people away. I steeled myself, as a matter of personal pride was at stake, and went back down and occupied a urinal a short distance from a man, in his thirties, whose full name I remember to this day. He started smiling and nodding, and then I was faced with an erect penis, a broader smile, and some very quick hand movements from him. Joe and I judged the moment, and then arrested him for importuning for immoral purposes.

He protested his innocence throughout, and even brought a doctor's note to court to say that it took him longer than normal to urinate, hence the lengthy period of time spent in the toilets. It was an all-female Magistrates' Bench and I cringed as I gave my evidence. He was duly convicted and that was the first, and last time, I ever got involved in that type of work. My team, of course, thought it was hilarious.

These toilets were known as the 'Silver Slipper' and they took their name from the sign over a ballet supply shop and dance studio opposite. It was a large Victorian underground public toilet, which was curved in shape. It was near to the Jaycee Cinema and the Victoria Pub, which was also popular with gay men, and the toilets were popular with the gay community from the sixties through to the eighties. In 1987, the toilets were demolished and filled in.

A colleague, Andy, who worked with me on Operation Red Card in 1987, reflected on his time working with the Plain Clothes Unit:

I was on the Unit in the eighties for six months, and we used to focus on the toilets in Station Street near to the Crown pub, Stephenson Street, Bristol Street and Kennedy Gardens near Snow Hill, looking for people engaged in importuning for immoral purposes.

It could be amusing, but equally sad at the same time, when you realised that some of the people we dealt with would finish up destroying their careers. During my time on the unit, I dealt with a major in the army, who worked in intelligence, a head teacher, and even a train driver who pleaded with us to let him go as he had a train to take out from Snow Hill. One day in Kennedy Gardens, we detained a man who turned out to be an ex-police inspector who had already lost his job, and who said, 'Do you know who I am?' and promptly tried to run off. He was in his late forties and I was well able to catch him.

We also used to execute search warrants at the adult book shops in Hill Street, looking for pornographic books and videos that breached the Obscene Publications Act legislation. It was a joke because, as fast as we took material away to examine it, the shop would be re-stocked again with new deliveries almost immediately.

Another officer, Ada Howles, was also on the Plain Clothes Unit during this period and recalls that things did not always go smoothly:

On one occasion, a member of the team had gone into a sauna to do some observations regarding allegations of prostitution. While he was there, he somehow got a huge splinter the size of a matchstick stuck in his bottom. He had to go to hospital to have it surgically removed.

On another occasion, we did a raid on a Chinese gambling den in Bromsgrove Street and seized a large amount of cash. Derek Bradbury had already smashed the front door in with a sledgehammer; one of the officers heard a noise inside one of the walls and we thought that it was a false wall hiding something. Derek was tasked again with putting a hole in the wall and, as he did so, we found ourselves looking into a cupboard. Suddenly someone in the premises next door opened the cupboard door from their side and we found ourselves staring at each other. It was hilarious.

Joe Tildesley also recalls the sauna incident:

> We were carrying out observations from a church opposite the sauna and
> 'Eddie' had gone in to try to secure evidence that sexual favours were
> being offered. Usually the officers would not be in for more than forty-five
> minutes but, after an hour had passed, I was starting to become anxious.
> Suddenly an ambulance turned up, with blue lights and two-tone horns
> blaring, and pulled up outside the front door of the sauna. Next thing was
> we saw 'Eddie' being taken out of the premises on a stretcher and placed in
> the ambulance, which sped off.
>
> I raced to the Accident Hospital, panicking, and when I got there found
> that somehow 'Eddie' had managed to get a 2-inch-long razor-sharp sliver
> of wood stuck in his bottom while in the massage room. He was in great
> pain and had to have it surgically removed under anaesthetic. I still have
> the piece of wood as a memento and have used it in a lot of 'after-dinner'
> speeches as a prop! We later raided the place, but left 'Eddie' in the office.

Ian Mabbett recalls his experiences as part of a small team of British
Transport Police officers tasked with dealing with problems of men
importuning in the toilets on New Street Station in the late seventies/
early eighties:

> A gay magazine advertised New Street station toilets as being a good
> meeting place and three of us were tasked with sorting the problems
> out. There were about twenty cubicles in the toilets, which were situated
> on the station overbridge, and some of them had holes in the dividing
> panels. Behind all the cubicles was a service corridor and we used to keep
> observations from there by looking through a radiator grill as people went
> into cubicles, sometimes two at a time. As soon as they were in, we would
> shoot round and one would look underneath, while one went over the top
> to corroborate the evidence of what we saw going on.
>
> As fast as we got one prisoner, the toilet attendant would phone up to
> say other people were in the cubicles. I remember that on one occasion
> we arrested a young serving police officer from a county force, and a
> schoolteacher who was charged with attempted buggery on a youngster.
> 'Rent boys', who were paid by men for sex, were rife on the station and we
> were forever ejecting them. Mostly they were compliant but two of them in
> particular were always aggressive towards us.

Bill Rogers, a retired BTP officer, also had similar experiences: 'I took a couple of guys from one of the toilets at Birmingham New Street, who were engaged in sexual activity. One of them was petrified and it turned out that he was a local magistrate.'

During observations for importuning in the toilets at the old Midland Red bus station, Bryan Davis recalls having to use their initiative:

> We only had room for one officer to keep observations by lying on top of a ledge. We used to close one of the toilets off with an 'out of order' sign and another officer would sit on the toilet inside. The two officers would each hold one end of a piece of string and, when two people were seen by the officer on the ledge to go into one cubicle, he would tug twice on the string to alert the other.

On 23 January, I was at Birmingham Magistrates' Court for the appearance of twenty-four of those arrested for public-order incidents in the city centre. The media headlines read, 'Clampdown on Terror Gangs of the Bull Ring' and the reporter's words spoke for themselves:

> Birmingham magistrates cracked down on trouble caused by gangs in the Bull Ring area of the city. Two men were sent to prison, and fines totalling £2,825 were imposed on seven youths. The court heard of running fights between gangs of skinheads, mods, Rockers and Hell's Angels. The chairman, Mr Meyer Palan, told one youth, 'Birmingham city centre is not a wild hick town, and you will have to learn that.'

Mr Anthony Randall, prosecuting, said special police patrols had made the arrests on Saturday afternoons in December and January. Gangs would congregate in the Bull Ring area, and there had been clashes between them in the funfair, and the open and indoor markets. Shoppers were jostled and knocked over by the gangs. Weapons used in the fights included an iron bar, leather belts and a pair of drum sticks. In one incident, a gang of more than 100 skinheads ran across the Bull Ring across the inner ring road, holding up the traffic. As they ran into Corporation Street, shoppers were pushed out of the way and fights broke out with rival factions.

Two of the defendants were sent to prison, another to a detention centre, and one remanded in custody for borstal reports. Others were fined and the remainder bound over to keep the peace in the sum of £100 for twelve months.

The first phase was done, but problems were set to continue for several months. We also started to see an increase in gangs of youths of West Indian descent gathering in the Bull Ring shopping centre and tension between right- and left-wing factions.

On Sunday 27 January 1980, I was in uniform on a reserve support unit for an Irish 'Bloody Sunday' march in Birmingham. This was organised to protest about the deaths of fourteen people in the Bogside area of Derry in Northern Ireland, shot by British soldiers during the course of a demonstration in 1972.

Such occasions had the potential to dramatically increase tension between the large Irish communities resident in Birmingham and factions such as the National Front, who turned out on this date to counter-demonstrate.

A total of 1,500 people gathered in Sparkhill on this day for a march to the Bull Ring. Some 800 police officers were deployed to keep the peace between marchers and rival factions, which included elements of the National Front. There were sporadic outbreaks of disorder and seventeen persons were arrested.

During this period, purse thefts started to get out of control in Birmingham Indoor Market and we turned our attention to this area. The stalls inside acted as magnets for shoppers but also thieves, who saw easy pickings. A few of the counters were occupied by butchers, who would do a 'shout' at certain times of the day, when large crowds would gather to get bargain meat-cuts and the like. Most of the customers were women, but what we quickly realised was that not all of our wrongdoers were purse thieves, and that some of them just wanted the close proximity of women so that they could indecently assault them in the press of people, or masturbate through holes in their trouser pockets.

When purses were stolen, they were often discarded in the gents toilets nearby. Our answer was to drill holes in the ceiling of the toilets so that we could keep observations. Not the nicest of places to frequent, but the job had to be done and, in February 1980, we started to make our presence felt there. We later obtained a 'buzzer' alarm, attached to a length of cord, which we could use when deploying a female officer as a decoy so that, if a thief tried to take her purse, the alarm activated.

On Friday 8 February, we supported Joe and his team in a raid on a 'sauna' in Deritend. Such premises were often just fronts for prostitution rackets. The plain-clothes team used to go in and do test visits to premises for a massage and to obtain a list of the 'extras' on offer before executing warrants. We went in quickly, finding one couple in the process of having sex, and, given my earlier bad experience, I extricated myself from the evidential chain as quickly as I could! Personally at that time I couldn't really see what great harm they were doing; the women were mostly local and the sauna was a safer environment than being on the streets. This was, however, well before the days of human trafficking and organised crime.

Joe Tildesley recalls some of his earlier difficulties in dealing with saunas:

There were five saunas in the city centre, which effectively operated as brothels. To prove this, we had to have evidence of at least two prostitutes operating from the premises. We used to raid them regularly but, actually, there were no powers to close them down and, in most cases, they just changed the name on the door and re-opened.

We had to prove that sexual acts were taking place on the premises, and also needed to find evidence relating to book-keeping. We did one raid that didn't go very well, so I went down to London for a couple of days to see how they did things. You needed to get in there to get the evidence of sexual services being offered when customers got to the massage table, but it was also necessary to do observations from outside to record the number of men entering the premises. This number never matched the records in the sauna and obviously the books would be full of fictitious names.

The owner of the sauna was supposed to pay VAT on their earnings, so obviously it was in their interests not to declare everything. The girls would pay the owner to work there and the average 'massage' was about £20. It was not unusual in some of the saunas for them to have 100 'punters' in one day, so there was big money to be made. Once we started doing things in a more structured manner, we got better results, recovering all sorts of evidence and taking photographs of the raid. We even started taking the floorboards up – you would be surprised what we used to find.

Patrols and arrests continued on Saturday afternoons and, on Tuesday 12 February, we spent time monitoring skinhead groups in Station Street, who were gathering for a concert by the group Madness at the Odeon in New Street. The band, from Camden Town in London, was formed in 1976 and had a cult following in the late seventies and early eighties.

Fifteen of their single records reached the UK top ten charts and fans were desperate to see the 'ska band' live on stage.

On Saturday 16 February, between five of us, we made ten arrests for public-order offences in the space of ninety minutes. It was an unrelenting process, and one which I relished.

Since my arrival on the DSU, the original team members had all moved on to other things and, while the officers I now had were less experienced, they responded well to direction and gave me fewer things to worry about.

Between 15 December 1979 and 1 March 1980, the five officers on the Digbeth Special Unit accounted for the arrest of forty-six persons, aged between fourteen and twenty-four, engaged in public-order incidents in the city centre. The majority were in the seventeen/eighteen-year age bracket, and still we had not totally broken the back of the problem, although our arrest ratios per officer were far higher than any of our uniform colleagues. On Saturday 8 March, we made four more arrests for public-order offences, including one we found with a rubber cosh, for possessing an offensive weapon.

On Tuesday 11 March 1980, Chelsea football fans started to gather in Birmingham for an evening game. Disturbances took place in the city centre, with confrontations between Chelsea fans and local West Indian youths. A serious wounding occurred in Station Street, and four Birmingham City fans aged seventeen, twenty-four, seventeen, and eighteen, were subsequently arrested and charged with causing grievous bodily harm to a nineteen-year-old Chelsea fan from Hackney, London.

We arrested a twenty-year-old Chelsea fan from Southall for a public-order offence in Station Street and, after documenting him, went back to Birmingham shopping centre to monitor the fans returning to New Street station. At 9.40 p.m., a skirmish took place at the top of the escalators leading down to the station, and I finished up in the middle of it. We dispersed the fans but, as we were doing so, I got bitten by an Alsatian dog being held by one of the 'Phillips' security officers who patrolled the shopping centre. He was profusely apologetic but, as the bite had pierced the skin on my leg, a visit to Birmingham Accident Hospital was called for on the way home so that I could have a tetanus injection. More humour for the team and another small dent to my pride.

On Saturday 15 March, we dealt with another four prisoners, one of which was for possession of an offensive weapon, and one for robbery at Hobsons Grill in the Bull Ring, following a lengthy foot-chase. Another twelve-hour day, but the results kept coming and, on Wednesday 19 March, thirty persons were dealt with at a special sitting at Birmingham Magistrates' Court.

I had primed our press office a couple of days before, and we again got some good newspaper publicity in an article headlined, 'skinhead Riot rocked Bull Ring shoppers':

> Shoppers and pedestrians were pushed aside as gangs of skinheads and rockers rampaged through Birmingham's Bull Ring Market area, a court heard. Mr Martin Jenkins, prosecuting at Birmingham Magistrates' Court, said it was a case of Saturday afternoon fever as rival gangs fought with each other in the crowded markets area ... One seventeen-year-old youth was sent to detention centre for three months for threatening behaviour and possessing an offensive weapon, a studded dog collar ... another seventeen-year-old was fined £400 for possessing an offensive weapon, a motorcycle exhaust pipe ...

On Thursday 27 March at 11.20 p.m., we again helped Joe and his team out with a licensing raid on a pub in Erskine Street, where illegal 'after hours' drinking was on offer. This was pretty common, and many licensees did regular 'lock-ins' to take more money. We found what we expected to find and the licensee, his wife, and a number of patrons were reported for selling and consuming alcohol after hours.

Joe's team were responsible for all licensing prosecutions on the division, but this proved to be a difficult area of work, as he recalls:

> Doing after-hours raids were not always popular with other police officers. I was never a drinker but there was a 'drinking culture' in the police service at the time, and there was potential for some conflict. I tried to concentrate on pubs where there was systemic underage drinking going on, but the manpower to raid a large city-centre pub in these circumstances was huge, and it proved very difficult to get the evidence we needed. In the space of two years, I only did one large raid on premises using the whole of the Special Patrol Group, but even then the end result was that the licensee just had to attend before the chief superintendent to receive suitable words of advice.

A week later, we covered a Genesis concert, again at the Odeon in New Street, which attracted large crowds. An English rock band formed in 1967, they eventually moved to pop music, and featured a number of musicians who became very famous, such as Phil Collins and Peter Gabriel. Their biggest commercial release at that time was a song called *Duke*, which spent two weeks at number one in the UK charts.

While we were out, we managed to arrest someone wanted for 'recall to prison', whom we had been looking for. This normally occurred when prisoners who had not completed the whole of their sentences were released 'on licence', but then breached the licence by failing to comply with conditions set, or by committing further offences. They literally went straight back to jail to complete their original sentence.

In April 1980, the West Midlands Police provided 100 officers to support Northamptonshire Police in dealing with a National Front march in Corby, which resulted in arrests. Also in the April 1980 edition of the *Beacon*, the voice of West Midlands Police, there was a centre-page spread on 'The Second City Beat' and the problems of policing Birmingham city centre. The article detailed the fact that the division had 456 licensed premises, including a pub at the wholesale market, which opened at 8.30 a.m. to 10.00 a.m. every day. There were also thirteen cinemas, and four live theatres.

Chief Superintendent Noel Jones, the head of F Division, said in the article:

It is a continuously changing population, and we are accountable to our public in a different way to divisions which are predominantly residential. Because of this, our policing is more intense over a greater part of twenty-four hours than in other places. The most prevalent crime on the division is thefts of and from motor vehicles and thefts from the person. There is also a problem with shoplifting, so special squads have been set up to deal with these areas. Just under 500 officers last year took 10,000 prisoners, with shoplifters and drunks making up less than 3,500 of that total. Although there is no football ground on the division, officers have a regular Saturday commitment throughout the season, with supporters arriving and leaving from the city centre. We are very much in the public eye here and, because policing is all about dealing with people, it is inevitable that young officers gain experience very quickly.

The article contained a number of photographs of staff at work, including one of me pointing studiously at a map accompanied by one of the team, holding a police radio. I had the longest 'sideburns' that you could get, which were more than 2 inches wide at the bottom, and my colleague had a full head of curly unkempt hair. The caption read, 'Digbeth has a unit made up of one sergeant and four constables to look at special crime problems. Sergeant Mike Layton discusses a case with PC Bryan Davis.' We were on the map in more ways than one.

One of our best arrests came on Thursday 1 May, when we detained a fifty-one-year-old man in the Indoor Market on suspicion of theft. We recovered two purses from him, plus others in his car and at his home in Moseley. The holes we had drilled to keep observations in the Indoor Market toilets had worked and we caught him rifling through a purse.

He appeared in court the following morning, and his arrest was reported in the press:

A fifty-one-year-old man who admitted stealing purses from women shoppers in Birmingham Bull Ring appeared before Birmingham magistrates. He admitted two charges of stealing purses and asked for thirteen others to be considered. After hearing that he had a criminal record dating back to 1941, the magistrates committed him in custody to Birmingham Crown Court for sentence. Mr Terence McGowran, prosecuting, said that police keeping observations in the men's toilets in the Bull Ring saw him looking through the contents of a woman's purse. Later, he admitted that he had stolen two purses that morning from the shopping bags of elderly women. He told police that, since coming to Birmingham from Sheffield in January, he had been stealing about twelve purses a week.

He was later sentenced to eighteen months in prison at Birmingham Crown Court when his solicitor David Hallchurch said that his mother had died the previous year and, since then, he had returned to his old habit of purse stealing. Over the years, I had come to realise that, for some criminals, prison represented a 'place of safety'. It gave them regular meals and a roof over their heads, as well as friendship and security. They had become institutionalised and actually felt emotionally lost when they were at liberty, so re-offending gave them a route back to a familiar environment – providing, of course, that we could catch them!

Skinheads were still particularly active, and racial tension was rising as a result of the activities of some of them who were affiliated to the National Front at that time.

We made three arrests in Manzoni Gardens at 3.35 p.m. one Saturday, when three white youths led a group of fifty black youths across Manzoni

Gardens in Birmingham City Centre, near to New Street Railway Station, looking for revenge for a race-riot by skinheads. Saturday afternoon shoppers scattered when the group ran at a handful of skinheads. However, being in the right place at the right time, we prevented them from landing any blows. The previous night there had been clashes in Small Heath, Birmingham, between skinheads and black youngsters, which had led to police intervening.

On this particular day, the group had formed up in Digbeth and moved to the Bull Ring, where they recruited more black youths. When they reached Manzoni Gardens, some of them were dispersed by uniform officers, but a number charged across the open area, shouting, until they were split up by my team and arrests made. A seventeen-year-old told us after his arrest that he was angry that some of his friends had been beaten up in Small Heath, and that he had heard that there were skinheads from London in the city centre preparing to march.

At a subsequent hearing at Birmingham Magistrates' Court, a nineteen-year-old from Handsworth, a seventeen-year-old from Alum Rock, and a sixteen-year-old ex-public-schoolboy from Edgbaston admitted using threatening behaviour. Each was fined £50 and ordered to share costs of £25.

During the following week, I liaised with Laings Security in the Bull Ring shopping centre and arranged to have the keys to some of the service corridors, which overlooked Manzoni Gardens and parts of the Outdoor Market area. From these, we could get a good view of what was going on, without revealing ourselves.

On Saturday 21 June 1980, I started work at Digbeth police station at 9.30 a.m. and sat down with the team. We knew that a persistent group of skinheads met in Manzoni Gardens every Saturday afternoon and, when confronted by the police, usually spent the rest of the afternoon playing 'cat and mouse' with them, causing trouble along the way. It was good sport for them, but not today; I gave specific instructions that we were going to gather evidence against them for obstruction of the highway and that, if the opportunity arose, we were going to arrest all of them. The officers looked at me a bit quizzically, but we prepared thirty sets of blank forms in anticipation and, in the afternoon, set off for the service corridors.

At 2.00 p.m., we saw the group gathered in Manzoni Gardens as expected, and they began to occupy all of the wooden benches, blocking the pavement areas as they generally fooled around between each other. Members of the public gave them a wide berth as the group shouted at them. Eventually two uniform constables turned up and made efforts to split them up, but without great success. The bulk of the group then moved off slowly towards the Outdoor Market area in a column, and the two constables followed behind, continuing to try to engage with them but to no avail.

We made our way to the top of a spiral staircase, which led from the Outdoor Markets and up into the Bull Ring Shopping Centre, observing the group as they moved between shoppers and forced them to make way. Luck was with us, as they headed straight towards us. After blocking the spiral staircase for a while, they started to make their way up it towards us. As they reached the top, the five of us in plain clothes lined up and I shouted, 'Police – move over to the side and stay where you are'. The two uniformed officers joined us and we managed to contain them. I called up on the radio for back-up, and more uniform officers arrived, including a sergeant who was known for being somewhat risk averse. When I told him that we were going to arrest everyone, he said that he had to go to another job and then disappeared!

When I had sufficient staff, I announced to the skinheads that they were all under arrest for 'wilful obstruction of the highway' and we formed them into another column, this time of our making, to march them down to Digbeth police station. You could see the shock on their faces and they were subdued as a result. After a short walk, we had thirty-two people lined up in the cell corridors and a bemused-looking custody sergeant, who wasn't my best friend for a few hours.

All thirty-two of the skinhead group duly appeared in court on 22 July 1980, which was reported in the press:

> Thirty male youths and two girls appeared before Birmingham magistrates. The court was told how the week previous to this incident a gang of about 200 youths had gathered in Manzoni Gardens on a Saturday afternoon and set off to march through the Bull Ring shopping centre, chanting and pushing shoppers out of their way.

The magistrates heard how we had observed our group, with about twenty of the youths dispersing as the others marched on through the Markets area. With just one exception, those in court, aged between thirteen years and twenty-six years, pleaded guilty to obstructing the highway, and each was bound over in the sum of £200 for a year to keep the peace.

One female pleaded not guilty and, on principle, I insisted that we pursue the case. I later found a store detective who independently had watched events from a window overlooking the markets. With her evidence and ours, the defendant was later convicted. The message had gone out that we were not going to tolerate these groups gathering anymore and, while I was not naïve enough to think that the problem was solved, things did improve measurably.

On Friday 27 June, we helped Joe launch another raid at a sauna in Bristol Street and the female proprietor was arrested. I had a cold at the time and the police photographer covering the premises from the outside at the time took a nice picture of me blowing my nose immediately before we rushed in.

In July we continued to arrest offenders in the Indoor Markets and, at the same time, focused on vehicle crime. We had a favourite spot in Brunel Street, near to British Rail's signal box. One of the officers used to lie on the floor of a walkway, which spanned the dual carriageway, and pretended to be drunk with a can of lager in his hand. Using this tactic to carry out observations, we made seven arrests for vehicle crime on 31 July.

In August 1980, 600 officers from West Midlands Police supported Warwickshire Police in policing a National Front march. In the same month, I had an extended period of annual leave, during which the four PCs on the team sent me a picture postcard of the Bull Ring centre showing the area where we had made the thirty-two arrests. On the back, it read: 'Mike – Having a great time, wish you were here. All of us at 150 per cent and managing to cope. See you soon. Love from "Captain Beaky's Band".'

The postcard was a reference to the release in 1980 of a 7-inch single record entitled 'Captain Beaky', which reached number 5 in the UK pop charts and whose core words were:

The bravest animals in the land are Captain Beaky and his band
That's Timid Toad, Reckless Rat, Artful Owl, and Batty Bat
They march through the woodlands singing songs
That tell how they have righted wrongs.

Who said that police officers did not possess a sense of humour!

4

CHEQUE FRAUDS AND THE LOCARNO MURDER

On my return, we made an arrest for two robberies in the Indoor Market on 19 August 1980 and, three days later, helped Joe and his team out with a licensing raid on the Horsetrader pub in Smallbrook Queensway for underage drinkers. It wasn't a big job and, while relationships with most licensees were good, it was also necessary to show that we were impartial. In any event, underage drinkers generally spelt trouble, as they couldn't take their drink and caused problems.

On Saturday 23 August, Birmingham City FC were at home to Manchester United. In the afternoon, we made three arrests for public-order offences, two of which were football-related, where opposing factions faced off in Digbeth. One of them was a skinhead who was known for committing criminal damage in the city centre by creating graffiti. He was a nuisance, and I tasked an officer with doing a complete trawl of the main streets to collate all of the damage before arresting him.

His appearance at court prompted the headline, 'Skinhead scribbler "wrote off" £500', and was reported as follows:

> A scribbling skinhead ran up a £500 repair bill for his month-long spree of writing names and slogans on benches, buses and subway walls, Birmingham magistrates heard today. And the unemployed seventeen-year-old gave his brief answer to magistrates, who asked why he did it: 'I was bored.'

He went on to admit two charges of criminal damage, asked for seventeen others to be taken into account, and was remanded in custody for medical and social enquiry reports. Prosecuting solicitor Mr Raymond Plunkett said the cost of removing the graffiti amounted to just under £500. Mr Plunkett told the magistrates that, when a particular word began to appear frequently in the city centre, police had increased their efforts to arrest the person responsible. He was found to be in possession of a felt-tip pen and admitted that he used it for marking walls. In a statement he said, 'Over the last month I have been coming into the city centre every day. Many of my friends hang around the Manzoni Gardens area. I used the pen to write on walls. I wrote everywhere, also on buses when I came into town'.

At 11.25 p.m. on Saturday 30 August, our Brunel Street tactic worked again when we observed four drunks from the Northfield area walk along a line of parked vehicles, kicking at the bodywork. We were waiting for them at the end of the line of cars and their night out ended abruptly.

I spent the rest of the month with the team, and members of the Special Patrol Group, who were more commonly known as the SPG, doing vehicle crime observations, and the prisoners kept coming. In the main, the SPG had limited CID experience in their ranks but they were generally highly motivated and, with a proper briefing, would do a good job. They did an even better job if you arranged for them to be fed as well, courtesy of the force. A police officer with a full stomach is a more efficient officer!

In September, 170 officers from WMP again supported Warwickshire officers to police an Anti-Nazi League march.

On Friday 19 September 1980, I booked off duty at 8.00 p.m. and caught the number 23 bus home to Harborne. I had a car, but didn't use it all the time, as it was difficult to park at work. I sat downstairs, minding my own business and staring out of the window into the darkness. I was tired and just wanted to go home but, as was my usual practice, I always carried my handcuffs with me when on public transport.

At 8.44 p.m., as we got to Harborne high street a forty-year-old local white male got on. He was as 'drunk as a lord', and immediately refused to pay when requested by the driver. The air was thick with slurred words, all beginning with 'f' and 'c', as the other passengers stared intently out of the windows. I knew it was going to end in tears, if I didn't intervene. Without introducing myself, I stepped forward and, in one lucky motion, managed to handcuff him, telling him that he was under arrest for being drunk and disorderly. I was now the recipient of the 'f' and 'c' words.

'Driver, take this bus to Harborne police station,' I announced, as I made sure that my new-found friend was not in a position to head-butt me.

By the time I had finished processing him, it was 10.00 p.m. and I was even more tired, but there was simply no way that I could let it go. The reality is that, as a police officer, you are always on duty, in one form or another, and even the law requires you to act. Police officers who have not intervened in the past have even faced criminal charges of misconduct in public office.

On Thursday 23 October 1980 at 5.30 p.m., we responded to a report of a street robbery by a skinhead youth in the Bull Ring. We got a description from Laings Security staff and did a search of the area. Twenty minutes later, we found the culprit, a sixteen-year-old living in a hostel in Sparkbrook, and arrested him. This was to be my 'swansong' on the DSU.

On Monday 27 October 1980, I was transferred to the CID on the FI Sub-division at Steelhouse Lane as a detective sergeant. The police station was a large three-storey building, with loads of character. It was remembered for different reasons by Alex, who worked with me on Operation Red Card in 1987, as he reflected,

> I was at Steelhouse Lane police station in 1980, and lived in single men's quarters on the top floor after joining as an ex-police cadet. The small rooms consisted of one wardrobe, one sink and one bed – that was it. My first experience was the sight of 'Dogbreath', who also worked on Red Card, lounging around in his boxer shorts. It was not a pretty sight. Sometimes we used to hold the morning parades in another officer's bedroom because he couldn't get up on time. The inspector would have us standing around his bed, holding our 'appointments' – namely police pocket notebooks and truncheons – while he read out our postings. It was all very relaxed.

Initially, I was allocated a fairly quiet area covering Aston University in Gosta Green and the surrounding areas, and given just one detective constable to manage. The university started life as Birmingham Municipal Technical School in 1895, before being given university status by Royal Charter in 1966.

It was soon clear that I was being presented with a bit of a challenge, not only to get results on an area with relatively low crime, but also to manage an officer who had a reputation for voicing his opinions quite loudly! I had never been to university, and found it quite a novel experience visiting the students' guild and mixing with the academic staff. The students were generally focused on having a good time in the first two years, and then worked their socks off in third year to get a good pass. They weren't focused on crime prevention, and we had to work hard to reduce opportunistic thefts.

My first case involved the theft of a cheque book containing thirty-eight cheques, and someone had been enjoying some fine wines and meals at restaurants in Birmingham as well as purchasing some expensive clothes. The restaurants proved to be a mistake for the thief, as I managed to get a good description from the Celebrity restaurant at 3 King Alfred's Place, just off Broad Street. It was described as a place that offered a large and exclusive menu, with some speciality dishes prepared at tables and an atmosphere complemented by cabaret attractions.

I got a bit more information when I found that they had also visited the sauna in Bristol Street. Finally we had the names of not one but two suspects, one of whom was arrested with a female in Erdington on Tuesday 11 November 1980. I was pretty new to cheque fraud, but it was prolific in the city centre, and could be interesting work when you started looking at handwriting and the forensic opportunities that handling cheques presented.

After lodging the prisoners, we linked up with a CID officer from the Cheque Squad and visited shops in the city centre where some of the cheques had been used. One of the shop staff was already a suspect, as it was clear that he knew the thieves by name and had been allowing them to push the cheques through his shop in exchange for a cut of the proceeds and some of the goods. He would wait for another day, but we took his receipt books away and charged the male we had in custody. The second suspect was more elusive.

At this time, I got to know another detective called Arthur. We actually became neighbours at one stage and he was a dedicated family man. Arthur was a short, quiet and unassuming individual, who adopted a serious approach to his duties. He did, however, have a great way with people and somehow was able to calm anyone with an aggressive streak in them. Before you knew it, they would all be drinking tea together.

On Tuesday 18 November 1980, I had some information that our second suspect had been at either Folkestone or Dover, and I liaised with the Special Branch units there, but with no luck at that point. By now someone had decided which side of the fence they wanted to sit on, so I was confident that I would get him in due course. He was a professional criminal, whose name reminded me of a jewellery heist, and I was looking forward to seeing him in the flesh, although at this point I thought he was out of the country.

Routine arrests continued, with the occasional irritation. Because the central lock-up was attached to Steelhouse Lane police station, whenever someone damaged the cells, it was 'custom and practice' for us to deal with them. It was a fairly regular occurrence, often committed by people who wanted to vent their frustrations and anger on anything or anyone.

The central lock-up was like a mini prison, with landings and metal walkways that you could see through below. There were lots of uniform officers walking around, long chains attached to their belts with heavy keys on the end. Most of the officers were middle to late service, and many of them had been in there for a long time. While it was a volatile and claustrophobic environment, most of the officers liked it and got used to the prisoners shouting across the landings to each other through the hatchways of cell doors. There was plenty of overtime and, at the end of their duty, they could walk away with no paperwork worries.

Due to its additional cell capacity, the central lock-up had played a major part in the response by the West Midlands Police in the previous month to a national prison officers' dispute. This had led to more than 3,500 prisoners at one time being lodged temporarily in police cells throughout the UK, and lasted until the end of the year.

On Friday 28 November 1980, we made a couple of arrests for theft, and it turned out that they were wanted by the Royal Ulster Constabulary for burglary. When we had finished with them, we lodged them over the weekend so that the RUC could come and get them. The following Monday, I did a split duty and went to Elmdon Airport to pick up two officers who were flying over from Belfast. The unwritten rule remained that visitors needed to be looked after and, following my experiences on my CID course, I knew that it was going to be a late finish as they wouldn't be going back until the following morning.

We got back into Birmingham, I booked off duty, and a group of us found somewhere that was still open. I paced myself and watched with interest. One of the two RUC officers drank beer, quite a lot in fact; however, after a while he slowed down and, while he was swaying a bit, he was okay. The second drank gin and tonics, one after the other, but showed no signs of being under the influence of alcohol until the point where he literally fell over and lay on the floor comatose. We eventually deposited them at their accommodation and, in the morning, they were handcuffed to the prisoners prior to the trip back to the airport. They were given strict instructions to look after the officers, one of whom left his coat behind, which had to be posted to him.

The Broad Street area continued to act as a magnet for some forms of criminality, much of which was fuelled by the effects of alcohol; Paul Newbold, who retired from the West Midlands Police after serving many years in Birmingham city centre, recalls one incident where he single-handedly made seven arrests:

Back in the early 1980s, I was a beat officer for the Broad street area. A few days before Christmas in that period, I decided to go into the Granville pub, situated in Broad Sreet at Granville Street, to check that there was no problems. The time was about 1.30 p.m. On my way in, I became aware of a group of young men leaving the pub who were quite loud and jovial, but not disorderly. One particular member of this group was about 6 feet, 7 inches tall and well-built.

I was in this pub for two or three minutes, when I heard via my radio that a GPO van had just been stolen from Granville Street/Tennant Street. I rushed outside to find a bewildered GPO engineer, who had been down a manhole fixing telephone wires when he heard his yellow Commer van start. He had left the keys in the ignition! He looked out of the manhole and saw the van being driven away by a group of lads, some of whom were hanging out of the back doors, shouting and laughing. He gave me a brief description, characterising one of them as being 6 feet, 6 inches tall and standing out from the rest.

I searched the area and, nearby, right outside the Accident Hospital, I saw the same group of men who I had seen outside the pub getting into a taxi. There were seven of them trying to get into the taxi. I went up to them and said, 'Where's that f–ing van!!', and told them that they were all being arrested on suspicion of theft of a motor vehicle. One of the lads inside the taxi said that it was on the road pointing down Bath Row. I called via my radio for a couple of 'panda' cars. Within a few minutes, the cars arrived and the prisoners were taken to Digbeth. The GPO van was found nearby intact.

At Digbeth I interviewed all seven in their cells. One of them admitted driving the van and was charged accordingly. During the course of one of the interviews, I asked another man whether they had permission to take the van. This man said that 'Buzby' had given him permission. Buzby Bird was a character used in television commercial adverts for the GPO in the 1970s and 1980s. They were all charged and bailed.

A couple of weeks later, my wife was on nights at the Birmingham Maternity Hospital and was having a general chat about families with another female member of staff. This lady was describing the antics that her two sons had got up to. My wife, on listening to the incident, thought that it sounded familiar and spoke to me when she came home from work. Having clarified that this was the same incident, it caused a lot of laughter for years to come. I got to know the two sons and the very tall man, who was known as 'the Lurch'. Looking back, I don't know how I managed it!

In 1980, a total of 166,031 crimes were recorded in the force area, which included thirty-six murders and twelve manslaughter/infanticide cases, all of which were detected except for one of the manslaughters. A total of 1,460 sexual offences were recorded.

On Wednesday 7 January 1981, I booked on at 9.15 p.m. and, in the early hours of the morning, I teamed up with Clive from my DSU days, who by now was now a detective constable. I had some information about our missing cheque-fraudsman, who was back in the country. We went up to Five Ways, did the rounds of the Peppermint Place and Maximillian's nightclubs, and then checked the Albany, Market, and Midland Hotels, but with a negative result.

I knew that we weren't far behind him, and my informant was plotting his movements for us. At 6.40 a.m., I went with other officers to an address in Hall Green, in a quiet cul-de-sac, where we found our target hiding in one of the rooms. The occupants denied he was there when they eventually opened the door, but I was sure that he was and, with the back and front covered, I wouldn't take no for an answer. Although he had never met me before, he knew me by name but, unlike me, had not been looking forward to our first meeting. He had no idea as to how he had come to be arrested and I didn't enlighten him.

He had been busy while on the run, and had continued to do cheque frauds, using stolen books while abroad, and had made at least one trip to Amsterdam. He was a typical conman, very plausible, smart-looking, and bright. We took him back to Steelhouse Lane police station and, by the time I booked off, I had done a thirteen-hour tour of duty.

I went out with the Cheque Squad at 6.40 a.m. on Monday 12 January 1981 and arrested another individual in Marston Green who was linked to the cheque-fraud enquiry. The reality of life was that, when people were facing a prison sentence, loyalty for most went out of the window; if they could spread the load by making sure that they weren't standing in the dock on their own, then they did so. I rarely witnessed 'honour among thieves'.

Another member of the fraud team came in three days later, and we now had four charged as co-accused. The job got bigger and bigger as we uncovered more links to other stolen cheque books through handwriting analysis and identifications using a chemical ninhydrin process – this turned the paper a sort of pink colour as it revealed fingerprints, which could be matched against the suspects. At the same time, my informant was keeping me updated on what was being discussed between them after arrest. I met the informant over the next few days, and other suspects involved in the cheque fraud conspiracy were identified, including a twenty-year-old Asian female.

Working with the Cheque Squad, we arrested another male in Knowle shopping precinct and then, on Thursday 29 January, I went with the female sergeant in charge of the Cheque Squad, and other officers, to an address in Stanmore Road, Edgbaston.

What the Cheque Squad sergeant did not know about fraud would not have filled a cigarette paper; but she was not known for smiling, smoked heavily, and guarded her team, and her role, jealously. We found our female suspect, who was arrested and spent the day at Steelhouse Lane police station being as un-cooperative as she could be in the presence of her solicitor. At the end of the day, she was bailed from the police station, pending the outcome of handwriting analysis on some Barclaycard vouchers. Her day would come, as I knew that, together with her co-accused, she had been having a taste of the good life at hotels and casinos in Birmingham.

On Tuesday 10 February 1981, I assisted at Bridge Street West police station with the interview of a suspect for a rape in Newtown, who was later transferred to the central lock-up. Bridge Street West was a very small station on the edge of Newtown, which was home to a few permanent beat officers and a small team of CID staff. It was an old building with just four cells and permanent office constables who were all long in service and real characters. Rumour had it that one of them used to prefer a 'liquid lunch', and would routinely walk across the road in full uniform to the pub opposite and come back balancing a tray bearing glasses. They knew everyone and everyone knew them in the area. I liked the place and, in due course, was to come to know the building and the area well.

On Tuesday 24 February 1981, the female was re-arrested and, after another interview, which was recorded by way of contemporaneous notes, she was formally charged. You had to be good at writing in those days, and some interviews could take hours with breaks in between. The trick was to write your question first and then ask it, otherwise you gave the suspect extra time to think about a response if you did it the other way around. It was laborious work, which had to be read over and signed at the end by all parties present. If you didn't get it right, it would be challenged at court and, if the notes were not signed by the suspect, they had less evidential value in the eyes of the legal system. It was also important to maintain eye contact with suspects to help you gauge responses, as well as giving your partner the chance to ask questions, but in a controlled manner so that you didn't finish tripping each other up.

Interviewing people was really an art form; some were good at it, and others never got past the starting post. Some suspects elected also to make written statements under caution, where they gave an account in their own words, which were written down and signed, or, in a few cases, signed police pocket-book entries. There were always those who sat in silence throughout or mimicked the criminals that they had seen in films or on television, replying, 'No comment', to each question and exercising their right to remain silent. Some prisoners and solicitors thought that by doing this the interviews would be wound up quickly, but I was stubborn and always spun it out for as long as I could so as not to give them the satisfaction. I never showed my frustration, as to do so would have made them think that they had won part of the psychological battle.

The beginning of March saw another week of night duty. After coming on duty on Saturday 7 March 1981, I spent half the night assisting senior CID officers from another division after four people were stopped in a suspect vehicle in relation to a murder enquiry, which two of them later admitted to being involved in. I was concerned by the twenty-three arrests during the course of the week, which was a bad week for woundings; just keeping my pocket note book up to date as we went along was a challenge that had to be met. Records in your police pocket note book had to be made at the earliest possible time after the event, and a record kept of where and when. Failure to do so would lead to an almighty grilling by defence solicitors, and you ran the risk of losing a job at court.

On Friday 13 March 1981, I went with a team of officers to Handsworth to assist them in the arrest of two persons, aged seventeen years and twenty years, for burglary. The older of the two had a real reputation for hating the police with a vengeance, and was a good-class criminal. Sheer weight of numbers was to persuade him to come quietly, but the look on his face told it all. It was not to be our last meeting, and next time it was for something far more serious.

My informant in the cheque-fraud case was still putting jobs in, and my opinionated detective constable was working hard and keeping his nose clean, so all was going well. The informant put a really good job in relating to cheque frauds from thefts at Aston University and, on Thursday 19 March 1981, I started the day just after 8.00 a.m. and finished duty at 8.00 a.m. the following day. During that time, we arrested seven people, including four members of the same family, after executing search warrants and recovering stolen property at an address in Ettington Road, Aston. I was exhausted, but well pleased, and we still had a fifth member of the family to find, who was somewhere in London.

On Monday 23 March 1981, I went to Stoke Newington in London with a DC from the Cheque Squad called John. He was a really eccentric character, with a gruff voice and a bald head, who dressed, and acted, like a solicitor in black suits with a waist coat. He enjoyed a drink and was very humorous after he had had a few. It was not unknown for him to sleep under a desk in the office rather than to go home. He was, however, tenacious and a good investigator.

We liaised with a detective sergeant from the Divisional Crime Squad and starting looking for our fifth family member, who was believed to be in the area. This was not, however, an area to go stomping around in, unless you wanted to cause a riot.

We spent the day visiting C6 London Cheque Squad and the bank inspectorates at Midland and Barclays banks, collecting cheques and exhibits in connection with the case. Later that day, we obtained a search warrant from a local magistrate. In those days, out of hours warrant applications required a visit to the home address of a local magistrate. It was not unusual to stand in someone's kitchen with a bible in one hand, swearing the oath, and then to find a cup of tea presented to the other. We would give the grounds for the warrant application and, if the magistrate agreed with the evidence, they would sign the papers and that was it. I never had one refused throughout my service, but you had to have your facts straight, as smashing the wrong door down had the potential for dire consequences.

At 6.20 a.m. the next day, John and I went with the Metropolitan Police to the George Downing Estate in Stoke Newington and executed the warrant. We recovered stolen property and arrested the twenty-seven-year-old family member for which we were looking, together with his nineteen-year-old girlfriend. We lodged them for a while with the local police while we did some further enquiries at New Scotland Yard and National Westminster Bank Fraud office and then drove back to Birmingham with them. They weren't very happy. On the next day, we did some further enquiries in relation to hire vehicles that they had been using to commit crime and with Barclaycard fraud office. They had been a very active team and numerous offences were disclosed. Both were charged later at the end of a fifteen-hour day.

For the next few weeks, I was buried under paperwork and attendances at court. You could be the best detective but, if you couldn't keep your paperwork up to date, you were doomed. Some people did struggle and, in some cases, stress took its toll as they suffered in silence, too afraid to ask for help from an organisation that had not yet really got to grips with this type of illness. The answer to stress was to go for a drink!

Malcolm Halliday retired as detective sergeant and became an expert in covert policing. He was a CID officer based at Bradford Street in 1981 and recalls a particularly horrific murder at the end of March:

> A twenty-one-year-old man who had right-wing leanings, and was known to have attended National Front Meetings, had already attacked someone with a crossbow and tried to run someone over with a car. He then went on to abduct a woman, whom he tied up and put into the boot of her car, before making his way to the Socialist and Trade Union bookshop in Digbeth High Street. When he got there, he rammed the car into the shop and set fire to petrol he had with him. The staff in the bookshop escaped but, tragically, the woman who had been abducted died in the fire. He later got sentenced to life imprisonment.

On the day of the murder, the twenty-one-year-old responsible changed into military fatigues and, on arrival at the bookshop, used a full five-gallon drum of petrol to start a fire.

Dave Faulkner also remembers the incident:

> I was on duty as the office PC at Digbeth in the afternoon, when I was suddenly aware of a big bang outside. I thought that there had been a road accident, and immediately ran outside and down Digbeth towards the coach station. A car was embedded in the window of the bookshop next

to the Civic Hall, and was actually on fire. I ran towards the car, while another officer ran down a side street and found someone trying to hang himself, who turned out to be the murderer. At this stage, no one knew that there was a person in the boot of the car. It was an horrific crime.

Dave 'J' was on the CID at the time and recalls,

I was nominated to liaise with the husband of the deceased. He was a really nice guy and it would just be impossible to know how he was feeling. We brought him back to Birmingham with us from Hertfordshire to assist with background information on his wife, but we actually confirmed her identity by comparing dental records with those of the deceased.

Richard Barnes was subsequently sentenced to life imprisonment by a judge, with no recommendation about the length of sentence he should serve. He showed little remorse for his actions.

In April 1981, I was involved, with Arthur, in the arrest of a team of four people, who were involved in burglaries in the area, and the recovery of stolen property, and that of another two for theft of West Midlands Travel passes and deception.

On Thursday 14 May 1981, one of my informants put someone in for supplying cannabis and, while the offender did not live on my area, I wasn't about to hand the job over.

On Thursday 28 May, I responded to a call from a uniform officer and attended some premises in New Street, in relation to a scam whereby someone had set up a bogus company and invited people to send money for a non-existent service. The postal address was just a mailbox drop-off point in Temple House, and the uniform officer was with the potential offender and wasn't quite sure what to do. Within five minutes, the thirty-four-year-old was under arrest for deception, and a large sack, filled with hundreds of letters containing cash, was recovered. The case attracted interest from the press and the Force Commercial Branch, and he was later charged with criminal deception and kept in custody.

I was amazed at how trusting people were with their money. The scam was simple, as told in the words of jobless fifty-year-old Ray Rowlands, who thought that things were looking up when he saw an advert for a £100-per-week van driver. Hopeful applicants were told to send a self-addressed envelope for an interview for the job that also boasted expenses. His hopes were dashed, however, when the reply from Enby Products asked for £1 for an interview. The letter blamed a 'terrific response' for the need to charge a nominal interview fee. The address for Enby Products was, in fact, Adminaid Management Services Ltd, a legitimate agency that rented accommodation addresses. Several thousand responses were received.

On Saturday 30 May 1981, we liaised with the Force Drug Squad and went to an address in Ladypool Road, Sparkbrook, in relation to my drugs information. We arrested a nineteen-year-old for cultivating cannabis plants, and had all the lighting and drugs paraphernalia photographed *in situ*. We had the bonus of a second arrest for burglary and spent the day at Bradford Street police station dealing with them.

On Tuesday 2 June 1981, I was posted to a murder investigation, following the death of taxi driver Douglas Brunt in Hurst Street, in the early hours of that morning outside the Locarno Club venue, which resulted in the arrest of twenty-nine people. Douglas Brunt was stabbed to death, and two other men seriously injured, when a taxi drivers' fancy-dress ball turned into a pitched fight, with a forty-strong gang of bikers using knives, chains and wooden clubs as weapons. Women were caught up in the fighting as they left a party at the Locarno Ballroom at 2.15 a.m., which had been attended by about 300 drivers and families to raise money for charity.

Mr Brunt, aged thirty-one and married with two children, fell dying after being stabbed in the arms and heart while trying to help a fellow taxi driver, who was beaten with chains and suffered head injuries. A third taxi driver was stabbed in the back, and the two injured people were detained in the Accident Hospital.

The fighting occurred when the bikers left a rock concert at the nearby Romeo and Juliet's club in Hurst Street and started to harass women in fancy dress. Mr Brunt was hailed as a hero by his family and colleagues, as he tried to intervene to stop the violence. It was a chaotic situation that took some time to unravel, made more difficult by the fact that most of those arrested were wearing similar clothing and, in the main, were initially totally un-cooperative. The killer was among those arrested, but no one would shed light on who it was.

My first job that day was to interview two of those arrested with Arthur and, by midnight, both had been charged with affray and possession of offensive weapons. One of the two was the so-called chairman, or president, of the Birmingham chapter of the United Bikers of Great Britain and was known as 'Ugly'. The second wasn't very difficult for witnesses to identify, as he had his right foot in plaster and was on crutches.

Seventeen persons were charged with affray by the following morning. Nine of the accused were bikers from the Birmingham area, two were taxi drivers and six were unrelated to either. All of them were bailed to appear in court on the 1 July 1981.

More than £500 was raised in twenty-four hours by the TOA Taxi Drivers' Association in aid of the taxi driver's family, and emotions were running very high. Within days, three further bikers were charged with causing an affray and bailed.

I remained on the investigation for the next three weeks, and was given the job of creating a sequence-of-events chart, which, although basic, started to plot the movements of those involved as I sifted through the various witness statements and records of interview. I displayed the whole thing on a wall within the incident room, so that officers could brief themselves, and I was so proud of it that I took a photograph for posterity. This was seen as quite an innovative approach, as we did not yet have the luxury of crime analysts to do this sort of intelligence and evidence mapping for us.

For each of the suspects, I mapped their movements, clothing and what potential witnesses had said about them. For example, 'Ugly' was described as 5 feet, 11 inches tall, of slim build with shoulder-length straggly brown hair, with tattoos on both arms and a fresh injury over his left eye. He had a full beard and was wearing black leathers and a denim waistcoat, as well as a blue shirt, a white t-shirt, dirty jeans and boots. He was believed to have been in possession of a 3-foot length of chain and a chain belt, with which he had threatened the arresting officer. There was no code of silence among them and various things were said about different people during police interviews, as the reality dawned that someone was facing a murder charge.

Although this group dressed in what was seen as traditional Hell's Angels clothing and were referred to in the media as such, a number of them actually came from an off-shoot organisation known as the United Bikers of Great Britain. They had their own hierarchy and structure, and became more visible in their activities as they vied for power with other groups. We worked twelve-hour days and gave up our rest days, but we got there in the end.

Ada Howles, a constable at the time, recalls,

I was seconded onto the enquiry and remember taking the victim's clothing to the forensic laboratory in Gooch Street, so that they could try and work out what size and type of knife was used. Afterwards, myself and DS Roger Bache went out and bought a knife from a shop with similar dimensions. I also later sat in with one of the detective chief inspectors and did the contemporaneous notes for the interviews for some of the main suspects.

On Monday 8 June 1981, Martin Fox, a nineteen-year-old trainee technician was charged with the murder of Douglas Brunt. He made a three-minute court appearance before the Birmingham Stipendiary Mr F. H. Hatchard and was remanded in custody for a week. Fox had been one of those originally charged with affray but, after the enquiry team carefully pieced the evidence together, there were sufficient grounds for other officers to re-arrest him during the weekend and the charge followed.

5

AN UNUSUAL CRIME, RIOTS AND THE GPO ROBBERY

On Thursday 25 June 1981, I saw Chip in the central lock-up, where he was in custody and waiting to appear at court on charges. It was more of a social visit, and he knew that he was on his own, but we had known each other a long time and he was still keen to put information in. I saw him again a week later, and he gave me some information regarding a murder in Bedfordshire and about a person who was already in custody. It was very good information, and I later made contact with a detective superintendent from that force area, and arranged to get everything down on paper. Later that day, they sent a detective sergeant up to Birmingham to collect the paperwork and it was another nice little result.

On the night of Friday 10 July 1981, continuing into the following day, the Handsworth Riots occurred and lasted on a smaller scale for several more days. They were described by many as 'copycat' riots, referring to events in Brixton, Toxteth, and Moss Side. Trouble spread from Handsworth to the city centre, Wolverhampton and Coventry, resulting in a total of 599 related arrests being made, most of whom were for people under twenty-five years of age. In all, eighty-five police officers were injured, as well as four civilians, and 541 shops raided. Damage calculated at nearly £750,000 was caused to buildings and vehicles, which included eighty-seven private vehicles and thirty-nine police vehicles.

Four police stations were attacked, and the then-chief constable of the West Midlands Police, Sir Philip Knights, described it as 'the worst outbreak of civil disorder since 1919'. The officer for whom I have used the pseudonym 'Alex' commented:

When it started, I was on foot patrol on what was Beat 15 at the bottom end of Newtown, which borders with Handsworth. I had a call at teatime to come back into the station. We had no proper riot helmets. We had plastic things that fitted on the front of our normal helmets, which were rubbish. They hired coaches, as we didn't have a lot of vans, and deployed us in Soho Road; we did cordons while the Special Patrol Group took prisoners. Later on, we had a load of khaki helmets delivered to Steelhouse Lane.

On the Saturday afternoon I was with another officer in St Phillip's churchyard when we arrested someone for looting a jeweller's shop. There just happened to be a newspaper cameraman nearby, and we appeared in the *Sunday Mirror*, holding the prisoner under the caption, 'Still smiling', as we led him away. We worked all hours while it was going on but, in the city centre, it was just copycat stuff.

Joe Tildesley was by now a sergeant on the Special Patrol Group during this period, and recalls,

We were on standby for trouble and were deployed to the Handsworth Road. We had no riot shields to start with, just second-hand riot helmets from Northern Ireland. The chief inspector in charge of the SPG was a really imposing figure, who led from the front. He lined all of us up and said words to the effect of, 'We are going to clear Handsworth Road. I don't want too many prisoners but we will clear the road'. With that, more than 100 officers charged forward in the darkness and that's exactly what we did.

Dave Faulkner was aged twenty-five years, and had been a police officer for three years, based at Digbeth at the time. He recalls the first night of the riots:

I was living with my mum in a council house in Handsworth and was making my way back home from rugby training. I drove past Newtown Swimming Baths at about 10.15 p.m., and I remember the night sky was 'on fire' and literally lit up in front of me. I took a detour to get home and, eventually, when I was next on duty I got deployed to the Bradford Street area and Digbeth to cover for officers who had been sent to Handsworth.

On Sunday 12 July 1981, I was engaged all day in the central lock-up at Steelhouse Lane police station regarding prisoners who had been detained in connection with the riots. On the next day, I went to Court Number 2 in the Magistrates' Court with other officers, so as to assist with applying for remands in custody for many of those charged over the weekend. It was a huge operation, with 'all hands to the pump', and I eventually finished after 10.00 p.m. I was engaged with senior officers in the city centre in contingency planning, and spent a couple of days on standby with officers in the central lock-up the following week to deal with any further arrests. However, the real work was being done by the uniform officers on the ground.

During the months of September and October 1981, we spent a lot of time keeping observations regarding a spate of building-society robberies in the city centre, near to St Phillip's churchyard. The routine arrests and the paperwork that went with them carried on apace with prisoners for robbery, wounding, assault and deception.

I spent some time working with Arthur during this period, and an informant gave us some good information regarding a burglary at factory premises in Nechells, where microwaves valued at £3,000 had been stolen, and also regarding some robberies in the Handsworth area. Two days later, Arthur and I teamed up with one of the force headquarters' CID units, and four arrests quickly followed in the Nechells area. We went to Loughborough in the afternoon to search two addresses, and to look for another suspect with a negative result. However, by the end of the day, three of them were charged with the burglary and bailed. It was a quick and clean result, illustrating the value of good informants.

You could spend months and days, as I had done previously, doing a hard slog on an investigation, but one phone call from someone with inside knowledge made it so much easier; criminals hated it because most of them simply had no idea who the informant might be. We would also lay false trails to put people off the scent, but the absolute rule was that you never, never disclosed your source. Even in court, if you were challenged, there was a system in place to protect their identities.

One evening, Arthur and I went to the Black Horse pub in Woodcock Street on a routine enquiry and, when we got there, we literally fell over a twenty-one-year-old and a seventeen-year-old, both from Chelmsley Wood, trying to break into a car in the street. We lodged them overnight and both were interviewed and charged next day.

On Friday 20 November 1981, I was tied up all day with all available CID officers, working in the vicinity of Chamberlain Square, city centre, for a visit by Her Majesty the Queen. Dubbed the 'Queen of Smiles' by the local newspaper, everywhere she went, on what was her thirty-fourth wedding anniversary, she appeared to be in a happy and relaxed mood. Prior to coming to the city centre, she had visited BBC Pebblemill and an employment preparation scheme in Nechells for handicapped adults. Hundreds of youngsters gathered in Chamberlain Square to greet her on a lunchtime walk-about, prior to visiting the Council House nearby.

Royal visits put everyone on their 'mettle', as police balanced the public's expectation that they would be close enough to royalty to engage against the fear of the unexpected act that could lead to a breach of security. Senior officers would be visibly stressed on such occasions, as reputations were clearly at stake. Our job was to provide a watching brief and to look for any unusual activity in the crowds. As it was, despite Birmingham being swept by a gale, the visit was a great success and passed off without incident.

It was not quite such an uneventful day a short distance away outside the city's Holiday Inn; the employment secretary, Norman Tebbit, narrowly avoided two eggs that were thrown at him by a group of forty protesters, some on bikes, following his famous speech wherein he said that, 'some people should follow the example of his father and get on their bikes to find work'.

On the next day, Arthur and I had a trip to Leeds with other officers to bring back three persons arrested on our behalf for theft, and then did a detour to York Central police station to collect another one, who was wanted on warrant for failing to appear at court for theft. With four pairs of handcuffs and two officers per prisoner, it was a bit like a coach trip.

On Wednesday 9 December 1981 the first signs emerged of problems between two factions of Iranian and Iraqi students at Aston University. An Iranian was assaulted as political disagreement turned to violence. The investigation was handled by the local permanent beat officer, but I made it clear to him that he needed to take a firm line and to put the message out that violence from any quarter would be met by arrest. Some of the Iraqis were interviewed two days later, and my message was passed on.

On Saturday 12 December 1981, all available CID staff were directed to a robbery involving the theft of a considerable amount of cash from a Securicor van in Union Passage in the city centre. Two security guards were attacked and three cash boxes, containing £45,000, were stolen as they were carrying them from the Boots store in Union Passage. One of the guards was coshed to the floor in front of hundreds of Christmas shoppers. The attackers made their getaway in a silver Ford Grenada parked at the rear of Marks & Spencer. The attacker with the cosh was described as being a white male in his early twenties, with straight, mousey-coloured hair and a moustache. The second man was a West Indian in his mid-twenties and was wearing a beige bomber jacket. The good thing was that we had witnesses, and were soon able to compile 'photo fits'.

For the next three days, I was heavily involved in enquiries regarding the robbery, which led to the recovery of a vehicle in Ladywood believed to have been used in the crime, and to the arrest of a number of suspects taken into custody at Kings Heath police station – one of whom was well known to me from my Ladywood days. On Wednesday 16 December 1981, I went to Coventry to search some of the addresses of those in custody, and arrested the common-law wife of one of them. At another address, we recovered £100, which was believed to be from the proceeds of the crime.

Without much of a pause for breath, I was then put onto an enquiry relating to a serious wounding on a man and four other people. On Saturday 19 December 1981, at about 2.30 a.m., Tracy Ashton, a twenty-five-year-old printer from Kingsthorpe in Northampton, got into an argument with a teenager as he was returning to a coach after a works Christmas outing at the Locarno Ballroom in Hurst Street. His attacker was with a group of youths, and a brawl developed, during which the teenager produced an open razor and stabbed Mr Ashton five times in the chest abdomen, groin and chin. A detective said he was 'cut to pieces' and had lost a considerable amount of blood. The worst wound had penetrated the left wall of his heart. He had to have emergency open-heart surgery and was detained in the major injuries unit at Birmingham Accident Hospital on a life-support machine in a critical condition. Four of his friends were also injured in the ensuing fight.

An incident room was set up at Digbeth police station, which I spent nine days on, with a couple of days off for Christmas in the middle. This is how you got your experience as a detective. You could have as much theory as you liked but, when it came down to it, by being 'bounced' from job to job you learnt how to cope with extreme stress.

In 1981, a total of 188,230 crimes were recorded in the force area. Crimes of violence resulted in forty-two deaths, of which thirty were classified as murder, and twelve as manslaughter. All of the offences, with the exception of one murder, were detected. Offences of wounding continued apace, with over 6,500 recorded, but most worrying was the prevalence of street robberies, now referred to as 'muggings', which numbered 1,552 offences.

In January 1982, Dave Rischmiller was coming to the end of his term as a police cadet prior to becoming a constable, and performed a three-month attachment at Steelhouse Lane. He recalls,

> We were paired up with a regular officer and went out on patrols in the city centre. The culture of policing at the time was very different. On each shift at Steelhouse Lane, there were two inspectors, which was very unusual. One of them worked inside, while the other went out on patrol, and they rotated each week. The problem was that the two inspectors didn't get on with each other, and refused to cooperate over anything. Whoever's turn it was to work inside would be like 'a bear with a sore head', because they didn't like being tied to the office, so the staff would get a hard time. We had lots of Scottish officers and an Irish contingent. Many of their families had come to the Midlands in the fifties and sixties due to unemployment, or after leaving the armed services. The Scottish influence was strong and, due to my father's connection to the force, I was actually a member of the West Midlands Police pipe band from the age of twelve years, playing the bagpipes.

Another DC was doing some work with me by then, a tall thick-set officer of Irish descent, with a passion for rugby and a thick moustache that covered his lips. Paul was a bit of a character, but definitely someone to have next to you in a confrontation.

In the early eighties, Bryan Davis recalls being assaulted:

> I walked into the Jarna Indian restaurant by Park Street one night while on duty. As I entered, I came face to face with a guy who was holding one of the waiters up against a wall. I dived in, but what I didn't realise was that he was with two other mates and I got a right 'doing over'. The fight spilled out into the street, but I was unable to make a call on the radio as I struggled to hang onto one of them. Fortunately, a taxi driver was passing and he ran into Digbeth police station to tell them what was happening. The 'cavalry' arrived as everyone ran out to get to me. I finished up with a broken nose and two black eyes and spent the night in hospital with concussion.

On Monday 1 February 1982, I went with Paul and an experienced female DC to Edward Road police station in Balsall Heath to meet the local detective inspector regarding an allegation of rape. It was to be the start of a fascinating enquiry, with some surprising twists and turns.

The complainant was only sixteen years of age, of very slim build, but very 'street-wise' and quite a determined individual. She had gone into the local station to report being abducted and subjected to a gang rape, so our first step was to take a detailed statement from her. We then arranged to take her clothing for forensic analysis, and took it down to the forensic science laboratory. You had to be very careful when doing this to avoid cross contamination, so everything had to be bagged up separately and records kept of who had taken possession of what. This took us a couple of hours, and then we went for a drive with the complainant around the Newtown area to see if we could identify where the offence had taken place, as she wasn't familiar with the area. This was not going to be an easy one to solve.

Later that evening, we went back to Balsall Heath to take two witness statements of 'early complaint,' one of them being from her boyfriend. In such cases, it was really important to establish when the victim had told someone else, and it was always something that the defence dwelt on in court. On the next day, we took the complainant to Lloyd House police headquarters to arrange for photo fits to be compiled. The allegation was that she had been abducted on the street, at a location that was still unknown, by three men of West Indian origin who had forced her into a car. She had been driven to another unknown location and then forcibly raped by two of the three individuals.

The following day, I went to Wolverhampton and was given some information by a Regional Crime Squad officer, who had picked something up locally and had the name of a suspect. Once again, I went through the process of identifying associates and looking at every detail of his antecedent history from existing criminal records. It all helped to build a picture.

On the next day, I was tied up identifying a suspect wanted for assault and stealing a motor vehicle. Little did I know that, in 1984, this individual would play a critical role in a murder enquiry involving a pub licensee.

On Monday 8 February 1982, together with Paul and Arthur, we linked up with the Regional Crime Squad in Wolverhampton and visited a number of addresses in the area. We now had the names of three suspects, but no one was at home. We stuck with it and, on the next day, executed search warrants at other addresses, but again with a negative result.

On Wednesday 10 February, we had our first suspect in custody, who had been arrested on our behalf by local officers. He was a twenty-six-year-old man from Willenhall. After taking his clothing for forensic examination, we interviewed him at some length and then spent the evening making arrangements for an identification parade next day. We used to arrange for 'stooges' from Aston University, depending on the age profile of the suspect, and, as a small sum was paid for expenses, students were normally happy to participate.

The process was always quite tedious and everything had to be done exactly right to ensure that any identifications made stood up in court. The officers involved in the case were not allowed to play any active part, and the whole thing was managed by an inspector. For many victims, it was a real ordeal as they were in the same room as the suspects and, sometimes, it was just too much for them to cope with.

The next day a form WC316 was served on the prisoner, and he agreed to stand on the identification parade. The complainant made a positive identification without any hesitation and he was formally charged with rape.

We still had two people to find, but things went onto hold when, once again, I was posted to a major-incident room at Steelhouse Lane on Saturday 27 February 1982, following the murder of a man of Greek Cypriot origin. I had actually been on a major-incident room course in Coventry in the preceding two days, and my new-found skills were immediately put to the test in one of the office functions relating to 'statement reading and action allocation'.

Savvas Andreou, a forty-two-year-old Greek Cypriot, was found hidden behind a wall in a car park in Park Street in the city centre at 8.00 a.m. that day, having been bound and gagged. Two post-mortem examinations subsequently confirmed that he had died of suffocation and had been dead since approximately midnight on the Friday, the day before.

Detective Superintendent Bob Roberts was put in charge of the investigation, and said to the media at the time:

He was very well known within the Greek community, and not well liked. But I do not think that those responsible for tying him up intended he should die. I say this so that, if it is on their conscience and they regret it, they should know that, if they approach me, they will be treated with understanding. This man has obviously upset someone to such an extent that they wanted to teach him a lesson. You could call him a Romeo.

In 1969, Andreou served two years in prison after twice being convicted of bigamy. Although described as only 5 foot, 5 inches tall, and of heavy build, he was said to be particularly successful with women, some of whom had children by him and came from different parts of the UK. He also owed money to many people and was a known 'petty criminal' who used several aliases.

On Tuesday 2 March 1982, the body of fifty-nine-year-old Savvas Loizou Savvitsikkis, another Greek Cypriot, was found on the back seat of an old maroon-coloured Mercedes car on a quiet country road in Alvechurch, Worcestershire. He had apparently committed suicide, and had suffered gunshot wounds to the head and stomach, inflicted with a Walther automatic pistol. Next to the body was a suicide note written in Greek. He was an unemployed welder and odd-job man who lived in Erdington, and had originally come to England from Famagusta looking for work. Other officers on the enquiry had been looking for him since the day before, in connection with the death of Andreou. He came from a close family and left a wife and five children.

Detective Superintendent Roberts ruled out any motive involving a woman at that stage, and indicated that the circumstances of both deaths would be the subject of a double coroner's inquest. He said, 'Enquiries will continue on a smaller scale. We have a lot of loose-ends to tie up, mainly to confirm the movements of both dead men.' It was also necessary, of course, to be able to confirm, by way of forensic tests, that it was feasible for a man alone to shoot himself twice.

On Monday 8 March 1982, I went to the forensic science laboratory in Nottingham with another officer to take the pistol for forensic examination and, on the way back, visited a Greek restaurant in Erdington in an effort to try and trace another Greek Cypriot whom we believed could assist us with some background information. I found him on the next day and took a witness statement from him.

On Wednesday 10 March, I visited West Mercia Police scenes-of-crime officers regarding their statements, and was then put on standby regarding another person that we were looking for, who was believed to be about to leave the country. The following day I went with other officers to Heathrow Airport to collect a suspect, a Greek Cypriot aged thirty-five years, who had been about to board a Cyprus Airways flight to Cyprus. I assisted with his interview and, on 16 March 1982, was involved in the interview of a second suspect, a thirty-three-year-old, also of Greek origin. The first was a restaurant owner in Birmingham city centre, and the second a fish-shop owner from Sparkhill. They came from a relatively small but very tight-knit community, where family links remained strong and were material witnesses to the enquiry.

On Thursday 18 March 1982, I reverted to normal duties and spent all day dealing with a second rape suspect, a twenty-four-year-old from Wolverhampton, who had again been arrested by local officers after we had circulated him as being wanted. We escorted him back to Steelhouse Lane, and went through the same process as the first. He duly took part in an identification parade, and was charged the next day with rape. After appearing in court, he joined his associate in prison on remand.

On Thursday 25 March 1982, I was contacted at home following the arrest of the third suspect, a twenty-five-year-old from Wolverhampton who was detained in Wednesfield. My plans for the day changed, and I went to pick him up with Paul and took him back to Steelhouse Lane.

Again, we went through the same process and, the following day, he was positively identified on an ID parade by the complainant, charged and kept in custody. So far, so good – but it was not the end of the story, and I had an extensive file to complete before they could be committed to Crown Court for trial. The complainant had remained resolute and, despite the fact that we still could not be certain where the offence of rape had taken place, she had proved to be a very reliable witness.

On Friday 2 April 1982, Argentine forces landed in the Falkland Islands and captured them two days later. The country was to be focused on the ongoing drama as it unfolded in the next two months, but our work carried on as normal.

On Thursday 8 April 1982, while out with Arthur, we came across a sixty-five-year-old lady on the Stratford Road, who had been the victim of a common assault by an unknown youth. She was very distressed; we took her back home and recorded the incident at the local police station. Time spent in the police service did not give you immunity from the sense of pain and injustice that other people inflicted on innocent victims; but, for the most part, you learnt not to let it get under your skin or to allow other people's pain to become yours.

On Friday 9 April 1982, yet another murder occurred in St Phillip's churchyard in the city centre. Eighteen-year-old Paul Kelly from

Handsworth was beaten during a pitched battle with a number of youths in the shadow of the cathedral. The fight broke out just before 10.30 p.m., near to the junction of Colmore Row and Temple Row. It was described by witnesses as a 'fists and boots' battle.

On arrival of the police, Kelly was found lying with two others, who were seriously injured, in Colmore Row. He was taken to the General Hospital and put on a life-support machine at that stage. As was normal practice, police sealed off the area and surrounding streets, and two suspects were subsequently detained and taken to Steelhouse Lane police station.

With the detective inspector, a silver-haired man who smoked incessantly, I spent the night interviewing the two, a seventeen-year-old and a nineteen-year-old, who were both apprentices. They were both later charged with wounding Paul Kelly with intent, as well as wounding two other people, and kept in custody for court.

At 7.25 a.m. on Saturday 10 April 1982, Paul Kelly lost his battle for life after nine hours and was pronounced dead by the doctors who had fought to save his life. His family were regular attendees at St Augustine's Church in Handsworth, and Father Gerald Jackson led prayers for Paul, who was said to attend Mass regularly. I have never been a religious person but, when people are suffering, they look anywhere for relief and I certainly saw over the years that the answer for some was their faith and their beliefs. For them, it brought real comfort.

On Wednesday 14 April 1982, I went to HMP Winson Green, together with Paul and a solicitor's clerk, to interview the second man charged with the rape. He elected to make a written statement under caution. Thus far, the three of them had remained uncooperative and this was the first sign that cracks were starting to appear. The maximum sentence for rape was life imprisonment and, while it was rare for this to happen, it was nevertheless serious business and 'food for thought', especially when most of your time was spent sitting in a cell with the stench of humanity closing in around you.

On Monday 19 April 1982, I was present in the central lock-up when both of the people I had previously interviewed in respect of the churchyard murder were formally charged and cautioned with the offence, as there was now evidence to connect them to the injuries which had led to the victim's death.

On Monday 26 April 1982, I again went to HMP Winson Green by appointment with Paul. This time, the third man charged with rape elected to start a written statement under caution, which was followed up the next day with a further interview, and a third two days later when the statement was concluded. Although we were not at the stage of admissions to rape, it was clear that they had decided that saying nothing was not doing much for their cause while all the time they remained in custody on remand.

This man came up with an interesting defence in that he now claimed that he could not have had sex with the complainant because, at the time, he was suffering from a sexual disease known as NSU (non-specific urethritis) and that, as it was contagious, if she didn't have it that would prove it. He claimed to have received treatment at the General Hospital. I went to see the complainant on Friday 30 April 1982 and put the facts before her, at which point she disclosed the fact that she had indeed contracted an infection some time after the attack, but that it had been diagnosed as syphilis.

That afternoon, I visited Ward 19 at the General Hospital, which was a separate building at the rear of the hospital, and specialised in sexual-health issues. I dutifully stood in the queue at the reception and, when I got to the front, announced who I was and the fact that I needed to speak to someone. The man behind me was a tall man of West Indian origin, who whispered 'Babylon' to the people behind, which was the 'in word' for police at the time.

The reception staff quickly ushered me through to see the sister in charge and my education commenced in relation to sexually transmitted diseases. Even though I was dealing with a very serious case, confidentiality was crucial to the hospital staff in maintaining patient confidence, so the last thing they wanted was me in the queue.

After taking a further statement from the complainant, and her boyfriend, who had also become infected, I was back at Ward 19 four days later to deal with a query, but this time they let me in through the back door. Following compliance with medical disclosure issues, all of these facts formed part of the evidence at the future trial of the three defendants.

All three men appeared at Birmingham Magistrates' Court again on Friday 7 May 1982 and were again remanded in custody pending committal proceedings. All three of them were jointly charged with abduction and rape as co-conspirators, even though the evidence indicated that, while two of the defendants had engaged in sexual intercourse with the victim without her consent, the driver of the vehicle had not actually touched her at any stage and remained in the driver's seat as a passive observer.

On Saturday 8 May 1982, I was engaged with yet another wounding in Paradise Circus, wherein a man had been stabbed by a twenty-two-year-old, who was later charged with a serious wounding after we had taken statements from no less than seventeen witnesses.

On Friday 14 May 1982, the rape case took another twist and turn. During the morning, the case was adjourned at Birmingham Magistrates' Court for 'old-style' committal proceedings to take place, where all of the evidence would be heard in full before a decision was made as to whether to commit the case to Crown Court. These were rare occasions in cases, where the defence solicitors would seek to test the witnesses and submit that there was 'no case to answer'. The view of the legal profession was simply that it was their duty to provide the best possible defence for their clients, and it was often a gruelling experience for victims. It was even worse for rape victims, who could be questioned at length about their private lives and sexual history, all of which was aimed at trying to discredit them as a witness.

In the afternoon, I was tied up in Wolverhampton with Paul, investigating an allegation that one of the witnesses in the case had been interfered with, and took possession of a number of letters written from prison by one of the three accused. I was later made aware of an allegation that the complainant and her boyfriend were also involved in a conspiracy to pervert the course of justice.

The allegation was that they had been paid money not to give evidence.

On Monday 17 May, I updated a senior solicitor from the prosecuting solicitors department about the nature of the allegations, and then saw the complainant with her boyfriend at Steelhouse Lane police station. He was of West Indian origin, as were the defendants and, by whatever means they had been traced to their home address and presented with money by persons unknown, as well as being threatened that harm would come to them, and other witnesses, if they gave evidence. We took further statements from them and, in the afternoon, I arranged with the social services for the victim to be re-housed.

These events had not helped the case but, despite taking the money, she was adamant that she was, and always had, intended to give evidence. The case would hinge essentially on whether she would be a credible witness or not at the committal proceedings.

On Monday 24 May, Arthur and I received some information concerning the whereabouts of a stolen car, which was said to be in a rented garage in Flaxley Road, Stechford. We found the owner of the garage and, later that evening, examined a Ford Capri inside. The next morning we found a suspect for the theft, a twenty-eight-year-old and, after confirming that the vehicle was in fact stolen, charged him at Stechford police station.

The following day, I obtained a witness summons at Birmingham Magistrates' Court for the doctor from Ward 19, who had treated the defendant charged with rape, and served it on him in the afternoon. The next day I had a case conference with the prosecuting solicitors department and, in the evening, met the parents of the rape victim, who had travelled down from Scotland to be with her.

On Wednesday 26 May 1982, my former colleague Tony Everett was facing his own challenge on the outskirts of the city. At about 10.00 a.m., a man entered a sub-post office in Bartley Green, armed with a sawn-off shotgun. After threatening an assistant, he shot the sub-post master, causing a severe hand injury, and then ran off, having stolen £500 cash.

A number of police officers, who initially attended the scene, were threatened by the robber with the gun, before he ran off to a nearby flat and held the occupants, a couple in their twenties, and their three-month-old daughter, hostage.

Tony, who was a member of No. 4 Regional Crime Squad at the time, was in the area and attended together with a detective inspector called Joe. Tony recalls,

> We just happened to be nearby and, when we got there, we were told by officers that the suspect had gone into a maisonette in Cromwell Lane and was believed to be holding a couple and their child hostage.
>
> I managed to warn other residents in the block to leave, and then gained access to the maisonette immediately above the one where people were being held. Eventually, I managed to engage the suspect by leaning over the balcony and getting him to talk to me from the window below. At first, he pointed his gun upwards towards where I was standing on a balcony, and I was thankful for the fact that I was standing on a concrete block!
>
> By this time officers armed with .38 revolvers, and wearing bullet proof vests, had cordoned off the area. It took me some time but, eventually, I was able to establish some sort of rapport with the robber and, during the course of the day I lowered cigarettes, and fish and chips, down to

the people below in a basket attached to a piece of rope. The suspect was petrified that he had murdered the sub-post master and that he was looking at life imprisonment. I managed to get the senior managers to get the injured man speaking live on the local BRMB radio station to confirm that he had received hospital treatment and was okay.

This appeared to reassure him, and he agreed to come out and surrender himself at 7.00 p.m. that day. At this time, he came out of the front door with the shotgun in his right hand and a large amount of paper money in his left. I ordered him to throw the firearm as far away from himself as he could, which he did, and, prior to armed officers moving in to arrest him, he threw the money up in the air. He was led away by three officers with a blanket over his head.

The hostages were released unharmed, at which point one of them commented to the media that, 'he was very good to us all through the day. He even let me feed and change the baby. We didn't know him from Adam, he just burst into the flat this morning. We feel a bit upset, but everything is going to be okay now.'

At the subsequent trial of the offender, Mr Justice Peter Pain commended a number of officers for their courage, including Tony, and the defendant was sentenced to twelve years' imprisonment.

Tony Everett was no stranger to dangerous situations during the course of his service. On one occasion, while on patrol outside the Crescent Theatre in Cumberland Street, city centre, he spotted a fire inside. He smashed a door in with his shoulder, and single-handedly tackled a blaze with a fire extinguisher, which was near to the costumes for a *Guys and Dolls* production. On another occasion, he found himself stuck on the roof of a derelict building, as he tried to rescue two young boys who were stranded there, and ended up being brought down to earth by fire officers using an 85-foot hydraulic platform. In yet another incident, one involving a car chase, he and other officers finished up rescuing the occupant from a canal after he had dived into the water, trying to escape, and got stuck in mud. This offender was later found to be on parole from prison, and was wanted for committing a robbery while in possession of an imitation firearm.

Tony recalls one final incident involving firearms which had a slightly more humorous ending:

A member of the public dialled 999 to say that there were men with guns outside the Birmingham Mint in Icknield Street, Hockley. Myself and

'Bunny' Jones attended and, as we were approaching, we spotted four men wearing pin-striped suits and carrying what appeared to be Thompson sub-machine guns. We quickly decided that we were going to drive straight at them, but then we suddenly spotted a couple of people with cameras. It turned out to be the pop group Paper Lace posing for publicity for their new record, 'The Night Chicago Died'. The guns were imitation and they got their publicity, which included a photo of myself and Bunny in the local paper examining the guns.

Perhaps the strangest violent incident of all was when Tony was actually assaulted in Ladywood police station itself. Following the arrest of members of a well-known family, a number of men stormed the front office in an effort to free them. A pitched battle ensued, during which Tony and two colleagues were attacked. Seven men, including a father and three of his sons, were arrested and later appeared in court.

On Friday 28 May 1982, the old-style committal proceedings for the rape case took place in Court Number 7 at Birmingham Magistrates' Court. The victim gave evidence and the case was adjourned. More visits to Ward 19 followed and a witness summons for yet another doctor, who was required to give evidence in relation to the infection caught by the boyfriend.

On Monday 14 June, we all duly attended at Court Number 13 at Birmingham Magistrates' Court for the resumption of the old-style committal proceedings. Other witnesses gave evidence and, at the conclusion, all three were remanded in custody to Crown Court for trial. On that same day, fighting officially ended in the Falkland Islands, following the liberation of the capital Port Stanley by British Forces and the surrender of Argentine Forces.

On 17 June 1982, my detective inspector alluded in my annual appraisal to the fact that I 'did not suffer fools gladly and could occasionally appear intolerant of people ... '

On Thursday 1 July 1982, I went to Moseley to serve the 'absolute witness order' on the rape complainant, which meant that, as the three defendants were pleading 'not guilty', she would have to give evidence again at Crown Court. Despite everything, she remained resolute about standing in the witness box again. There was a simplicity about her that I knew would make it easier for a jury to deliberate on her evidence and, above all else, she had 'guts'. The next day, I served a similar order on her boyfriend in Edgbaston, although the relationship was no longer a strong one and I was not entirely convinced that he would turn up at court.

On Tuesday 6 July 1982 I spent all morning on my day off in Birmingham Crown Court Number 6, where the affray trial in relation to the 'Biker' murder in Hurst Street, June 1981, was taking place before Judge Toyn. A number of defendants were indicted with specific serious public-order offences, including the two that I had interviewed. It was to be a contested trial and the court was packed with defendants in the dock, a host of barristers, and family and supporters in the public gallery. It was a very tense atmosphere, and we had a visible uniform police presence, as the potential for rival factions to turn up to confront them was very real, as well as trying to make sure that witnesses were not intimidated as they gave evidence. Some of these people were seriously violent individuals, and there was no doubt that they would be totally focused on witnesses as they stood in the witness box.

It was a trial that would inevitably go on for some days and, at some stage, I would be required to give evidence; however, for the time being, I left it with the officers in the case who would need to be there at all times.

The next day, I attended a serious robbery at the Midland Bank in Dartmouth Street, where one person had been arrested at the scene by a headquarters CID team. This sort of robbery was becoming more prevalent and, in the most serious cases, some criminals were prepared to carry loaded firearms, with the preferred choice for many being sawn-off shotguns yet again.

Later that evening, I met an informant, who gave me the names of two individuals involved in the theft of the West Bromwich mayor's chain of office, which I passed on to the local detective inspector next day. In September 1981, regalia worth thousands of pounds, including the mayoral chains of the former Tipton and Wednesbury councils, were stolen from a plate-glass showcase in the foyer at West Bromwich Town Hall. Three eighteen-carat gold and jewelled chains and pendants worth more than £20,000 were stolen, despite automatic alarm systems linked to West Bromwich police station being activated. The property was never recovered.

On Friday 9 July 1982, Paul and I went to Huyton police station in Liverpool to interview three locals in relation to the theft of a motor vehicle. We dealt with the three, and drove back in the dark. It was nearly midnight before we got back to Steelhouse Lane and tiredness had once again set in.

On the same date, Judge Toyn directed that three of the defendants in the Biker trial be formally found not guilty on a charge of affray. All three had denied the charge, although they did agree to be bound over to keep the peace for two years, in the sum of £200. The jury were also directed to find another one not guilty of possessing an offensive weapon, namely a pair of crutches, but his trial on a charge of affray continued, along with those of nine others.

At this time, I started working with another CID officer, who was of short build and could be quite intense. He was very hard-working and articulate but, on occasions, came into conflict with colleagues. After someone threatened to take him outside and put him straight, I had to give him some advice about modifying his style.

I was back at Birmingham Crown Court on Wednesday 21 July 1982 for two days in relation to the bikers. I had given my evidence, which was largely uncontested. On the afternoon of the second day, eight defendants, who had been found guilty by the jury, were given various sentences, including prison. In the main, it had been a good result and both of the people I had interviewed were among those convicted.

Postscript: 'Ugly' came to notice again in the press on 5 March 1987, when Birmingham Crown Court heard how seven armed men in a hatchback car planned to attack a rival gang of bikers. Police found a loaded sawn-off double-barrelled shotgun with seventeen cartridges, eight knives, four metal bars, two wooden staves, a wrench and an axe. All seven men were known as 'apprentices', 'prospects', or full members of the United Bikers of Great Britain. Ugly was among them, and the prosecution claimed that, when a rival gang known as the Motorcycle Tramps had tried to take them over, Ugly had asked for help and five members of the Bristol Chapter responded.

All seven were stopped in the car at 1.30 a.m. on August 28 1986 in a routine stop-check in Kings Heath in Birmingham. All of them were subsequently convicted of conspiracy to inflict grievous bodily harm and carrying offensive weapons. Ugly was sentenced to four years' imprisonment, which was reduced on appeal twelve months later to three years in prison.

Defence and prosecution lawyers moved in small circles and knew each other well. The police moved in and out of both elements and, in many respects, I came to know the defence solicitors better. I played everything 'dead straight' with them, and expected the same from them, even though we all had a job to do. I gave respect and expected it back – this was not personal – it was a job. On occasions, we used to use the same pubs for a drink after work and there was often a lot of friendly 'banter' between us.

On Wednesday 28 July, I was on nights and went to a flat in one of the tower blocks at Six Ways Aston, following an allegation of abduction. The complainant was a single woman, who knew her tormentor and was in fear of him. Following a call, I raced back there two hours later with uniform officers and detained a twenty-five-year-old man who had damaged the front door of the woman's flat. She was shaken, but refused to make a complaint; however, as it was council property, we didn't need her complaint and we got around the problem by arresting him for criminal damage.

In those days, abusive relationships and domestic violence were vastly under-reported to the police, who had neither the training, nor indeed sometimes the inclination, to investigate them properly. I hated the power that such offenders gave themselves, although simultaneously it was obvious that in essence they were nothing but cowards.

During the course of that week, I worked with a DC called Joe, who was a 'real grafter'; we were run off our feet dealing with over sixteen prisoners for various offences of wounding and thefts. The nightclubs we covered ensured a steady flow of prisoners for this type of crime.

On Saturday 31 July, Joe and I got involved with a job at Bradford Street, where some juveniles had been arrested for burglary and a serious wounding had occurred at one of the local pubs. The acting inspector had the name of a suspect, but some information had also come in that a shotgun was hidden at an address connected to him in a flat in a tower block in Highgate. I spoke to a senior officer regarding the availability of firearms officers, but the information did not reach the threshold for deployment, so off we went 'mob-handed' to see what we could find. Just before 2.00 a.m., we gained access to the flat, where two brothers were present, and we recovered a shotgun from the kitchen. They were duly arrested and, at the same time, other officers traced the suspect for wounding. We left three good prisoners lodged in the cells for the day-turn CID to deal with.

Also on Saturday 31 July 1982, John Swain was on a late-turn, working on B Unit at Digbeth, when he showed just how some police officers develop a 'nose' for detecting criminals. He recalls,

I was asked by one of the sergeants to bring some chips into the station. I was a bit put out because, as an officer with a few years' service, I felt that it was a bit demeaning, so I decided to carry out a stop-check before I went back in.

I saw this brown Austin Princess car parked in Bell Barn shopping centre in Lee Bank with four West Indian youths sat inside. Three of them were wearing overalls, and one was wearing a yellow top. One of them was holding a half-full bottle of brandy and, as I approached the car, I felt that there was just something not quite right. As I was talking to them, I noticed a stick protruding from under the rear seat and, when I checked it, I found that it was half a snooker cue with tape wrapped around one end.

At this point, I quietly asked for some back-up and a fast-response Zulu car arrived shortly afterwards. The more I looked in the car, the more I found; there was another wooden pole with a taped end, a cocked air-gun, a length of rubber hose, a bread knife, and even an open lock knife. It was like a robber's kit.

All four of them were arrested, and it transpired that, when I came upon them, they were planning to rob the garage in Bath Row, but the driver was insisting that he didn't want to be the get-away driver. They were eventually charged with conspiracy to rob. I never did get the chips!

The best stop-check I ever did was when I was out with a probationer constable, showing him the ropes. We stopped someone in Bristol Street and I asked him three questions. The first was, 'Are you waiting for someone?', to which he replied, 'No'. The second question was, 'Have you just been down a passageway to urinate?', to which he replied, 'No'. The third question was, 'Have you just done a burglary?', to which he amazingly replied, 'Yes'.

It transpired that he had just gone round the back of the Ambassador Sauna and had tried to break into the place. We took him to the police station and I gave him a piece of paper to write down what crimes he had been involved in. He proceeded to write down details of thirty burglaries. Now that was a stop-check!

On Sunday 8 August 1982, I went with uniform officers to an address in Great Hampton Street, where we arrested a twenty-two-year-old woman on suspicion of wounding her three-year-old son. She was released 'process to be decided'; after liaising with a doctor from the Children's Hospital, and social services, an interim care order was applied for, enabling the child to be removed to a 'place of safety'.

I spent my thirtieth birthday investigating a robbery in Duddeston Manor Road, in the vicinity of Revesby Walk, in Nechells. Two men attacked a twenty-two-year-old post office employee at 10.25 a.m. as he walked from his van to the nearby Revesby Walk sub-post office. He was struck on the back with a cosh, but was unhurt, and a bag believed to contain several thousand pounds was stolen. The two offenders were waiting for him as he arrived and then ran to a Rover motor vehicle, believed to have been driven by a white youth, before switching to a Fiat saloon car in the Dolman Street area. The offender with the cosh was described in newspapers as 'coloured', aged twenty-eight to twenty-nine years, 6 feet, 2 inches tall, of stocky build with a small beard and moustache. His partner was also described as 'coloured', aged nineteen to twenty years, 5 feet, 8 inches tall, and clean shaven.

I spent two hours taking a statement from an eyewitness who lived in a tower block nearby. We arrested two women, one of whom lived in the same tower block, and a man aged twenty-two years, shortly afterwards and lodged them at Steelhouse Lane police station. Later that evening, we had the names of two good suspects and started doing some research. I knew both of them, and it was not going to be easy. It was the two men who I had been involved with on 13 March 1981 in Handsworth.

On Monday 16 August 1982, I went to see a witness in Nechells regarding the Fiat motor car that had been used in the robbery and arranged to take a witness statement. The following evening, I sat down with the DI and the DCI to plan our next move.

On the morning of Wednesday 18 August 1982, I formally arrested one of the two suspects, aged twenty-one years, on suspicion of the GPO robbery. If anything, he was even more anti-police than when we had met eighteen months before and he was openly hostile during his interviews in the presence of a solicitor. In the afternoon, he was served with forms to attend an identification parade, charged with the offence shortly afterwards, and kept in custody.

The second suspect, an eighteen-year-old, was also arrested and charged during the course of that day, and both appeared at Birmingham Magistrates' Court next day. They were remanded in custody to police cells for three days for further enquiries. They were strongly suspected of having committed other similar robberies in the force area. They also needed to be eliminated from a murder enquiry in Nottingham. We spent hours tracking down additional witnesses and taking statements, and the evidence against them slowly grew stronger. We also had a police witness: a mounted police officer, who just happened to be nearby at the time of the robbery and saw the suspects fleeing.

On Monday 23 August 1982, our first suspect took part in an identification parade at Steelhouse Lane police station, where witnesses from robberies on three other divisions also attended. Two of our witnesses positively identified him as being one of the two robbers. While this was a positive step forward in terms of the evidence chain, a hard slog continued for several weeks as we continued to trace witnesses in the vicinity of Duddeston Manor Road, some of whom were very reluctant to get involved.

Dave Faulkner also had dealings with the first suspect on another occasion, and can vouch for his hatred of the police:

He was one of two brothers, and both of them disliked the police intensely. I was out with some officers doing observations at Masshouse Multi Story Car Park, when we saw him trying to break into a white Escort Cabriolet car, which we believed later they were looking to use on a robbery. I recognised him straight away and a foot chase started. Two other officers got to him first, and he kicked one of them unconscious before we managed to arrest him. I interviewed him later. It was a one-way conversation – I did the talking and he sat there in silence.

On Wednesday 8 September, I was engaged with the local resident beat officer for Aston University when seven Middle-Eastern students were arrested following a disturbance between two opposing Iraqi factions in the Vauxhall dining centre. It seemed that they had forgotten the message to behave. All of them were charged with assaulting each other, as well as public-order offences, and kept in custody overnight for court.

The following day, I went with the beat officer to arrest an eighth person in student accommodation at Stafford Tower and, on Monday 13 September, another two arrests followed from the campus for wounding from the same incident, and then finally an eleventh person for assault.

Although they were from two factions, I charged all eleven as co-accused, which meant that, when they appeared in court, they all had to stand next to each other. They simply hated this and soon got the message that we would not allow politically motivated violence anywhere. In many ways, it was an easy enquiry, as they simply all wanted to complain about each other, even to the extent of claiming damage to the gold chains around their necks during the fighting. Eventually, a twelfth defendant was added to the list. The arrests caused quite a stir and, at one stage, I had to come in on one of my days off to complete a report for the deputy chief constable.

On Wednesday 6 October, the two original robbery defendants, together with a third man arrested in the intervening period, were committed in custody to Crown Court to stand trial. I obtained a banker's order for one of them on the same day, so that I could examine his accounts.

In October 1982, the Special Patrol Group became known as the Operations Support Unit. Mike Cresswell remembers his two-week attachment to the CID during this period:

> During the first week, I was working with Mike Layton and his team. Most of the CID were well dressed, but I had not been in plain clothes before and so had to borrow some of my father's old clothes. In the first week, we were non-stop and I worked five twelve-hour days. For the second week, Mike was on leave, things were quieter and I finished up spending a bit more time in the pubs!

On Friday 15 October, the twelve Iraqis appeared in Court Number 12 at Birmingham Magistrates' Court and the case was remanded. I had already liaised with the prosecuting solicitors department, and we had agreed that in due course we would deal with them by way of a 'bind over' if they agreed to keep the peace.

Further evidence was still coming to light regarding the armed robbery, and the witness list got visibly longer.

On Thursday 21 October, I gave evidence at the trial of the two individuals charged with murder in St Phillip's Churchyard.

On Friday 29 October 1982, the Iraqis appeared at court, and agreed to be bound over in the sum of £250 for two years; they were ordered to pay £25 each towards legal-aid costs. They had been previously served with immigration forms, and their passports seized while on bail, so they knew that it would not be wise to engage in this type of activity again.

6

STOLEN VEHICLES AND
MEETING 'GEORGE'

November 1982 was another month of regular visits to court. The good thing was that Steelhouse Lane police station was next to the Magistrates' and the Crown Courts, so I didn't lose time travelling. I got to know all of the police and civilian ushers who worked there well. If they didn't like you, the chances were you would be right at the end of the list of court cases for the day, so it was worth cultivating relationships. It was like a small community in its own right, and an intriguing place where justice was played out. It was also a place where informants were fostered and the fabric of society was protected.

Bill Rogerson, retired BTP officer, also recalls,

> There was a Sergeant Watts at the court and a PC called 'Paddy'. I got on really well with the sergeant but, if you caught Paddy on an off day, especially when you were halfway through a week of twelve-hour nights, woe betide you, because you could be there until late afternoon.

December 1982 started off in a fairly uneventful way with the usual round of crime reports, some bomb hoax calls to three city-centre stores, and a multi-agency case conference at the Children's Hospital regarding the allegation of wounding on the three-year-old boy. These were always difficult cases to deal with, as the absolute need to protect a child was balanced against the desire to keep families intact. Placing a child on the at-risk register was not taken lightly, and removing a child from the parents and placing it in care, either on a temporary or permanent basis, raised real dilemmas for support workers, who frequently worked long hours with heavy caseloads and limited options. Every risk had to be reviewed, based on facts and evidence.

We now had a new detective chief inspector, who was a tall guy, very bright, and also extremely flamboyant. He used to fiddle with anything that had moving parts attached to it, and things would often come apart in his hands.

On Monday 13 December 1982, the two defendants charged with the GPO robbery appeared in Crown Court Number 8 for 'plea and directions'. They both pleaded 'not guilty' and were remanded for trial. I sat in court while the proceedings took their course and, as usual, received icy stares from the defendants in the dock – I was the enemy.

On the same day, Arthur and I attended the General Hospital regarding the sudden death of a patient on one of the wards. The next morning we did a formal identification of the body with a family member, and then attended the post-mortem held in the Central Mortuary at Newton Street. By now, I had seen many dead bodies over the years, but I never believed anyone who said that they had become immune to it and I know I never did. When the life and spirit has gone from a body, it is possible to put your professional head on and switch off. What is often harder to deal with is the real sense of pain and loss from loved ones who are left behind, especially if the individual has died at a young age.

On Wednesday 15 December, an attempted robbery occurred at a Trustee Savings Bank in New John Street West, Newtown. I did a search of the area with other CID officers, and we recovered the vehicle used in the offence in Gerrard Street. Scenes-of-crime officers attended, and we called for a dog handler, but there was nothing for it to track. I left the enquiry with a DC called John who worked on the Bridge Street West team. He was a strong-minded, able detective, whose career path was to cross mine a number of times over the years.

As the Christmas week approached, we spent more time keeping observations near to bank premises and night safes in the city centre, as they presented easy targets for opportunist thieves, who would prey on unsuspecting shop staff members sent out with large amounts of cash takings to deposit, with little or no apparent thought for security.

On Thursday 23 December 1982, we dealt with a prisoner in the central lock-up who had assaulted two members of staff, and Christmas Eve passed off relatively quietly with an arrest for criminal deception at one of the stores.

Assaults on police officers were depressingly routine, and Mike Cresswell recalls the time he was assaulted as a probationer, while on a traffic attachment at the end of 1982:

> I was out with an experienced traffic officer when we pulled a car over; the driver was obviously drunk. He was a nasty piece of work and I was going to handcuff him, but was told not to bother by the other officer, who obviously knew better! I got in the back seat with the prisoner, and then the other officer let his wife sit in the back seat with us as well. Big mistake!
>
> The prisoner started playing up and, while I had his arm in a lock, I couldn't control his head; he promptly head-butted me twice. I head-butted him twice back and that seemed to calm him down until we got to the station. The moral of the story is don't always accept advice from an officer with more service! The prisoner got six months for assaulting me.

In the following days I was made aware that someone was putting pressure on one of our witnesses for the GPO robbery. A case of arson followed in Duddeston Manor Road, and the person responsible was charged and kept in custody as 1982 passed.

A total of 210,688 crimes were recorded by West Midlands Police during 1982, which represented an increase of 11.93 per cent over the 1981 figures, and included 134 cases of rape. Crimes of violence resulted in forty-five deaths, thirty-nine of which were recorded as murder, and six as manslaughter. All of these offences were detected. By now, offences of wounding had exceeded the 7,000 mark. Offences of robbery increased yet again, with a total of 1,732 recorded; so-called street robberies were still very prevalent.

The first week of January 1983 was particularly busy with a variety of jobs. We dealt with a twenty-two-year-old from Erdington on a Monday, who was found in suspicious circumstances in the nurses' home of the General Hospital. He was kept in overnight and charged next day with a breach of the peace.

On Tuesday morning, I went with a female officer to arrest a woman for theft and deception who worked at Debenhams in Bull Street. In the afternoon, we assisted with the arrest of three people detained by court security for being in possession of stolen property in the court building; rather a strange thing to do in the circumstances. On Wednesday, I was tied up with the arrest of a man for stealing cash from machines in the university sports centre, and likewise on Thursday in connection with an arrest for DHSS frauds. On Friday, I took some further statements from my rape victim, and another witness, and spent Saturday looking without success for a burglary suspect.

On Monday 10 January 1983, I went to a case conference at Number 5 Chambers Fountain Court with Mr Barker, prosecuting QC, for the forthcoming rape trial. The following day was spent warning witnesses to attend.

On Wednesday 12 January, the trial of the three defendants for rape started at Birmingham Crown Court Number 6. All three pleaded 'not guilty' and, although I was the officer in the case, I was not allowed in court to listen to the proceedings as I was giving evidence in relation to the arrests and interviews. I arranged for one of my attached officers to sit in court behind the prosecuting solicitors, so that he could deal immediately with any queries as they arose. It was a slightly cumbersome system, where the prosecuting barrister would pass a note to the prosecuting solicitor if he, or she, wanted something, and they would pass the note to the police, who would deal with it and then reverse the process. There were often bits of paper being passed here and there, but always with solemn faces as befitted the occasion. It didn't go down too well for a judge to see you smiling or being flippant. Likewise, my attached officer was not allowed to give me any information at all in relation to what witnesses had actually said when giving evidence. To do so could compromise the case.

The trial entered its second week and, once I had given my evidence, I was allowed to remain in court to see the proceedings come to a conclusion. The victim, as expected, had been given a hard time by each of the three defence barristers in turn, but remained resolute and all of our witnesses turned up and gave evidence.

On Wednesday 19 January, the jury, having considered all of the evidence, returned 'guilty' verdicts in respect of all three of the defendants for abduction and rape. After their antecedent history had been read out, and mitigation speeches made by the defence, all three were sentenced to five years in prison. The judge made no distinction between the two who had sexual intercourse, and the driver who had not. He was a big guy, but swayed visibly as the sentence was read out.

It was a real result, after all the twists and turns, and a complete vindication of the victim who had finally seen justice done. We had been through a journey together and I admired her courage. She thanked me outside the court and, apart from dealing with a subsequent claim from the Criminal Injuries Compensation Board and arranging for the return of forensic exhibits, I had little further dealings with her.

She had endured a horrifying ordeal, abducted from a street, and placed in fear as she struggled vainly in the darkness of a car surrounded by three men who were complete strangers. At the point of rape, she may well have feared the worst, and yet she had come through the experience with her head held high and shown an inner strength that I have only witnessed on rare occasions. I felt nothing for the defendants, who had shown no remorse throughout and tried every trick that they could think of to get the case thrown out.

I now had another two DCs working with me: one a tall slim officer who could be very opinionated, but who was very enthusiastic and well able to convert prisoners to informants; and Malcolm Halliday, who was a real character. We were quickly back to business as normal and started looking at a number of individuals for fraud, and thefts of blank excise licences.

On Sunday 23 January, I received an anonymous telephone call to the effect that a man wanted for deception by the police in Bournemouth was receiving treatment on a ward at East Birmingham Hospital. A quick check with Dorset Police confirmed that he was in fact wanted but, while in hospital, we couldn't touch him until he was discharged. We kept it all low-key and the hospital agreed to let us know before he was released.

On Wednesday 26 January, we went into Birmingham city centre and visited Park View Hotel, and the Boot nightshelter, trying to trace two individuals whom we wanted for a burglary at some premises called Discount Jewellers in Moor Street. It took us a lot of footwork but, at 6.25 p.m., we found the two: a twenty-two-year-old, and a nineteen-year-old, both of no fixed abode, in Dale End, and arrested them. We took them back to Steelhouse Lane, and they later admitted the burglary, where more than £2,000 worth of property had been stolen, as well as other offences. Because of their backgrounds, both were charged and kept in custody to appear at court next morning.

This was always the tedious part of the job, because you simply could not go home until the overnight remand file had been completed. This entailed completing a summary of the evidence, on an initial WG534 proforma, and attaching statements from witnesses and records of police interviews. If you were asking for a remand in custody, you had to outline what the objections to bail were and to attach records of previous convictions. If you wanted bail conditions such as a condition of residence, sureties, curfews, or a reporting condition at a police station, you had to outline everything. If there was a compensation claim, you had to provide a statement with details, and so it went on. We finished at work at 11.00 p.m. and were back in the office for 8.00 a.m. the next day.

The following morning we set up outside the DHSS offices in Staniforth Street, waiting for a couple of suspects to sign on for their benefits. The DHSS managers were usually very helpful, but normally they did not want people to be arrested on the premises as, in their view, it compromised their staff and raised safety issues. We could live with this by having someone inside ready to give us the nod when they had signed on and were about to leave, but you had to box them in very quickly outside if you wanted to avoid a foot chase, and the potential embarrassment of losing a prisoner.

At 10.15 a.m., we made two arrests but had to lodge them both quickly in the cells in order to assist other staff dealing with a robbery on a Securicor van in Newtown shopping precinct. We did a search of the area and recovered the vehicle used on the job in Alma Way Newtown; we then did some house-to-house enquiries looking for witnesses, before returning to the station to deal with the prisoners. In the evening, we had intended arresting our hospital patient, but his discharge was delayed so I made alternative arrangements.

On Tuesday 8 February 1983, we made a breakthrough regarding the excise licence enquiry when an informant made a test purchase and pointed out the receiver's address to us in Winson Green. We also had the name of a car-sales pitch in Handsworth thought to be involved. In the afternoon, I had to attend a briefing at the police training centre Tally Ho, having been nominated to participate in a joint training exercise with the military at Hereford.

Also on this date in 1983, the world of horseracing was shocked to hear of the kidnapping of Shergar, the Irish racehorse that won the Epsom Derby by ten lengths in 1981. The horse, a bay colt with a distinctive white blaze on its head, was stolen from Ballymany Stud, near the Curragh in County Kildare, Ireland, and was never seen again.

Dave 'J' recalls a lighter moment connected to this case:

At the time we had a detective sergeant, who came from an Irish background and was always playing tricks on people, so a few of the staff decided to get their own back. They managed to put a completely false telex message together, which purported to be from the Garda Police, requesting that sensitive enquiries be made in the area, and that preferably they should be conducted by an officer of Irish descent as there was a strong local Irish community. The upshot was that this detective sergeant was led to believe that Shergar was being kept at the back of the Sydenham pub in Sparkbrook, and he eventually visited the place only to find some retired pit-ponies that were kept there by some travellers. He didn't know the real truth for ages until a senior officer eventually put him wise.

On Wednesday 16 February, yet another armed robbery took place outside Lloyds Bank in Colmore Row, involving a Security Express van and the theft of £16,000 in cash. Two armed robbers grabbed a firm's payroll from outside Lloyds Bank, Eden Place, in the afternoon. As the Security Express guard was crossing the pavement, he was confronted by a man about 5 feet, 8 inches tall and in his mid-thirties, dressed in navy-blue clothing and wearing a peaked cap. He initially produced what appeared to be a sawn-off shotgun, and tried to take the cash bag away from the guard. He was then joined by a second man, also in his mid-thirties but much taller, who was brandishing a handgun and who successfully snatched the bag. They ran down Eden Place pedestrian area to a red Ford Cortina, whose registration plate began with the letters WFD, which then sped off in the direction of Paradise Circus. We did another search for the suspect vehicle, but this time it was a fruitless effort.

On Thursday 17 February, I went with a uniform inspector and a serial of officers to the Royal Army Ordinance Corps in Herford to take part in a joint exercise aimed at being prepared for acts of terrorism. We threw ourselves into a scenario, involving the initial search of an area for an explosive device, which was conducted by uniform staff drawn from several areas. Eventually, as events played out, a 'hostage victim' was discovered with a device attached to them and the army bomb-disposal experts were called in to disarm it, while police cordons were put into place.

It was all very serious stuff and the military used these exercises as part of the re-accreditation process for their staff. My role as a CID officer was to advise on the forensic recovery and evidential aspects of the investigation. The senior officers present were in particular put under a lot of stress, as there were strict procedures between the military and the police as to who was in charge at what point, and handover procedures that had to be followed, particularly if there were live terrorists to be dealt with.

The next day I went with a female officer to return clothing to the rape victim, who seemed to be doing well, considering. On Sunday 20 February, the vehicle used in the Colmore Row robbery was found in Newtown, and we did the usual enquiries.

John Swain started working on the Plain Clothes Unit in February 1983 and, like others, did his fair share of observations in the Station Street area for people engaged in 'cottaging'. John recalls,

On one occasion, I had just been down to the toilets and, when I came back up, I walked over to the doorway of the Scouts shop and stood there. This bloke came over and stood next to me and tried to engage me in conversation. He told me that he had just come down from Lancaster, and then asked me if I would like to go somewhere. Before giving me a chance to reply, he suddenly grabbed my 'goolies', at which point I quickly said, 'Yes – Digbeth police station!'

Another favourite spot for couples to go to was a space above the lift shaft on the top floor of the Albany multi-storey car park, where we often made arrests for gross indecency. On another occasion, I was working in plain clothes and we did some observations in Station Street on a stolen car. In those days I was using an old Morris Oxford, and we were watching a new Toyota. The thief came back, and somehow managed to get into the car and pull away before we could stop him. Fortunately, the driver's window was open by 2 inches, and I literally pulled the glass from the window and clung on as he dragged me along. I then managed to grab the steering wheel, and steered him into the outside wall of the parcels yard situated on platform 12 of New Street Station. In the process, he knocked over a pedestrian and I got injured, but we got him.

On Wednesday 2 March, I was on duty in the afternoon at Steelhouse Lane police station, when I was asked to deal with a man who had turned up at the station in a distressed state. He was a thirty-eight-year-old from the Streetly area, and it soon became apparent that he was in severe financial difficulties. It took some time to calm him down and to get to the bottom of things, but finally he disclosed that, in order to try and resolve his problems, he had become involved in criminal activity. He ultimately gave me some information in relation to the theft of two motor vehicles from a large car outlet in Digbeth.

Above: The site of the Crown pub in Hill Street and previous location of the 'Silver Slipper' toilets. (Courtesy of Bary Crowley)

Below: Photograph taken by Paul Rainey of mounted police officers at a colliery during the miners' strike. (Scan 01870002)

Above: Officers deployed to miners' strike preparing for public-order duties. (Paul Rainey)

Below: Officers playing cards in a rest period during the miners' strike. (Paul Rainey)

Above: Digbeth police station. (West Midlands Police Museum Group)

Below: Police cadets on parade outside Tally Ho police training centre, Edgbaston, Birmingham, *c.* 1979. (West Midlands Police Museum Group)

Left: Police officer in public-order kit, holding truncheon and shield. (West Midlands Police Museum Group)

Below: Winson Green Prison, opened in October 1849. (West Midlands Police Museum Group)

Above: Central lock-up, Steelhouse Lane, Birmingham. (West Midlands Police Museum Group)

Below: The 'Battle of Digbeth', 1978. (West Midlands Police Museum Group)

A meeting held by the National Front at Digbeth Civic Hall on 18.2.78. precipitated the use of riot shields for the first time by West Midlands Police.

Above: The 'Battle of Saltley Gate', 1972. (West Midlands Police Museum Group)

Below: Two police officers talking to a group of youths in Birmingham city centre. (West Midlands Police Museum Group)

Police cadets outside Tesco in Birmingham city centre. (West Midlands Police Museum Group)

PC Dave Cross in old police uniform, next to a police vehicle outside the WMP museum. (West Midlands Police Museum Group)

Left: Two mounted police officers, including PC Kay Weale, outside Victoria Law Courts in Birmingham. (West Midlands Police Museum Group)

Below: Search teams in Handsworth after the 1985 riots, including PC Mo Barlow. (West Midlands Police Museum Group)

An hour later, he was formally arrested by a colleague from Digbeth police station to be dealt with. In my experience, people often expressed a real sense of relief when finally owning up to criminal behaviour, especially when it was not their usual lifestyle. As a police officer, I made no excuses for exploiting this knowledge to get to the truth.

On Thursday 3 March, we had an early start and went out as a team to Mansell Road in Small Heath, where we made three arrests for criminal deception after working with DHSS fraud investigators. Another two arrests were made elsewhere, and that gave us five people to deal with, all of whom had been involved in making false benefit claims. All five were charged and kept in custody for court the next day.

The following morning my team made another two arrests. We were on a roll, but there was no time for complacency, as we got tied up working on a robbery at the Midland Bank in Great Hampton Row in the afternoon.

On Sunday 13 March, while on night duty, John and I dealt with a burglar, before finally assisting uniform colleagues regarding the arrest of a man suspected of the theft of £400. He had been arrested by a PC and then lodged in the cells at Digbeth, but he wasn't admitting anything. John and I took 'the bull by the horns' and paid him a visit.

When people are taken into custody, they are always searched by the arresting officers, both for their own safety – e.g. to remove belts, shoe laces or anything that could form a ligature – as well as ensuring that they are not carrying concealed weapons or drugs. The police also have responsibility for ensuring the safe-keeping of a prisoner's personal effects, all of which have to be listed in detail on the custody record. The process also assists in establishing the identity of the individual, especially if drunk and fighting. Finally, a search of the arrested person can provide evidence relating to the offences for which they have been arrested. Searches needed to be comprehensive, but measured and proportionate. Strip searches were not the norm, but we had the power to carry them out if necessary.

In this case, we were pretty confident that our man was the thief. He was strip-searched and the stolen money was found in his underpants. He had literally been sitting on the evidence in a cell for a few hours.

On Tuesday 22 March 1983, I attended yet another robbery, with the DI, on a Securicor vehicle in Newtown shopping precinct and spent a couple of hours with witnesses. This type of offence was occurring with depressing regularity, and usually consisted of two active robbers, at least one of whom would have some sort of weapon, and a third member of the team in a waiting getaway car, which would normally be stolen and on false plates. The robbers would do the snatch, and drive a relatively short distance away, where they would dump the stolen car and switch to a second vehicle.

On this occasion, the circumstances were slightly different, however, as two robbers escaped with £4,800, contained in a cash box, on foot, after their getaway car failed to start. The thieves snatched the box from a security guard and ran to a nearby multi-story car park, where they tried to start a Datsun car but without success. They then made off on foot, still carrying the box, which was later found, minus its contents, in an alleyway near Six Ways Aston. Both of the robbers were described as black. One was aged about nineteen years, of very slim build with permed wet-look hair. The second was aged about seventeen years, of slight build and 5 feet, 6 inches tall. No one was physically hurt in the attack but, in my experience, security officers very often suffered from severe stress as a result of their ordeal, sometimes leading to long-term sickness and, in extreme cases, feeling unable to perform the role again.

On Monday 28 March 1983, we picked up an enquiry relating to the theft of a JCB and road-laying machine from Heneage Street. In the afternoon, an informant gave me some information regarding two West Indian youths who were suspected of stealing a W-registration Ford Capri car from the Bournville area, and setting it on fire in Newtown. Finally, at the end of the day, I went to a magistrate's house in Edgbaston to swear a search warrant out for an address in Smethwick, where I believed that there were some stolen musical instruments.

On Tuesday 29 March, I went with four officers to Piddock Road police station in Smethwick and, after liaising with the local CID, went to an address in Thomas Street to execute the search warrant. We recovered a saxophone, which we believed to be stolen, and arrested a twenty-one-year-old. We went to some shop premises that specialised in musical instruments and, shortly afterwards, arrested a nineteen-year-old on suspicion of theft. Two further arrests followed during the course of the afternoon on suspicion of theft and handling stolen property.

The following day, we started searching for a suspect whom we believed had been involved in the theft of a motor vehicle. At 5.30 p.m., we saw the seventeen-year-old from Handsworth driving his own vehicle in Lea Hall Road. We took him and his vehicle to Bridge Street West police station, and later got the complainant for the theft to come to the station to have a look at it. He was able to positively identify parts on the vehicle as having come from his own, which was valued at £6,000. The suspect was later charged with theft.

On Thursday 31 March at 3.45 p.m., I went with two of my team to Birch Road East in Witton in response to a call from the complainant for the JCB theft in Heneage Street. In a factory unit, we found the stolen JCB, which was valued at £7,000. At 6.45 p.m., we arrested a thirty-eight-year-old at an address in Solihull for the theft and, after searching a transport yard with a negative result, we dealt with him at Steelhouse Lane.

The next day, I got another search warrant for a garage in Newtown, where we had information that there were three stolen vehicles, and we executed the warrant on Saturday 2 April, but found nothing. It didn't mean that the information was wrong; it just meant that, by the time we turned the place over, the property was gone. I was satisfied with the quality of the informants we had that were providing regular updates and, as they only got paid on results, they had nothing to gain from misleading us.

On Monday 18 April 1983, another robbery occurred in the afternoon on a post-office van in Lower Temple Street, where £25,000 was taken and, yet again, a stolen vehicle was used. Two men described as burly and wearing balaclavas attacked two post-office workers in Birmingham city centre, just after they had collected the cash from WHSmith newsagents. They were threatened with pick-axe handles by the men as they were about to load the money into the post-office van in a nearby underground service delivery area, and the cash bag was stolen. One of the post-office workers also had an alarm device taken from him before he had chance to use it. The robbers then escaped in a stolen Evening Mail van, driven by a third man.

My detective chief inspector, Richard Chidley, said to the media, 'This was a very well planned and executed robbery', and confirmed that we were investigating similarities with another raid on Barclays bank in Colmore Row, when a similar amount of cash was taken earlier in the year.

During the course of the robbery, which occurred at 4.30 p.m., one of the suspects removed his balaclava so that the post-office workers could hear him better and, in the half-light, they saw his face. The stolen van was taken from Pershore Road, Stirchley, at 11.25 a.m. the day before, and was subsequently found abandoned on the car park of WEB Coating

Systems Ltd in Lower Tower Street, Newtown, which was about a ten-minute drive from the scene of the robbery.

On 1 May 1983, Sinn Fein held a march and rally in Birmingham to commemorate the deaths of some hunger strikers, which passed off without incident. At this time, I started looking at an emerging trend whereby large groups of black and white youths were engaging in thefts from shops in the city centre. I spent time in the Birmingham shopping centre and submitted a report to senior managers on the issue. I remained interested in street-gang activity and was always looking for something new to get my teeth into.

Dave Faulkner recalls one of his experiences with Zulu Warriors in 1983:

> It was a Saturday afternoon, at about 12.30 p.m., and we received a report of a number of youths associated with the Zulu Warriors gathering in the Bull Ring. Next thing was they were doing a run through, 'steaming' through the open markets and grabbing clothing from stalls as they ran. I just happened to be in the right place at the right time, and one of them ran straight into my arms, carrying seven pairs of trousers. He was just sixteen years old then but I got to know him well over time.

On Monday 9 May 1983, the trial started at Birmingham Crown Court Number 8 of four defendants charged in connection with the Revesby Walk GPO robbery in Nechells, which went on until Tuesday 17 May 1983. It involved the defendant who had been prone to serious stares. He was found guilty by the jury, and two other defendants involved in the actual robbery pleaded guilty. A fourth defendant on the periphery was found not guilty and discharged. Justice was served and some seriously nasty criminals were sent to prison for six years.

The following day, I saw Chip again, after some time, and he gave me some information regarding a burglary at Hockley Flats, where property valued at £6,000 had been stolen. I passed it on to an old colleague at Ladywood, as I simply didn't have the time to action it.

On Thursday 2 June, at 4.40 p.m., we attended a musical-instrument outlet and turned our attention to two individuals aged seventeen years from Erdington, who were trying to sell some amplifiers. They were unable to provide any satisfactory responses in relation to ownership and were arrested. We later identified the amplifiers as having been stolen during a house burglary in the same road as one of those arrested the previous day. They were both charged with burglary, and their recent possession of the property following the break in would be a strong factor in helping to determine their guilt. A lot of people tried to wriggle out of a conviction for burglary by claiming to have 'bought property at a good price from an unknown man in a pub', so every little helped.

On Thursday 9 June 1983, I worked a 6.00 p.m. to 2.00 a.m. 'first night watch' to provide a low-profile policing presence at Birmingham Council House and Birmingham Art Gallery, with another CID officer to cover the counting stations set up for the general election.

On 17 June, the detective inspector commented on my annual appraisal: 'He becomes more patient as he matures and can be relied on to supervise and guide with tact and authority ...' In normal circumstances, the words might have been motivational, but I was not totally convinced.

I went out with Malcolm Halliday on Tuesday 28 June 1983 and arrested a twenty-year-old from St Paul's Square in Hockley on suspicion of burglary dwelling house. He went by the alias 'Chuck Rogers' – there was no accounting for taste.

Friday 1 July marked a change in direction, and I had decided that we would start to get proactive with some of the professional gangs of thieves operating in the city centre. This meant 'dressing down', and getting out and about on the streets in pairs, focusing on the shopping areas around Corporation Street and New Street.

It felt a bit like the old DSU days, although I knew that I would only be able to fit the observations in around the conventional work. We had our first break in the afternoon when a description was passed over the radio of two suspects, one of whom had assaulted a member of staff in one of the stores. I was with two officers attached to the CID and we were close to the ramp leading from New Street up towards the shopping centre and New Street station.

Almost immediately we saw two individuals matching the description crossing the road towards us. They were obviously in a hurry and kept looking behind themselves constantly. This meant that they were not focused on us and, as they reached us, we hustled them into a doorway, arrested them on suspicion of assault, and handcuffed them. One of them, who became involved with the Zulu Warriors, was quite anti-police, while the second was in a state of shock. By the end of the day, one was charged with the assault.

'Nick' was fourteen years of age at the time and was already an established 'Bluenose' Birmingham City football fan, having attended his first home game at St Andrew's at the age of ten. He was also very familiar with the city-centre shoplifting scene and recalls,

I had a bit of a difficult upbringing and found myself mixing with the wrong crowd. We used to go into Birmingham city centre in groups of up to six people, looking for designer gear such as Farah. The Co-op store and Rackhams were favourites, but you had to be careful to keep an eye out for the store detectives, and the women were the worst. A favourite trick was to go into a changing room with a pair of sports trousers to try on and then come out wearing them under your own. You had to watch, though, that they didn't make a rustling noise as you walked out!

Sometimes little teams would head out from New Street station to places like Worcester, fill a big bag up, and come back on a train. People rarely paid for a train ticket. I got detained once for keeping watch when a mate stole a Pierre Sanger cardigan and I got a caution. That was enough for me – it frightened me to death, and the store detective was built like an Amazonian woman.

Nick was never a hardened football hooligan, but witnessed the weekly ritual of football-related violence at fairly close quarters during this period and, in the years ahead,

I went to all the home and away games, and already knew some of the Junior Business Boys. They were predominantly a youth group aligned to the Zulu Warriors – the 'up and comers'. The worst act of violence that I witnessed was in Coventry city centre, when I saw one of those big beer mugs with handles on come flying through the air into a crowd of fans and literally watched the glass disintegrate into someone's face.

When a home game was on, I would go with my mates to New Street station, buy a platform ticket, and stand on the bridge watching fans travelling through, just to see what was happening. I was never into drugs, but some of the kids used to sniff glue from plastic bags. The first memory I have of seeing some serious hooligans was a bunch of West Ham ICF (Inter City Firm) fans, who were really well dressed in suits, nice sports gear, and raincoats. Everyone in those days liked the fashion aspect.

The worst violence was always when Birmingham City played the Villa, with fighting everywhere and even CS gas being sprayed by fans. After matches at St Andrew's, we would congregate by a small park, before walking back into the city centre to see what was about. People started carrying small telescopic umbrellas to use as weapons as well as newspapers that were rolled up very tight.

Joe Tildesley was a sergeant on the Special Patrol Group between 1981 and 1983, and recalls the atmosphere that pervaded football matches in those days:

> I was mostly on E serial, and then later L serial for a while with ten officers. Football seemed to occupy three days a week, with terrible incidents of violence all blurring into one another. It was relentless, and not unusual for just my serial alone to make up to twenty arrests in a high-profile game, without counting the numbers of people we threw out of grounds. Leeds, Millwall, Chelsea, Manchester United, and the 'Blues' fans were the worst to deal with. I remember on one occasion getting a really good kicking when we were trying to deal with a pitch invasion at a ground. I got isolated from my serial and got pushed from behind onto the floor before they put the boot in. We had a black officer on my serial and he suffered terrible racial abuse. What he put up with was nothing short of remarkable.

One of the attached officers who worked with me was a well-built officer with ginger hair by the name of Barrie. He was an excellent officer, who was both fearless and routinely enthusiastic. He had an easy way with people, and I enjoyed having him on my team. By the end of his service, he was a detective chief inspector and an expert in covert policing tactics.

While working together, we met and cultivated probably the most prolific informant I was ever to work with, even better than Chip. For the purposes of this story I will refer to him as 'George'.

On Saturday 2 July 1983, we hit the city centre again, looking for three suspects, two of whom were brothers who were wanted for theft and robbery. Four of us went out together and, at 2.20 p.m., one of them, a sixteen-year-old on the run from a remand centre, was arrested. We stop-checked six youths acting suspiciously in Rackhams, and I spent the rest of the day interviewing the suspect in the presence of a social worker and visiting his mother in Bordesley Green. At the end of the evening, I met George in a local pub, who promised further information. Anything to do with informant meetings had to be shown in red in your diary and mine started to show a lot of very positive red ink.

On Wednesday 6 July, I went out again with one of my team, patrolling the Bull Ring and Birmingham shopping centres and keeping a look out for a number of youths involved in till snatches. We dealt with a prisoner for theft an hour later and then, just before we were due to finish, our prospective Zulu was arrested again for theft, together with another future Zulu who was well known for the size of his waist and his skills as a professional shoplifter. He would never admit to anything but he did have a sense of humour. There followed a till snatch at McDonald's, which we went to before going home.

On Thursday 7 July, I took the team into the city centre looking for two brothers that George had pointed us towards, who were believed to be involved in the snatches. At 3.30 p.m., we found the first brother, a twenty-year-old from Erdington, in Stephenson Place, and arrested him on suspicion of theft from a till at Tesco. Half an hour later, we found the second brother, a twenty-one-year-old from Newtown, at the same location and arrested him on suspicion of theft from McDonald's. We didn't have enough evidence to charge the first brother, who was bailed to return to the police station at a later date. After speaking again to the security staff at McDonald's, I was satisfied that we had enough evidence and charged the second brother with theft, keeping him in custody for court next day.

On Saturday 9 July, I sat down with the DI to look at how to deploy a serial of officers from the Operations Support Unit to assist the observations into city-centre street crime and then briefed and posted them. Within three hours, they had produced three prisoners for theft.

We had another DCI at this time, who was a bit of a 'worrier', and, instead of being pleased about the results we were achieving, he was more concerned about the number of hours' overtime being worked. Not exactly motivating stuff, but I let it ride. I took him with me to see the informant the following week, so that he could make a payment and this seemed to reassure him as George proceeded to put two more jobs in.

On Wednesday 3 August, we went to Hall Green and arrested a sixteen-year-old for theft of travel tickets. We recovered some of the tickets and, when interviewed in the presence of his parents, he admitted the offence and was charged. The following day, a further arrest for theft followed. A further target from Birchfield was suspected of stealing Armani jumpers from a shop called 'Max's'. I went to see a local magistrate in Edgbaston to get a search warrant, and we later recovered £750 worth of stolen property at his home address, which the shop manager identified.

On Friday 5 August, we brought yet another job to fruition with the arrest of a twenty-one-year-old from Bordesley Green, who admitted two offences of theft on my division before I transferred him to Stechford police station to be dealt with for affray and a wounding with intent to commit grievous bodily harm, commonly known as a Section 18 wounding. I was in almost daily contact with George, and my workload for a time was almost exclusively based on his information.

On Saturday 6 August, I saw George again, and he gave me specific information relating to a further ten suspects.

7

GETTING TO GRIPS WITH THE BORDESLEY FIRM

On 10 August 1983, I interviewed another member of the city-centre criminal fraternity based on further information from George. He was represented by a solicitor with whom I got on very well; he always did a good job for his client, but was very balanced in his dealings with the police. The suspect admitted an offence of theft and was charged and bailed. I met George twice that afternoon, and he gave me information on a further six suspects, plus an offence of robbery, as well as theft of clothing from C&A, a large city-centre store.

On Monday 15 August, I went to Nechells to investigate a burglary at Droitwich construction site, where property valued at £15,000 was stolen. The following day, I liaised with the detective superintendent in charge of the Regional Criminal Intelligence office and then came in on my day off to liaise with him and Shaw Taylor, a television presenter, and to film an item on the offence for *Police 5*, as it was known.

On Friday 19 August, I met George again and I walked away with information on two burglaries and three more suspects, one of whom was to cross my path in years to come regarding a murder enquiry.

On Tuesday 23 August I sat up at the unemployment offices in Staniforth Street with Malcolm, the Scottish DC, and arrested another city-centre target for theft, a twenty-year-old from Erdington who was a lifestyle criminal. We were lucky, because we found two rings in his possession that we later identified as the proceeds of a crime at a jewellers. He admitted several offences and was charged and bailed. The process led to an accomplice, who was arrested and also charged with the same offence.

The following day, George put another job in: this time at Redditch, where a theft and assault had taken place, plus a theft from Tesco and the activities of an organised team of shoplifters from Stechford. On Tuesday 30 August, I took a CID officer from Redditch police station over to Stechford and arrested our suspect. I waved goodbye to him as they took him away to be dealt with locally. The good thing with many of these jobs was that there were often witnesses to the crimes and, once identified, many of the targets knew that it was game over. By the next day, Redditch CID had the name of a second suspect for the same job and we added him to the list of people for which we were looking, which was getting ever longer as George added still more jobs.

On Sunday 4 September, we had a manic day. We started off dealing with an allegation of attempted rape, with one person in custody who needed to be interviewed. Finally, the most we could possibly prove was an assault occasioning actual bodily harm at which point the complainant declined to prosecute and the prisoner was refused charged and released. Later in the day, we interviewed and charged a person for theft and then assisted uniform staff regarding the arrest of thirteen Asian youths for public-order offences, going equipped to commit crime and possession of offensive weapons. For good measure, we then picked up two for burglary, which fortunately we were able lodge overnight, otherwise it was going to be yet another long day.

George continued to make contact on an almost daily basis and, on Tuesday 6 September, we struck again with the further arrest of our prospective Zulu. He admitted the theft of a wallet, which we later recovered, and he was charged and bailed.

The following day, another city-centre criminal from Nechells was arrested and charged with theft from the person. I was spending as much time in Stechford and Bordesley Green as I was in the city centre, but we were having some great results, and they had no idea what was going on. Information followed on eight more individuals on the same day, including a potential robbery at a post office, and within twenty-four hours a further five suspects and information on jobs in Coventry and Paignton.

On Tuesday 13 September, I took a team of officers to Glebe Farm in Stechford and arrested two brothers, and two others, on suspicion of robbery and theft; arrangements were made for the Paignton suspect to be detained. We recovered a stolen driving licence and suede coat, and finished the day with two charged with theft, one bailed for an ID parade for a robbery in Bull Street, and one refused charge. We were unrelenting in the manner in which we went after them, and there was no let-up in the flow of information.

Two days later, another twenty-year-old from Bordesley Green had his moment with us, and he went on to admit offences of theft, including the theft of clothing from Tesco in August. He was charged and kept in custody. We made a further arrest the following day in Stechford for deception.

On Tuesday 27 September 1983, George was waiting with another batch of information regarding some burglaries and a robbery at a post office in the city centre. My detective chief inspector was no longer complaining about the overtime.

Around this time, we were engaged in a lot of elimination enquiries regarding a suspect vehicle linked to the Caroline Hogg murder investigation, and they all needed to be followed up and dealt with quickly. Caroline was a five-year-old child who went missing on 8 July 1983 from a play area in Edinburgh, and was last seen walking away with a 'scruffy man'.

Her body was found in a ditch in Leicestershire ten days later, 300 miles away, and sparked a nationwide murder hunt, which was not solved until 1990 with the arrest of van-driver Robert Black, who was later convicted. More than 189,000 witness statements were taken and, for each enquiry we received, we had to confirm ownership of the vehicle and confirm the individual's movements on the day of the murder. Any one of those enquiries could have provided a breakthrough and, although it was tedious work, it had to be done in a methodical and painstaking manner lest you forgot the hideous nature of the crime.

At the beginning of October, George came up with some further information on a serious affray at the Yew Tree pub and some substantial cheque frauds; I was again using my red pen. More was to follow regarding ten more individuals and another fight at licensed premises. There was no doubt some turf wars were going on, as gangs tried to take over pubs as their exclusive territory in which to deal in either drugs, stolen property, or simply to provide safe meeting places at which to plan their next jobs.

Joe Tildesley remembers a similar situation that year when he was still working with the Operations Support Unit:

My serial of ten officers were a wonderful group of 'crime fighters'. We would be out in the van and someone would just shout up, 'Stop that car!', and we would routinely find drugs and stolen property. Somehow we managed to get some information on a guy who had escaped from prison and was wanted for armed robbery. We should really have handed the information over but, because we also had CID officers working alongside us, we decided to keep it, even though it really was out of our league. That's when it all started to go wrong.

Eventually, we identified an address in Sheldon where we believed the escapee was staying. We got a search warrant and, at 5.00 a.m. one day, we smashed the door in with a sledgehammer. The male occupant came to the door just as it went in, closely followed by a pregnant woman. They had dialled 999 – we had hit the wrong house!

I was mortified, but quickly one of the CID officers insisted on knocking on a few doors either side of the house. We got lucky and stormed into another house. As the CID officer ran into the upstairs bedroom, the wanted man was in bed with a pistol in his hand. After a struggle, he was disarmed and arrested. There were to be no commendations, as six months later four of us appeared before the deputy chief constable to receive 'written advice' for the way in which the job had been handled.

We all felt bad about smashing the wrong door down, so we had a collection for some flowers for the pregnant woman. I gave the money to one of the officers to get the flowers and, for some totally inexplicable reason, he went and got some from the cemetery. The couple realised and it all made the papers. It was a disaster.

On Wednesday 12 October 1983, acting on some of George's information, together with an attached officer, I arrested a twenty-three-year old from Bordesley Green for burglary at some insurance offices in Alum Rock Road. He was interviewed and police-bailed pending comparison of some fingerprints found at the scene. Another three new jobs followed the same day and we recovered some stolen property: two coats from waste ground in Stechford, where they had been abandoned. It was clear that some of the team were fearful of getting a knock on the door.

On Thursday 20 October, together with Regional Crime Squad officers from Manchester, we plotted up on the unemployment benefit offices in Corporation Street and, after an hour and a half, we arrested a forty-two-year-old from Aston who was wanted for a recall to prison, criminal-deception offences, and for interview in relation to a murder in Liverpool.

In the afternoon, I went to HMP Winson Green, where two of our city-centre criminals were on remand. They both wanted to make statements admitting further offences, and I was happy to oblige them. Before I finished, I passed one of George's jobs over to the CID at Nuneaton and gave them the names of the two suspects, although I also undertook to look for them.

On Tuesday 1 November, Malcolm and I spoke to another informant, who identified a suspect for a burglary at Vogue Menswear in Corporation Street. We went into the Birmingham shopping centre in the afternoon looking for him and, just after 5.00 p.m., found the suspect – a twenty-year-old from Kingstanding. He was arrested, interviewed and admitted the job. The next day, we went to Digbeth and arrested a sixteen-year-old from Castle Vale for the same job and charged and bailed him.

On Monday 7 November, we carried on making enquiries regarding the Vogue Menswear burglary and, the following day, arrested a sixteen-year-old from Ladywood for receiving stolen property. We were contacted in the afternoon by the CID from Market Harborough, who were looking for one of our city-centre criminals for burglary. Two of the team found him at an address in Rednal next day and he was escorted back to Leicestershire.

Later that day, I spent several hours with a detective sergeant from No. 4 Regional Crime Squad. There was a growing realisation that we had 'got a tiger by the tail', and other people were starting to take an interest in our results.

At the end of our discussions, we had identified a group of forty-three persons who were engaged in professional shoplifting expeditions throughout the UK. Many of them had grown up together in the Stechford and Bordesley Green areas of Birmingham, and were lifetime friends. This was big business and, when confronted, some of them had shown a propensity for violence.

On Thursday 10 November, we sat up outside the unemployment benefit offices again and, after an hour's wait, arrested another burglar. An evening meeting with George yielded another three jobs in Birmingham, Redditch and Mansfield.

As a result of the murder of a female on Tuesday 15 November, I was posted as the 'statement reader' on the incident room at Steelhouse Lane police station. A murder enquiry was launched after the body of an unidentified woman was found in an alley. Described as slim, and aged between twenty to thirty years, she was found behind the Ventair factory in Oughton Road, Sparkbrook. She had been dragged through piles of rubbish and waste bins in an effort to hide the body, which was spotted at 4.30 p.m. on Sunday 13 November 1983.

The victim was later identified as twenty-seven-year-old Mary Choudry, a local prostitute, who had last been seen alive late on the evening of Friday 11 November 1983, walking in the Kingswood Road area of Moseley. She had a five-year-old son and lived alone in a council flat in Highgate. It was believed that she had been strangled, sexually assaulted, and robbed of her black suede handbag.

Prostitutes could be a great source of intelligence, as they passed information between themselves in an effort to stay safe. Clients, on the other hand, were quite the opposite and would generally do their utmost to avoid contact with the police, fearing exposure to family and friends. The enquiry was headed by Acting Detective Superintendent Alan Watson, who made an appeal for people to come forward in strict confidence. It would not be an easy enquiry and forty officers were put onto the investigation.

The role I was given entailed reading every single statement taken from witnesses and highlighting 'actions' that needed to be raised as lines of enquiry or to deal with continuity of evidence and corroboration. It was a tedious task, which required great concentration and patience. Buried within a statement might be that small lead that could lead to an offender, so there was no room for error. I worked four twelve-hour days and both of my days off, before finally being able to take two days' holiday.

On Thursday 24 November 1983, I went back to normal duties and attended the sudden death of an elderly male in one of the tower blocks in Newtown. A police surgeon also attended as a precautionary measure, but there were no suspicious circumstances. I always felt sad in these situations. There is an inevitability about death but, when it comes suddenly and when the person is alone at the time with no one there to add comfort in those last moments, it seemed to me to be all the more tragic. Being surrounded by family photographs and memories of the past made these situations all the more poignant.

In 1983, Dave Rischmiller was a probationer constable based at Bradford Street police station, when he was given a rather unusual task:

> I was sent to the General Hospital to sit with an assault victim who had head injuries and was expected to die. I was told that, if he woke up, I was to tell him that it was expected that he was likely to die and that I should

take a 'dying declaration' from him as to who his attacker was. I was just nineteen years of age and wasn't relishing the idea of passing on such a message, but he didn't wake up while I was with him.

As a young police officer, Dave was only too aware of the success of his father, John, who became a detective chief inspector and was well known throughout the force.

Malcolm Halliday recalls a slightly different experience in respect of a dying declaration:

Manzoni Gardens attracted a hard core of alcoholic vagrants. I was working one weekend when two of them had a fight; one of them smashed a bottle and thrust it with great force into the throat of the other. He was not expected to survive but, when I went to see him, he proved to be very difficult. He insisted that, if he lived, he would not make a complaint but, if he died, he would provide us with the name of his attacker. He survived and, as expected, there was no prosecution.

Violence was just a routine part of our work, but some of the worst injuries I ever saw were actually inflicted by the 'alleged victim' himself. I was called to a block of flats and, when I got there, I saw this guy with severe head injuries to the point that you could see his brain. It turned out he had Munchausen's syndrome and had hit himself with a hammer and coal axe.

On Friday 25 November 1983, I met George with the DI to make a payment and this time he gave information regarding an arson attack at a city-centre nightclub. Four days later, another of the suspects he had put in was found at an address in Smallheath. We knew that he had stolen a video recorder in Birmingham city centre, but he was also suspected of similar offences in Burton on Trent, and Worcester. He later admitted several offences of theft and was charged and bailed.

On Tuesday 6 December, I met a new informant on New Street station for the first time. I had known him when he was in short trousers, but this was the first time that 'Ben' had made a commitment to provide information. He also knew a lot about what was going on in the city centre and some of the same people that George knew. It was useful to have that cross-reference and, by the end of our meeting, seven persons suspected of receiving stolen property from the markets area had been identified.

During the course of that week, I attended two robbery scenes at building-society night safes in the Bennetts Hill area. There was no let up to the criminal activity that was taking place within a very compact and built-up area and we were constantly responding to major crimes with scarce resources.

On Thursday 8 December, Mrs Ann Whelan, the mother of Michael Hickey, one of four men convicted of the murder of Staffordshire schoolboy Carl Bridgewater, decided to stage a sit-in protest on the roof of Victoria Law Courts in Corporation Street. I spent nearly three hours getting cold outside, watching events and supporting uniform colleagues before she came down. She unfurled a banner calling for an independent public enquiry, but was finally persuaded to finish her protest by Chief Inspector Percival 'Pip' Postans, who climbed 40 feet up a ladder to the roof to reach her. She had, however, achieved her aim, with crowds of curious onlookers gathered in the streets below, as well as press photographers being present. Mrs Whelan, from Hollywood, was arrested for criminal damage as she climbed down and appeared in court that evening.

George had tailed off a bit in terms of the supply of information. This was a warning sign that he was either getting involved in criminality himself or his nerve was going a bit. He knew the rules on the first issue and I could understand the second. He was in deep trouble if he was ever to be found out, and we both knew he would suffer severe consequences. I was always very careful where I met George, but you could not cater for the unexpected and, whenever we were in a pub, I had one eye on the other customers. If you chose somewhere too quiet, you would stick out like a sore thumb and, if it was too busy, you couldn't take in everyone that was there.

On Thursday 22 December, I interviewed a security officer in the morning regarding thefts from some city-centre offices, saw George at lunchtime for a pre-Christmas chat, and, late in the afternoon while doing a circuit of the city centre, helped an off-duty PC out with the arrest of a youth for assault in Edgbaston Street. We recovered some stolen property from the security officer who was charged with burglary.

Bryan Davis recalls one of his experiences as an 'attached CID' officer in 1983:

I went with another officer, who was also attached, to collect a prisoner from Marylebone police station in London. When we arrived, the guy in charge of the CID turned out to have just been on a course with a West Midlands officer and treated us like royalty. He insisted on taking us for a drink before we went back on the train and, by the time we were on our way back with the prisoner handcuffed, he was definitely the most sober of the three of us.

In 1983 a total of 210,051 offences were recorded in the West Midlands, which included forty cases of murder and two of manslaughter. Only one of the murders remained unsolved. Offences of wounding continued to rise, with 7,211 reported, as well as robberies, which rose to 1,780 recorded crimes.

Wednesday 4 January 1984 started off with a bang, with a good team effort as we made an arrest for deception in the morning, another for theft of a motor vehicle, and a third for theft, followed by an address search. The following day I was tied up in the central lock-up interviewing a couple of our elusive suspects who had been arrested on other matters, one of whom was charged, and one refused charged. During the day, two of my team, DC Malcolm 'Doc' Halliday and PC Pete Wilson, were assaulted while trying to make arrests for car crime. One juvenile was detained and dealt with by the British Transport Police, as the original crime was on their jurisdiction.

Malcolm recalls the incident well:

I was out with Pete doing observations on a car park at the back of a nightclub in Bristol Street. We were dressed in 'scruffs', trying to blend in, when we noticed a Mini with four youths inside acting suspiciously. I got a set of keys out of my pocket and started to try car doors to make it look as if we were car thieves; in fact, I nearly got one key stuck in the door of a Jaguar motor car, which made me sweat a bit! We edged closer to the vehicle but they suddenly started to move off.

Pete and I tried to block their escape route but they simply drove through us. I got hit on the knee, and fell to the floor, while Pete grabbed the driver's door and pulled it open. The driver put the car in reverse and the door hit Pete and he was left lying on the floor. At that stage I thought that he was very seriously injured.

As they were trying to escape, they got held up by a skip lorry and I somehow managed to get to the car again and threw my police radio at them, and then dived in through the back window. I almost managed to reach the driver but the two kids in the back and front seat passenger kept 'battering away' at me and eventually pushed me back out. I had a good look at the driver, however, and recalled that he had his hair cut like a girl. They then drove off with the door hanging off, and I ran to a call box in the nightclub to dial 999. Fortunately, Pete wasn't too badly hurt and I subsequently identified the driver on an identification parade and we found fingerprints in the car.

I maintained excellent relationships with my old force, the British Transport Police, and regularly met former colleagues at New Street station.

We continued enquiries the next day, looking for other suspects for wounding Pete Wilson in the Selly Oak and Kings Norton areas. On Saturday 7 January we had a breakthrough when some anonymous information was phoned into Bournville Lane police control room. I liaised with the BTP and we put a plan together for the following week.

Just before 7.00 a.m. on Monday 9 January, I briefed officers and we went looking for those wanted for an offence of wounding on the officer. Together with two other officers, I went to St John's Children's Home in Gravelly Hill, Erdington, and arrested a sixteen-year-old. He was taken to Steelhouse Lane, and from there to the juvenile court, where I got him remanded in police custody for a day. I interviewed him in the presence of his mother and he admitted stealing the car.

During the course of the day, we made five further arrests, including two brothers from Kings Norton. All six were charged with stealing the vehicle and one of them, a fifteen-year-old, was charged with wounding the officer. It was a good joint effort by the two police forces.

On Friday 20 January, I liaised with the BTP again regarding a robbery at Duddeston Manor railway station. They were looking for a suspect and only had a first name but, fortunately, by the end of the meeting we were able to come up with a full one. In the afternoon, we dealt with a burglar from Castle Vale who was charged with a burglary at an oriental-carpet shop.

The following day, I went with one of my team to Union Street, where we detained a twenty-four-year-old from Stoke on Trent on suspicion of criminal deception relating to a 'gold' chain that had been falsely hallmarked. We put him 'on the sheet' (custody record) at Steelhouse Lane police station and then took him to Newton Street, where we found his wife and a child sat in a car, and recovered more property.

Later that afternoon, after lodging him in the cells, we took his wife back home and searched their home address, with support from the local

CID. We then took photographs of the premises and recovered further items, before returning to Birmingham. We had a lot to sort out and, with the authority of the DCI, lodged the prisoner overnight. The following day, I made the decision to hand him over to the CID at Hanley to be dealt with. We had one offence of attempted deception. but he was facing serious charges in their area.

On Tuesday 24 January, I saw another potential informant who provided 'street' names for two robbers who were active in Birmingham shopping centre. We confirmed the location of one offence and, the following morning, went to an address in Warren Road to make enquiries regarding a possible robbery. The enquiries proved negative, but little did I know at the time that this individual was to become my number one target, known as 'Francis', on Operation Red Card three years later in 1987. A quietly spoken individual, he was to join the ranks of the 'Zulu Warriors' and immerse himself into organised football violence.

George made contact in the week and put two of the usual suspects in again for theft at an elderly persons' home.

On Sunday 5 February, I spent twelve hours with the night DC interviewing six persons from the Kingstanding area, who were arrested following a fight in the Crown pub in Hill Street. All of them were interviewed by way of contemporaneous record and charged with affray and other matters. Two days later, a seventh accused was added to the list and yet another outstanding city-centre suspect was dealt with.

Malcolm Halliday has his own memories of performing night duties:

It was always non-stop havoc and I never went through a week of nights without a death or a rape happening. I recall one job, while I was at Steelhouse Lane, when a security officer had been driven at after he disturbed someone at Bristol Street Motors near to Belgrave Road. As it happened, the vehicle had been stop-checked near to the Silver Slipper toilets in Station Street, so we knew quite quickly who the owner of the vehicle was. After a search of the area was made, a 'near-naked' man was found at the bottom of a wall, which he appeared to have fallen from.

I remember visiting to check on the injured man's condition in hospital and asking one of the nurses if he had been sexually assaulted. Her curt response was, 'I am here to try to save his life – not to look up his backside!' He later died in hospital.

The suspect was arrested next day, and alleged that he was about to have consensual sex with him, when the victim said that it was going to cost him some money. He got upset, a struggle ensued, and the victim fell over a balcony and landed at the bottom of a wall.

The case was later adopted by then Detective Inspector Richard Bryant, and the suspect was subsequently dealt with for manslaughter.

Jon Lighton joined C Unit at Steelhouse Lane in January 1984, and quickly found himself immersed in the weekly cycle of violence and public order that was a routine part of policing Birmingham city centre. He recalls,

I was told by a sergeant when I arrived that, if I allowed anyone to abuse me or threaten me in any way, I would make it twice as hard for the next bobby to deal with them. Like my colleagues, I took the advice and adopted a strong approach to troublemakers, including those who insisted on coming up to me to say, 'Evening Cuntstable'.

We used to put a public-order van out on Thursdays, Fridays and Saturdays, with a sergeant and up to ten constables on board. In those days, we had no cages for prisoners, so the violent ones were just restrained on the floor of the van until we could get them to the station. We were always flat-out going from job to job. Even when we had a break, we regularly got called to attend jobs where clothes-shop windows had been smashed and the contents plundered. It was as if they knew when the shifts changed and refreshment breaks happened.

Two flash-points for trouble were the Parisian pub in Cannon Street, and the Windsor pub, which was a 'Blues' pub and run by a retired police officer. There were fights outside on most Saturday nights at closing time and, after responding to one shout for assistance, I vividly recall finding two policewomen actually sitting on top of a drunk to restrain him in the back of a police car as his friends milled around the vehicle.

I recall on one occasion going to Faces nightclub at Five Ways when there was a Caribbean night, and someone stole all the money from the tills and stabbed the bouncers. The ambulance service couldn't get into the club to treat the injured, and it finished up with officers turning up from all over the force. As we went in, I found myself isolated behind the reception desk as people pressed in around us. It was pretty scary stuff. There was another club nearby called Maximillian's, which had steep stairs at the entrance. If you had a shout there, you would often find yourself in the middle of people fighting and falling down the stairs as they were ejected by the door staff.

Maximillian's nightclub was at Five Ways, just off Broad Street and, in 2011, a person called 'Glynis – novice Brummie' said on social media that, 'Maximillian's had an illuminated dance floor!! Caused many an accident when the DJs used to put it on flash and the drunken dancers would fall over'.

Jon went on,

> Although our boundary was New Street, we were also often called to support officers from Digbeth, and I regularly found myself in John Bright Street fighting with crowds who had turned out from the nightclubs there, or outside the Locarno in Hurst Street. You just never quite knew what to expect. On one occasion, I was with another officer when we came across two women fighting outside the Nightingale club in Albert Street. We grabbed both of them and, as we did so, a wig fell off one of them – they were both men dressed as women!

On Thursday 9 February 1984, George put another two jobs in, and I spent some time in the city centre, liaising with the BTP, who were experiencing a rise in robberies and thefts from the person on New Street station.

On Saturday 18 February 1984, I was on standby in the office in relation to problems created by visiting West Ham supporters and dealt with yet another night-safe robbery at a bank in the high street.

On Monday 27 February 1984, I was posted to Bridge Street West police station – another opportunity and another challenge.

8

MURDER IN HOCKLEY
AND THE MINERS' STRIKE

On Tuesday 28 February 1984, I was tied up with the arrest of two good-class burglars from Nechells. My new team were weighing me up, and it was a time for tactics and reflection. I picked up John, one of the DCs, and we went out to one of the prisoners' addresses and found some of the stolen property – a good start. In the afternoon, I saw another of my informants with another Irish DC Alan, and met another potential informant in the early evening. At one point, we did an enquiry in Wheeler Street, Lozells – my birthplace.

Newtown was a busy inner-city residential area, with a diverse population, but a great place to work; there was plenty of scope for getting into the criminal fraternity. It suffered from a lot of burglaries and vehicle crime, as well as robberies and domestic violence.

Just to the north of the city centre, Newtown was bordered by the Jewellery Quarter, and the University of Aston; to the west there was Hockley, and to the north Lozells and Aston. In the late sixties, a large project took place to construct sixteen tower blocks, which featured heavily in our crime statistics.

On Friday 2 March, I went to a sudden death in Inkerman House within the Newtown shopping precinct. There were no suspicious circumstances, but you had to be very careful not to jump to conclusions in these situations. The first priority for a police officer is the 'protection of life' and, thus, when someone died you had to make comprehensive enquiries to satisfy the needs of HM coroner and relatives of the deceased.

On Wednesday 7 March, I went with Alan to do some follow-up visits to burglary victims. We went to a house burglary in Hospital Street, then to Lozells Road regarding a burglary at a Ladbrokes betting shop, and then off to Mossborough Crescent to see a witness regarding a burglary in one of the tower blocks. We went back into the office for a short break, then visited a flat in Rea Tower and saw another victim in Unett Street. From there, I had a sergeant's meeting with the DCI, did an interview of a suspect for fraud with Alan, and finished the evening off familiarising myself with one of the local pubs on the section.

On Thursday 8 March, together with John and other officers, I went back to Rea Tower. Our enquiries regarding a burglary in one of the flats had paid off and we went to another flat two floors up from the burgled premises. It was typical of a number of flats I had visited, wherein the registered occupant had allowed the premises to be used as a 'crash pad' for local criminals, who would gather to take drugs, store stolen property, or have casual sex. Whenever you got into one of these places, if you had the patience to unravel all of the connections, a good result was normally achieved.

At 8.20 a.m., we arrested an eighteen-year-old and a seventeen year-old on suspicion of burglary and took them both back to Bridge Street West. They were lodged in the cells and I went to Teviott Tower with John, and an attached officer, and arrested another eighteen-year-old, who was likewise made a 'guest' at Bridge Street West. There was only a small cell block at Bridge Street West, so you needed to be careful about how you lodged the prisoners, because they could easily shout to each other in an effort to get their stories straight.

In the afternoon, I went with Stuart, and other officers, to Rea Tower and made a fourth arrest of a sixteen-year-old on suspicion of the burglary. We also found a fifteen-year-old in the flat, who was on the run from Tennal Assessment Centre in Harborne.

Tennal was a children's home operated by Birmingham City Council, and many of the residents were vulnerable and came from deprived backgrounds. Years later, a police investigation, codenamed Operation Camassia, led to convictions for child abuse at the home, and many former residents from the seventies and eighties came forward to make complaints. It closed that year.

The first two were later released on police bail, pending further enquiries, and the second two were charged with a burglary in another tower block. Our absconder was returned to the home. It had been a good day for us, and my team had worked well. They were all good interviewers and knew which 'buttons to press'.

On Friday 9 March, the enquiry continued with the further arrest of a twenty-two-year-old for burglary. We were looking at a number of burglaries in tower blocks where the victims were lone females. We searched some bins around Geach Tower, looking for some abandoned stolen property, and later arrested the mother of one of the young burglars for assisting an offender. She was interviewed in the presence of a solicitor and released, process to be decided, while the burglar was charged.

Another arrest for burglary came the next day and more enquiries in yet another tower block – Martineau Tower. On Sunday 11 March, we arrested a nineteen-year-old female from Schofield Tower on suspicion of receiving stolen property, and she was police-bailed.

On Monday 12 March 1984, Arthur Scargill, the President of the National Union of Mine Workers, declared a national strike and called for action by all NUM members in all coalfields throughout the UK. While it would not directly impact on me personally, it did mean that, in the coming months, many uniform staff would be drafted away to other duties, making it more difficult to sustain workloads. Policing large-scale demonstrations was never to be the same again.

Birmingham was no stranger to miners' disputes, and large numbers of officers were involved in what became known as the 'Battle of Saltley Gate' in February 1972, when confrontations took place between the police and picketing miners at the West Midlands Gas Board coking works in Saltley. Initial attempts by 2,000 striking miners failed to close the plant but, after Arthur Scargill requested local unions to support the pickets, 10,000 trade union members marched from factories to the coking plant, and the police were obliged to close the plant for safety reasons.

Dave Cross was on duty during the picketing at Saltley and recalls,

I can best describe it as several days of very friendly banter with the miners, until coking wagons arrived, at which point there was a great deal of pushing and shoving. We got fed with hundreds of pork pies, many of which were shared with the pickets.

Regrettably, on one occasion a chief inspector was knocked down by one of the lorries as it was leaving the plant. The moment he was injured, all the pushing stopped and he was treated by officers. I arrested the lorry driver for breach of the peace and careless driving, but he was later found not guilty.

Retired PC Tony Everett was also on duty at Saltley during this period, and recalls a day when bottles, stones, and meat pies, 600 of which had been provided to pickets by members of another union, were hurled at lorries loaded with coke from the plant. On 7 February, 1,500 miners' pickets, attempting to blockade the depot, struggled with 500 police officers, leading to fourteen arrests, and two officers requiring hospital treatment for leg injuries and broken ribs. Tony recalls,

> We spent a lot of time sitting around in vans and, first of all, everything was very well-tempered. We were deployed right at the front gates in Nechells Place, but the mood changed dramatically during the day, leading to serious disorder.

Numerous officers from the West Midlands subsequently swapped the streets of Birmingham for other 'far-flung' places in the UK to become involved in the policing of the miners' strike in 1984. A number of those officers have provided recollections but, far from revealing lots of lurid tales of extreme violence, their recollections are, in the main, far more simple, routine, and strikingly similar. Their accounts also go some way towards describing the police culture and mentality during this period, when Margaret Thatcher was determined not to give in to the miners' demands and the police were tasked with 'holding the line'. They also illustrate the sharp contrast between my work as a detective and that of the front-line uniform officers.

An officer, whom I have given the pseudonym 'Liam', recollects,

> My memories of the miners' strike are that alcohol was drunk, women were chatted up, overtime was gambled away, and we did some policing. Sleeping in the vans was a nightmare, travelling around the various coalfields in Yorkshire and Nottinghamshire. The funniest thing was the variety of uniforms that police officers on mutual-aid turned up in, all different shades of blue and black. Mostly we looked a right mess.
>
> One Monday morning, we turned up at a mine in South Yorkshire, having travelled three hours from an army barracks where we were staying. We were already pretty tired. We were met by a local superintendent, who said that, at 5.00 a.m. each morning, we would line up and he would blow a whistle. At this stage, local miners would come forward and start pushing and shoving. Two other forces turned up with us; there were officers from Greater Manchester Police, who were all

over 6 feet tall and built like heavyweight boxers, and some officers from Norfolk who came in a posh coach with tables in, and wore Gucci public-order gear. After the briefing, we lined up Norfolk in front, then West Midlands Police, then GMP.

The whistle was duly blown, and about 200 miners came forward, some big lads among them pushing and shoving. They were punching and kicking out. In the middle, we were being squashed and suffocated by the ferocity of the attack, but the Norfolk officers really took a beating, with helmets being pulled off and some officers visibly becoming distressed. After a few minutes, the whistle was blown again, and the miners pulled back, jeering as one or two of our colleagues were physically sick in the bushes nearby.

No one was happy with the actions of the miners; in fact, we were seething. We all huddled together, nursing our injuries, and got our breath back. There was great camaraderie among us and, within one hour, you would have thought that we had all known each other for years. We discussed tactics for the next day and a plan was decided upon.

The following morning we lined up again; this time we were in the front, Greater Manchester Police in the middle, and Norfolk at the rear. The whistle was blown again and once again there was an almighty rush forward from the miners present. This time, however, our cordon at the front separated and, as miners rushed through, they were met by the talents of the Manchester boxers. As the miners got stuck in the middle of the police lines, there was panic and they ran back to their assembly point, we having clearly established who was in charge. The local police superintendent was blowing his whistle frantically for us to stop and he actually started shouting at us, but we had made our point and they never came at us again like this.

We spent a week at a mine in Nottingham. They were totally different and we even visited them in their social club and had a drink with them. They gave us little copper tags, denoting which mine we were at, and arranged for us to have a look down the pit. We really sympathised with them, and just had small numbers of police at the entrance.

When we stayed at Harrogate training centre, we used to go to the Tambourine Bar, where scantily dressed ladies played a tambourine every twenty minutes to the record that was on. It was packed every night. In the training centre itself, I saw the biggest card school I have ever seen; officers who had just finished duty would go to one of the landings and gamble away hundreds of pounds.

At Grantham Army Barracks, two van-loads of officers from London were detained on their way back to the capital, having forgotten to return some hire televisions they had rented from a local company.

At Cleethorpes, the chalets were damp, with water running down the walls, but this was my funniest memory. On my van was an officer who thought he was a real ladies' man and thought all the women in Cleethorpes loved him. We got fed up of listening to him and so, one night, our sergeant paid a woman to keep him talking in a pub and to agree to go back to his room. Before he got back, all of his uniform trousers were removed from the room and, before things started getting complicated, the woman left.

At 3.00 a.m. the next day, while we were all in the van waiting to start the day, this guy turned up wearing a pair of beige trousers; he was immediately told off by the inspector and told to stay in the van all day. He was furious and, when we got to a police station in Yorkshire for breakfast, someone told him what the sergeant had done. He went ballistic and threw an orange at the driver's window, thinking that he was sitting in it, but actually hit the inspector who was covered in orange juice as it hit the grill and split open. The officer was immediately ordered back home to the West Midlands.

A lot of the time we did feel sympathy for the miners we spoke to. We did a lot of overtime and many of us bought a 'Maggie Thatcher car' or a 'Maggie Thatcher fridge' – enjoyable times and pleasant memories.

Another officer, 'Alex' commented,

I went twice to South Yorkshire and stopped at Wakefield police station. We slept in a locker room on camp beds. We always did nights and were deployed either inside or directly outside collieries. It was comical, because all of the pushing and shoving was just for the cameras. There was this unwritten rule that, if they managed to break though the cordon, they would run round and join the crowd again. We also used to collect all of our sandwiches in big bin bags and give them to the miners. It wasn't all aggravation. To be honest, we slept most of the time.

There was one funny incident I can recall. After we had finished, we used to go for a drink in a local pub that used to stay open for us, before going back to a locker room. Afterwards, we were all trying to sleep, when a good mate of mine, who was in a camp bed near to me, got up in his sleep and started urinating over an officer from another force. The officer woke up and was furious, and started chasing him around the room. It was bedlam, but hilarious to watch.

Andy told a similar story:

I went to Kerseley, near Coventry, a couple of times, where we did static points around the pit, and stayed in the barracks at Sutton Coldfield. I also went up to the miners' HQ in Sheffield. There was pushing and shoving, but nothing serious – sometimes just a lot of bad mouthing going on. My brother went to Orgreave and it did get nasty there. I remember that we were constantly fed Mars bars and poor sandwiches, and a lot of the beds we slept in had fleas, as the beds were in constant use from people changing over from night shifts to day shifts.

There was nothing else to do but have a pint and go to sleep after a shift. I was in a bunk bed at Sutton barracks with a good friend, John, in the bed below me. Next to us was a metal locker. In the middle of the night, I was still in my sleep and I needed to 'pass water', so I went into the metal locker, not knowing where I was. John woke up to feel a fine spray near him and just hoped that my aim would not change. I got back into bed and slept without realising anything.

'James' said,

I was on a Mobile Support Unit with the British Transport Police during the miners' strike and was deployed to Derbyshire and Nottinghamshire on public-order duties. Fortunately, there were no real issues for us on the rail network and nothing exciting to talk about.

In contrast, retired Major Investigation Unit Detective Debbie Menzel recalls,

I was in uniform at the time of the miners' strike and we girls were not allowed to go, so we ended up policing the streets of the West Midlands while the men went off to various places. On the division I was working, I remember once doing a whole set of night duties when the entire shift were women – happy days! Getting onto the CID was also very different, as they tended to have just one female detective in each CID office, so you had to wait until someone left.

Paul Rainey retired from the West Midlands Police in 2002 and became an expert in road-traffic investigations, as well as becoming a police driving instructor, and recalls,

I was a traffic officer when the miners' strike took place. Public order was not the sort of policing we normally got involved in, but we had done some basic public-order training and we were asked if we wanted to volunteer for picket duties. We had some kit, which really just consisted of pads, some of which were wrapped around the shins under the trousers. We still wore tunics in those days and some officers had helmets with visors on and carried long shields, but our kit was pretty basic.

Our names went into a hat and mine was picked. About twenty-four of us from Traffic travelled up by road in a convoy with some vans to West Yorkshire. We were in a coach and I took a number of photographs as the convoy moved along the motorway, with each vehicle displaying full headlights.

During the daytime, we spent a lot of time standing by on reserve and officers slept wherever they could – in the vehicles, or even lying full length in the grassy fields. Those who stayed awake played endless rounds of cards. At night we stayed in an old army camp, which was awful.

On one occasion, a group of at least eight mounted police officers from South Yorkshire were deployed to a colliery, where we were on standby. I watched them as they mounted up and made their way 'two by two' down a narrow lane to support officers at the colliery gates. I photographed them when they left, disappearing into the mist. When they came back, several of the horses had been injured and it was clear that they had been faced with a lot of violence by the striking miners, as officers dismounted exhausted.

On a couple of occasions, we were actually deployed in pairs to carry out ordinary patrols in some of the villages. It was an effort at trying to introduce some normality into the area and, to be fair, most people were okay with us. We even got invited into a couple of the pubs and, apart from the odd bit of muttering, the locals were friendly.

As time went on, I was nominated to become a driver for the superintendents, who were deployed from the West Midlands Police to act as public-order commanders. I used to pick them up on a Thursday and usually spent four days away. Some of the senior officers were very inspirational – I remember one, an ex-rugby player, who crowded us all into a big hanger-type building, and then jumped onto a table to address everyone before we went out. He certainly got our attention.

The only other act of violence I witnessed was during a game of cricket taking place in a field, as officers were on standby. One of the guys was called 'Robbo' and he fancied himself as a fielder. Someone threw a stone up in the air instead of the ball and 'Robbo' went in for the catch. Unfortunately it slipped through his hands, hit him on the head, and knocked him out!

Another retired officer Peter Keys recalls being on picket duty at Frickley Colliery in Yorkshire:

The pushing and shoving happened when the so-called 'scabs' were bussed in. One day, an officer fell down in the line. A miner blew a whistle and all of the miners stopped until he had got up and brushed himself off. The whistle was blown again and the pushing and shoving restarted. You couldn't make it up.

Frickley became known by the motto 'second to none', due to so few workers breaking the year-long strike. After it finished, a review by the National Coal Board reduced the workforce by 400 people.

Steven Jordan retired as a chief superintendent in the West Midlands Police in 2007, and has his own memories of the strike:

On day two of the dispute, West Midlands Police sent a large contingent to Nottinghamshire. I was the staff officer to my sub-divisional chief inspector, who had recently commanded the Operations Support Unit. I remember being at work until 2.00 a.m., running around with admin issues, then parading again for 5.30am, travelling with officers to Mansfield and sitting in a pit canteen – for hours. We deployed to the gates a couple of times. It was heavy rain for much of the day, and only a few surly pickets appeared at the gate. It reminded me of Owen's poem 'Exposure', in which he compared the hideous conditions in the trenches with the danger of enemy bullets: the catch line of the poem being, 'but nothing happened'. And nothing did happen. Eventually, we dragged ourselves home, shattered from sixteen hours of inactivity.

I also spent a week as a serial sergeant based at Wakefield. We were deployed twelve hours a day, 4.00 a.m. to 4.00 p.m. to a smallish pit in

West Yorkshire. Most of the time, we sat in the vans in abject boredom but, every morning at about 6.00 a.m., the coaches containing the working miners arrived. Ten minutes prior to their arrival, we would form cordons and the pickets would leave their huddles around braziers and form up opposite. The sound of heavy diesels would strike the ear and the shouting and shoving would start. There would be a great deal of pushing from the pickets, but no aggression towards the police at all. Occasionally, a picket would push his way through the cordon. He would then jog back round the end of the cordon, join his comrades, and push again. Afterwards, we would stand around chatting to the pickets. They were angry men but their anger was not directed at us in any way, and the relationship was remarkably cordial, notwithstanding the best efforts of the media to sensationalise the drama of the conflict. If we had spare 'doggy bags' (packed lunches in police speak), we shared them with the pickets, who accepted them with gratitude and good grace. The whole experience resonated for me with accounts of the 'phoney war' in late 1939.

Dave Faulkner also recalls his experiences during the miners' strike:

I got deployed on at least five occasions, sometimes for up to a fortnight at a time. We were basic public-order trained, and we just had long shields and heavy duty cork helmets, which just got knocked off at the start of any trouble anyway.

In the main, the accommodation we stayed in was awful. At Dawley in Staffordshire, we stopped in the MOD barracks in Sutton Coldfield, which, frustratingly, was just down the road from where I lived at the time. When we went to Driffield in North Yorkshire, not far from Catterick, we stayed at RAF Driffield in the old married quarters, which had been allowed to fall into disrepair. There wasn't even any running hot water.

The worst place was at Bolsover near Chesterfield, where we stayed in a derelict cottage hospital and slept on canvas beds with no heating. We had to find food from outside and, one night, after going out for a walk I came back and found the local MP, who is a well-known character, standing outside the place, and actually had a conversation with him.

I went to Orgreave shortly after the main riots. To get there, you had to drive down some narrow country lanes, and frequently the vans were bricked by unseen individuals hiding within the tree lines. It was a nasty place to be. On occasions, we would find ourselves on picket lines, being jabbed with sharp instruments, and one of our senior officers warned them that if it continued the shields would come out. They hated them and always got wound up when we deployed with them.

At all of the other locations, it was a bit of a 'pantomime'. We would have a chat with the strikers and when the workers arrived there would be some pushing and shoving, and then it would go back to normal.

At one location, there were a load of Metropolitan Police officers. They all had pony tails and looked like they were out of a fashion show. One day, West Midlands officers were called out to reinforce a picket line that was in danger of being breached. The Met officers were supposed to deploy as well, but they just carried on playing cards. Afterwards, some of our sergeants had a bit of a showdown with some of theirs over it, and things got a bit heated. The next day, somebody got a load of Fyffes bananas and scattered them around the inside of their coaches. One of the Met officers didn't see the funny side of things and turned on one of our sergeants. We all played rugby and there was a bit of a stand-off as we all gathered round Bob, who actually was very good usually at turning confrontation into comedy.

On another occasion, we were at a pit called Creswell in the East Midlands. The place reminded me of Cadbury's, with its own bowling green and social club. Bob got hold of a load of 'red noses' and, when the usual pushing and shoving started at shift changeover, Bob shouted, 'West Midlands – noses on', and we all stood there in uniform with the noses on. The pickets burst out laughing and stopped pushing.

Except for Orgreave, nobody wanted to hurt anyone – not us – not them.

On 18 June 1984, a mass picket involving up to 6,000 miners took place at British Steel's coking plant at Orgreave in South Yorkshire. Facing them were between 4,000 to 8,000 police officers, drawn from various counties. A small number of them had been trained in new tactics, following the Brixton and Toxteth riots, supported by up to fifty mounted police officers and nearly sixty police dogs. By the end of the day, almost 100 arrests had been made, and more than 120 pickets and police officers injured. It became known as the 'Battle of Orgreave'.

Steve Jordan has vivid memories of events:

Day one of the Battle of Orgreave was very violent and made the headlines. I went on day two. Wisely, they only sent supervisors and staff who were properly and recently public-order trained. This was a first! My training as an infantry platoon commander had taught me that, in the heat and chaos of 'battle', it is very difficult to keep tabs on those for whom you are responsible. On the bus on the way, I spent half the journey getting my serial to 'number off'. They tolerated it, but thought that I was probably a bit eccentric, and a couple of other sergeants clearly thought I was a bit of a 'prat'. There was muttering and laughter.

We arrived. The atmosphere was palpably tense. It was a hot day and the atmosphere was hotter! There was a charge of hatred in the air, which I had experienced in the disorders between the National Front and the Anti-Nazi League, but not before in the miners' strike. Also, it felt for the first time as though the police were the protagonists, not the people charged with preserving order between disputing sides. We lined up. It felt like a medieval set-piece battleground. The police were lined up and the pickets were in parallel lines about fifty metres away, so that they could build up momentum in the charge. There were even mounted officers to reinforce the sense of cavalry in the fight.

My serial was absolutely in the front line, with the police lines about six deep, so there was a lot of support behind us. I called on my colleagues to 'number off'. They did. I was satisfied. We were ready.

The guttural roar of diesels again presaged the conflict, this time signalling the arrival of the coking lorries.

We withstood the first charge. Several others followed, and continued throughout the day, whether the lorries were arriving or not. Weapons were wielded and some disgusting things were thrown at the police lines. This was up close and personal, and it was very hard for officers to maintain self-control against such attacks. Command and control was very hard. Radios were useless in the noise of battle, verbal commands were inaudible, and officers became separated from colleagues.

After every push, of which there were probably twenty that day, I called on the serial to number off. I was confident that they were all there. They no longer saw this obsession as mild eccentricity. At the end of a physically and emotionally exhausting day, we returned to the coaches. Most colleagues had suffered minor injuries, just cuts and bruising, myself included.

The PSU commander wisely thought to check that we were all there before we got onto the coach. I was able to say that my serial was all there without having to check again. The other two sergeants began madly counting. One was short of an officer; the other had lost two! After about two hours, we discovered that two of the three had returned to force on another coach, having been separated in the chaos. The third officer remained missing for some time.

I was pleased; I had fulfilled my duty to those I had been trusted to command. I counted them all out … I had de-bussed as a young supervisor, nervous at letting the side down, thinking that the older and cynical sergeants probably thought me an idiot. I returned much more confident about doing what I thought right, rather than making decisions that were culturally normative. The army motto, 'Serve to lead', still held.

Mike Cresswell's experience were somewhat more sedate:

I went up to Durham and it was pretty quiet. There was the usual pushing and shoving, and shouts of 'scab' on the picket lines, but nothing out of the ordinary. Some of the miners were really tough guys and, one day, I recall one of our officers, who was himself a strong rugby player, trying to move a picket. He took him by the arm, but the guy was solid and just went rigid and refused to move. He gave up in the end. We stayed in police training centres and old RAF camps; it was all a bit basic but, having served in the Navy, I was used to cramped conditions.

Bryan Davis had a slightly different experience:

I was on Traffic, and we went to South Yorkshire to do picket duties at one of the pits. Some of the miners used to be allowed to go down the mine to do essential maintenance work and we used to play cards with them regularly. One night, while the inspector was asleep in the van, the maintenance men asked my serial if we wanted to have a look down the mine. We all went down in a lift and got on a small train, which travelled for about a mile before we stopped, with a view to turning round to go back. At this point, the train broke down and we started walking back. At some stage, the inspector woke up to find his sergeant and the whole of his serial missing and the time to form picket cordons was approaching. We eventually got back just before 6.00 a.m. to form cordons and we all came out of the mine with black faces. Needless to say, the inspector gave everyone a real dressing down. To this day I have a piece of polished and varnished coal as a memory.

While all this was going on, everyday policing continued in Birmingham.

On Tuesday 13 March 1984, we had a change of direction, and Alan and I arrested an eighteen-year-old from Newtown for indecent assault on a female. He admitted the offence and was charged. Later that day, I saw George and he put a couple of jobs in. He was much quieter these days and he had been having his ups and downs; but we had a lot of history between us, so I wasn't ready to give up on him yet.

On Wednesday 14 March, we started doing enquiries at local schools regarding some robbery offences. We always tried to avoid arresting pupils in school because it caused problems for the teachers, who needed to build relationships, but sometimes it could not be avoided.

On Tuesday 20 March, three of us went to one of the big comprehensive schools and arrested a sixteen-year-old from Severn Tower, Nechells, for a robbery committed in one of the Metropolitan Police districts. He was taken to the central lock-up and lodged in one of the juvenile detention rooms to await an escort from London. We went back to the school in the afternoon and this time arrested a fifteen-year-old from Aston for an arson attack on the annexe at the school. The next day, we arrested a second youth at the school, aged sixteen years, for arson. George met me and put three suspects in for a burglary.

I saw George again on Thursday 22 March 1984, and he gave me some information relating to stolen credit cards from Marks & Spencer, together with the name of the suspect. We were back into a routine and the next day spent some time checking registers at scrap-metal dealers, including the one found not guilty at Henley-in-Arden Crown Court. He was now on my patch and I wanted to make sure that he knew it.

On Monday 26 March 1984, David Harris, the licensee of the Woodman Licensed House in Hockley, was stabbed to death in Wells Street by a man described as a West Indian male. I was at Bridge Street West police station at the time, trying to sort out a search warrant, and went straight to the scene to liaise with the detective chief inspector and the detective inspector.

We co-ordinated an immediate search of the area and, later that evening, I took a statement from a witness, who had rendered first aid at the scene. I hated violence and the futility of it all. Murders meant dropping everything else and putting a total focus into what you were doing, as the first twenty-four hours were vital. A murder incident room was set up at Steelhouse Lane police station and this was to become home again for a while.

The next day, I was committed to house-to-house enquiries in the area. This was a detailed process that had to be meticulously planned and scrutinised, and I worked with a uniform sergeant whom I trusted totally to organise it with me. We then started doing the rounds of local pubs, looking for any small lead. Leave days were cancelled and we went onto twelve-hour shifts. This was the norm.

Malcolm Halliday was one of the officers involved in completing house-to-house enquiries and recalls a couple of incidents:

I and a DC nicknamed 'Knuckles', due to the arthritis in his hands, visited one particular flat in Newtown and spoke to a family. One of the occupants was a Rastafarian guy and something just didn't seem quite right. While we were chatting, a little girl, aged about two years, handed me a pouch. When I looked inside, it was full of cannabis. I told her to 'give it back to daddy'. We were looking for a murderer, not for drugs, so we let it go; but we did mark the form up to the effect that we thought that the occupants were not telling the entire truth. At a later stage of the enquiry, it transpired that the guy had been repairing his car outside the block of flats on the day of the murder, when the person responsible came running up after the attack, covered in blood, and demanded to be taken out of the area.

Not long after the murder a woman was attacked by a black youth in the same area. He was intent on robbing her, but she fought back, and a load of CID officers who were making enquiries in one of the nearby pubs all ran out and captured him. He had picked the wrong person and the wrong place.

Subsequent to the murder a substantial reward was offered for information leading to the arrest of the offender. We also had a photofit picture of the suspect and, with each passing day, the potential lines of enquiry were increasing. We spent a lot of time getting round the pubs in the area, pushing the issue and looking for that small scrap of information that would lead us to the killer.

On Sunday 1 April 1984, a call was made to the incident room by an individual claiming to know who was responsible for the murder. I met this person later that day with another officer, and the suspect was identified as someone called 'Jakey', with a possible full name.

I saw the informant several times over the next few days, and the information given was reiterated both to me and a senior officer, as well as other background information being provided on the suspect. There was no contact by the informant then for some time and, despite extensive enquiries being made, all of these enquiries met with a negative result based on the details given.

On 17 April 1984, police officers throughout the UK were reminded of the frailties of human life and the potential dangers that they faced routinely. On this date, PC Yvonne Fletcher was one of thirty officers deployed to police a demonstration involving rival factions outside the Libyan Embassy in London. At 10.18 a.m., without warning, anti-Gaddafi supporters were subjected to automatic gunfire, and eleven people, including the officer, received bullet wounds. The officer was fatally wounded in the stomach and died later in hospital. An inquest determined that the shots had been fired from a Sterling submachine gun by someone from within the first floor of the Embassy. To this day, the murder of the officer remains a live investigation.

On Wednesday 18 April, a knife was found in the public toilets at Smethwick Magistrates' Court in the area adjacent to where security officers screened visitors. The knife was subsequently disposed of, in accordance with normal procedures. It was later to form part of the evidence chain in the murder of David Harris, although we were not to know it at the time.

On the same date, I did my work on the house-to-house section in the morning and then assisted Stuart, John, and Alan with observations in Great Hampton Row for a suspect vehicle, the occupants of which had been involved in the theft of a quantity of cyanide. Within fifteen minutes, the suspect appeared, was arrested, and later charged with the offence.

On Monday 23 April 1984, I covered my house-to-house duties again in the morning and then went to Tewkesbury police station with Stuart, looking for a receiver. With the local police, we searched some caravans next to some licensed premises, with the consent of the owners, and took possession of further property relating to the case.

The next day, acting on a lead in respect of the murder, I was despatched in the evening with John to Canning Circus police station in Nottingham to interview a potential informant. We eventually brought the informant back to Birmingham and identified an address in Handsworth where a potential suspect lived. Shortly after 2.00 a.m. the following day, we hit the address and arrested a twenty-three-year-old on suspicion of involvement.

By the time we had searched the address and got back to the station, I had done a sixteen-hour shift and it was time to leave it with other officers.

I had about five hours' sleep and was back in the office in the afternoon, ready to go again. This was still very much a live enquiry, and lots of officers on outside enquiry teams were following up different leads. The criminal fraternity never liked these situations, because it meant that they would receive additional attention from the police and their activities would be disrupted.

On Thursday 26 April 1984, a twenty-three-year-old man was arrested in connection with the murder of Mr Harris. He appeared at Birmingham Magistrates' Court the following morning. I was not involved in the arrest, but went round to the court with the DI to observe the remand. He was a well-built guy, who remained composed and listened intently to the proceedings. He was remanded to police cells for three days, and subsequently charged with the murder.

I returned to normal duties on Wednesday 9 May and started to play catch-up with outstanding enquiries. I saw George in the evening. On Thursday 10 May, I was busy assisting a uniform officer regarding an arrest for robbery, arresting a receiver, and then searching a second-hand shop in Lodge Road flats, Hockley, where we recovered a wedding ring, which was contained in a shopping bag adjacent to the till. The next day, we were busy searching scrap-metal dealers and made two arrests, followed by the arrest of a twenty-five-year-old on suspicion of a robbery in Farm Street.

On Saturday 12 May, Birmingham City FC played Southampton FC at home at St Andrew's football ground. The match finished in a 0-0 draw and, as a result, Birmingham City were relegated from the First Division to the Second Division. After the game, PC Andrew Thomas, aged thirty years, was hit on the head by a flying brick and punched and kicked by a gang of Birmingham City fans, who ran amok outside the ground. He was helping to escort a crowd of over 1,000 supporters, when some of them broke away, overturned a police van, began stoning mounted police officers and then turned on him. At the time he said to the press:

> I grappled with one lad, and then saw stars and collapsed. I looked up and saw about fifteen fans putting the boot in as I lay on the ground. Words alone cannot describe how I feel. I was treated like a punch bag. I shall be scarred for life and I ache from bruises all over my body.

The officer, normally stationed at Acocks Green, received eleven stitches to a gash in his forehead where the brick hit him. A lone Blues fan, who asked to remain anonymous, tried to protect the officer and was also beaten up for his trouble; both were treated for their injuries at the East Birmingham Hospital. In a separate attack, in Emmeline Street, Sergeant Graham Biddle and PC John Stevens were also assaulted by fans throwing stones.

In all, a total of twenty-six arrests were made, but none in connection with the attack on PC Thomas. The pain continued for the club when three Birmingham City players were arrested in a disturbance outside Peppermint Place nightclub in Broad Street at 1.30 a.m. on Sunday. Police were called to a taxi rank and they arrested three men, together with a fourth man. After being detained at Digbeth police station for some hours, they were charged and bailed with offences of assault and being drunk and disorderly.

On Monday 14 May, I was made aware of the wounding of the officer at St Andrew's football ground. I was convinced that there would be a connection with some of the E Division team and I made contact with George. I saw him next day and he was able to assist with the job and with an offence of rape.

The following day, I went with Stuart to Bordesley Green and arrested a twenty-year-old suspect for the wounding of the officer. He was having none of it, and we eventually had to police-bail him, pending further enquiries. This was always the frustrating part when you were arresting someone purely on the strength of someone else's information. You could hardly tell the prisoner that you knew that they had done it, and there were times when you just had to accept defeat and move on to the next job.

In the afternoon, we made our way to Erdington police station regarding the arrests of four youths for burglary, including the rape suspect, and an outstanding target from our tower-block burglaries. The alleged rape was on their area, so I shared my information and left that with them. The burglary suspect was interviewed for our offence in Rea Tower and charged.

On Thursday 24 May at midday, I assisted the DI in relation to the David Harris murder with an identification parade for the person in custody charged with his murder. The following day, George gave me a whole raft of information relating to five suspects and their involvement in a nightclub wounding and burglaries. Some of those named were our 'usual suspects', including the 'fat man'. It was clear that the only time that some of these people were not committing crime was when they were in custody.

Five days later, George gave me some valuable background information relating to the murder of a prostitute in Balsall Heath, which was passed on to the deputy senior investigating officer. Within days, he followed this through with further information relating to stolen vehicles being scrapped.

9

SOLVING THE MURDER MYSTERY AND YET ANOTHER MURDER

On Sunday 17 June 1984, I went into the office to deal with what was an unusual robbery, in that the victim was a CID officer stationed at Steelhouse Lane, called Cheryl, who had been robbed of her handbag a couple of days before. She was a fearless individual, who stood no messing from anyone, but it proved that even police officers were not devoid of feelings in such situations. The events are told in her own words.

> I can recall that I had been into the city centre on a burglary enquiry. I was obviously in plain clothes. Walking back to the office at Steelhouse Lane, I stopped at a set of traffic lights in Corporation Street, opposite the Law Courts. I can remember that, as I approached the crossing, I stood there looking at a car with three 'Scallys' in it and I thought, 'no way are they going to stop for me to cross the road'. The lad I eventually identified was in the front passenger seat. He was light-skinned and of mixed race, with an afro hairstyle. The driver was white and had short blond hair. There was a third person in the back of the car. The windows were down, and the mixed-race guy had his elbow resting on the door. I looked to my left, and the next thing is I was yanked into the road with my bag. I was holding it as a clutch bag with the strap wrapped around my hand. The mixed-race guy was grabbing at my bag and eventually the strap broke. The bag was pulled into the car and they sped off. I realised what had happened and thought, 'Fuck, they've got a police radio' – it had been in my handbag.
>
> I started to run after the car, but couldn't get the registration number. I ran to the station to report it. I ran into the controller's office and

gave them details of the car. I possibly had two or three letters of the registration number. I ran into the CID office and said, 'I've been robbed,' and burst into tears. A couple of the officers, one a detective sergeant called Dave, said I had to cancel my credit cards straight away and asked me about keys. I thought, 'Fuck, my house keys were in the bag – they'll be on the way to burgle my house'. They took me home and sorted out a new lock for the door. I was in shock.

I didn't know it at the time, but a witness had actually been standing at a bus stop nearby and saw the whole thing. They took the registration number of the vehicle and phoned it in when they got home in Lichfield.

I later found out that it was a stolen car. The blond 'Scally' was locked up the following day after a car chase. I think he had stolen a couple of cars, one was beige, and the one in the robbery was pale blue, not old and not new. Over the weekend, my credit cards were used at off-licences and jeweller's shops in Newtown and Aston to the tune of £1,500.

Some of the contents of my bag were found in Newtown Row and I think that the cards were eventually seized at one of the shops. The blond driver was charged with the theft of vehicles but not the robbery. The mixed-race guy was then arrested, and I can only guess as to how that came about ...

The mixed-race offender was a nineteen-year-old from Northfield. I interviewed him and he later told us where the bag had been dumped in Electric Avenue in some water. The Underwater Search Unit helped us out the next day to search for it, and we recovered the police radio.

Cheryl continued,

I had to attend an identification parade. The offender had a scar on his face and, when I went in to see the line up, they were all standing there with sticking plasters on their faces. They all actually looked like each other; it was uncanny. I walked down the line and looked at each one carefully. I was very sure though, and, when I got to him, he looked like 'a cat in a pair of headlights' and I picked him out.

I went to Crown Court and the case rested heavily on the identification evidence. I pointed to him several times in the dock and left the jury in no doubt that I was sure. He got eighteen months in prison, which was unusual, as it was his first time in custody. I suddenly realised what a victim felt like. I had been a police officer for six years and on the CID for two years. I had dealt with numerous witnesses for rape and robbery, but until then never fully realised what they went through as victims. It really shook me up; even the ID parade was really nerve-racking and, after that, I showed a lot more empathy towards victims.

I was no stranger to giving evidence at Crown Court, and it sometimes did have its lighter moments. I was giving evidence before a judge one day in relation to a person who had assaulted me by punching me in the chest. The judge asked the prosecuting counsel if there were any photographs of the injury. I went bright red, and people started tittering in the court. Those that know me will understand why! I also went on to become a victim of crime on other occasions, so the experience stood me in good stead.

On Thursday 21 June 1984, George contacted me again, and I met him in a local pub with a sergeant from the Force Stolen Vehicle Squad. He reiterated his information regarding organised vehicle crime, plus a jewellery snatch in Hockley.

On Friday 22 June, a robbery occurred in Newtown shopping precinct. We managed to locate a couple of witnesses and, on Monday 25 June, we made an early start and arrested two suspects on suspicion of robbery and supply of cannabis at a flat in Hodgson Tower, Guildford Drive, Newtown. They were aged twenty-one years and twenty years.

After checking the work time-sheets of the second, we eliminated him from the robbery; however, we liaised with two officers from the Central Drug Squad and, by the end of the day, we had sufficient evidence to charge one with possession of cannabis with intent to supply, and one with allowing his premises to be used for the supply of drugs.

We had a good witness to the robbery and spent some time taking her around the area, looking to make a street identification, but without any luck. She did spot one of the robbers a few days later in the precinct but, by the time we got to her, he had disappeared again.

On Tuesday 3 July, I met George; he identified a suspect for burglary and told me about an affray at a pub called the Broadway involving some of our city-centre crew.

On Thursday 5 July, I went to one of the tower blocks with one of the beat officers to investigate some robberies relating to pedal cycles. Local knowledge paid off and, the next morning, John and I went with two beat officers to a flat in Severn Tower, Cromwell Street, where we made three arrests on suspicion of robbery. Two of them, aged ten years and fifteen years, were absconders from a local care home. We made a further arrest of a twelve-year-old later that afternoon, who was also an absconder from the same home in Hospital Street. All four admitted offences of robbery, burglary, and receiving stolen property.

On Saturday 7 July, I spent the afternoon in Chamberlain Square with the DCI regarding a miners' march, which was led by Arthur Scargill. With peace in the pits hanging in the balance, the miners' president led a march of 5,000 trade unionists from Saltley Gates to the city centre, and used the subsequent rally to announce, 'We are going to win'.

He was involved in delicate negotiations with the Coal Board chairman, Mr MacGregor, but was clearly in a defiant mood, as supporters applauded him loudly and chanted, 'We will support you ever more'. Among those taking part was the Scottish miners' leader, Mick McGahey, and several Labour MPs. Every leading trade union official in the West Midlands was there, together with Derek Robinson, the former Longbridge convenor.

Ours was just a watching brief and there were no incidents.

On Wednesday 11 July, I had a meeting with the detective inspector at Steelhouse Lane police station to discuss the issue of the David Harris murder. We were still vexed by the issue of the identity of 'Jakey', and I was tasked with making further enquiries.

The next day, I went to the Salvation Army Hostel in Snow Hill and arrested a twenty-one-year-old male who was wanted for a serious wounding in Eire. He was taken to Ladywood police station, pending extradition proceedings. I then went to Glen Parva Young Offenders' Institute, which was built as a borstal in Leicestershire in the early seventies, to make enquiries regarding 'Jakey', but drew a blank.

Over the years, a small story has stuck in my memory in relation to Glen Parva, as told to me by one of the inmates. It may be true, or it could be a figment of the imagination of someone who had time on his hands:

> One of my cell mates decided that he was going to 'do a runner', but he wasn't that bright. He wasn't worried about getting through the fence but, because it was winter, there was a lot of snow on the ground. My mate was worried about being tracked in the snow, so he got some white paint and painted the bottom of his shoes to hide the footprints! He got caught.

When we got back to Newtown, we went to look for the original informant I had spoken to in the Harris case, but got diverted when we came across another two residents from Hospital Street carrying a stolen video recorder in Newtown Precinct.

On Wednesday 18 July, while on night duty, I once again saw George and he provided details of a robbery, plus four suspects for burglary and receiving. I saw him again on Saturday 21 July and he provided details in relation to a hit-and-run accident involving a small child. On Tuesday 24 July, I met a different informant with Alan and was given information regarding a burglary where microwaves valued at £2,000 had been stolen – yet more red ink!

On Friday 24 August, I got a telephone call at home at 6.00 a.m. and was called into the office in relation to the suspicious death of a male in Martineau Tower. I liaised with the DI, did some enquiries in Newtown, and then informed the mother of the deceased about her son's death. Delivering 'death messages' is just not a nice thing to do and, no matter how you put the words together, the result is the same – anguish and pain.

I had learnt quickly that, while it was important to show compassion, it was also like 'walking on broken glass', and there were some things that you never said like, 'I know how you feel', which normally provoked a very negative reaction from people – after all, how could you possibly know how someone else felt. It was also important to be careful about what you said, so as not to compromise an investigation. Families always have an absolute thirst for knowledge in these situations but, if you revealed something that could only have been known by an attacker, the integrity of that evidence would be damaged.

Likewise, saying things like, 'It would all have been over very quickly', might sound like a sensitive approach, but could lead to excruciating discussions about exactly how many minutes and seconds you actually meant by that comment. This type of discussion was best left to the medical profession and the coroners.

At 1.00 p.m., I went with two uniform officers to Guest Grove and arrested a nineteen-year-old for assault occasioning actual bodily harm, commonly known as a Section 47 assault, on the deceased in an incident prior to his death. He admitted the attack, and was charged and kept in custody, while enquiries continued to ascertain the final cause of death and whether there was a link with his injuries. I saw George again in the evening, and he put a burglar in for a case where a substantial amount of clothing had been stolen.

On Tuesday 28 August, after liaising with the chief security officer at a large factory in Newtown, I obtained a search warrant, which four of us executed the next morning at some car-repair premises in Well's Street, Hockley. Stolen property from the factory was recovered, and we arrested the service manager, a twenty-three-year-old from Aldridge, for receiving stolen property. We lodged him and then went and arrested one of the managers from the factory, who was responsible for internal thefts.

On Friday 31 August, we spent the day dealing with a prisoner wanted on warrant for failing to appear at court, a prisoner for deception, and two good arrests for theft from the person, a seventeen-year-old and an eighteen year-old from Handsworth. Thefts from the person were usually only one step away from a robbery, so it was always good to catch them early before the level of violence escalated.

I met George again at 6.00 p.m. on Friday 14 September 1984, but the meeting was cut short when a murder occurred on New Street station. Following an argument outside the front glass doors of the station, a knife fight took place between two West Indian males and one of them was fatally injured – twenty-two year-old Desmond Steve Hamilton of Billberry Road, Pineapple Estate, Kings Heath.

Rush-hour crowds saw a knife being thrust into the victim's stomach just before 6.00 p.m., as the station was packed with travellers. The fight occurred at the taxi 'setting-down point' near to the glass doors leading to the station booking hall. A group of five or six West Indian men became involved in a violent argument and knives were used.

The victim died in Birmingham General Hospital at 7.00 p.m. Some of those involved in the argument were located at the scene and needed to be interviewed. The suspect for the fatal stabbing was described as a West Indian, who disappeared with blood stains on his face. He was of Rastafarian appearance with dreadlocks, a beard and moustache, and was 5 feet, 8 inches tall. He had a 2-inch-long fresh scar on his face, which had not been caused in this particular fight.

Paul Majster, a detective constable with the British Transport Police at the time, commented:

> I was working a 6.00 p.m. to 2.00 a.m. shift with DS Dave Drury. We were the first CID on the scene when it happened and, being rush hour, it was chaos. We realised quite quickly that he had been stabbed with something like a carving knife. All we could do initially was to cordon the scene off. There was no senior BTP officer on duty, and the local police were soon all over it. Generally, we had a good relationship, but there were some who still regarded us as 'the railway police'.
>
> There was a transitional period where the BTP had some jurisdiction issues but, in time, things got better, although the custody staff at

Steelhouse Lane could be quite indifferent towards us when we took prisoners there and treated us as outsiders.

I made my way to the station to liaise with the acting detective superintendent and then took statements from two key eyewitnesses. An initial incident room was set up in conjunction with the British Transport Police at the station, and I worked through the night, finishing at 4.30 a.m. – a tour of duty of seventeen hours. I was back in work seven hours later, and spent all day following up leads regarding a suspect, a twenty-one-year-old, who was arrested by Detective Sergeant Peter Hempton from the BTP at Crewe later that day.

Richard Bryant, by now a detective chief inspector, recalls the incident:

> I had been on a sea-fishing trip to Aberystwyth that day, when I had a telephone call from Mick Davey to tell me that there had been a murder on New Street station. I made my way into work and then located myself with BTP for the next thirty hours. The BTP found officers from all over the country to assist and they did a great job. I completed the prosecution file and I remember that one of the key witnesses was a retired senior police officer, who was working for NatWest Bank and was walking past at the time of the attack. A week after the murder, I got told off by the chief superintendent for poor performance, in light of the crime figures; but, when I explained how busy I had actually been, he became totally supportive.

A meeting duly took place between Chief Superintendant Jim Hoath, BTP, and a senior officer from West Midlands Police to settle the question of who would have primacy for the investigation. The West Midlands officer was relaxed about it, but had recently been on a course at Bramshill Police College, at which BTP policy on murder and terrorism offences had been discussed.

He was able to quote BTP Standing Orders accurately: 'In cases of murder, the local Home Office force will, in ordinary circumstances, take primacy for the investigation'. There was a bit of a debate but, finally, the BTP ceded the job to West Midlands Police, much to the annoyance of the arresting officers, who saw it as a slight on their professional abilities.

The incident room was duly transferred to Steelhouse Lane, and we continued dealing with actions raised in the ongoing investigation, during which time I was partnered up with Alan. It was normal to work in pairs on such investigations on outside enquiries, but the trick was to balance where you stripped out resources so that the day job could be continued. Criminals did not stop committing crime when such things took place; indeed, the wiser ones with their 'noses to the ground' would seize opportunities, knowing that we were spread thinly. The suspect was duly charged with murder, and I returned to normal duties on 25 September. He was later convicted of manslaughter and sent to prison for seven years.

On Wednesday 26 September, Stuart and I saw another potential informant, and we identified a team of three burglars, two of whom we were already looking for in relation to tower-block burglaries, again in Rea Tower and Teviot Tower. Burglars loved these flats because most of the front doors installed by the council were flimsy, and invariably failed to withstand a kick, while on the landings of the flats the burglars were generally left to their own devices, as most people avoided getting involved. All of the flats had spy holes in the doors from which to look out, but many of the residents were elderly and lived in genuine fear of repercussions.

On Thursday 27 September, I got the team out early and we went to a flat on the sixth floor of Rea Tower, arrested two of the three, and recovered some cannabis plants. It was the same *modus operandi* as before, when they had done a burglary on the first floor of the same tower block. We lodged our prisoners in the cells, then went back out and arrested the third member – a fifteen-year-old, with a bad reputation, from Unett Street. They all admitted offences of burglary and receiving stolen property, plus the cultivation of cannabis. We kept two of them in custody, including the juvenile, for whom I had to complete an 'unruly certificate'.

Informants were key to our success, and now we had another one 'on the books' who had delivered a great result within twenty-four hours. We saw the informant again next day and more information was promised on burglaries and the 'ringing' of stolen cars in the area.

In October 1984, my interest turned towards scrap-metal dealers again – there was one in particular whom I believed was receiving stolen metal. Yet another informant was in the early stages of cultivation and was pointing us in the right direction. This informant also put someone else in for the theft of a motorbike and, the following morning, I went with Alan to Castle Vale, where we arrested a twenty-two-year-old in one of the tower blocks and recovered stolen property and parts of the stolen bike.

On Saturday 13 October 1984, Birmingham City FC played Blackburn Rovers FC at St Andrew's ground in Birmingham. While I had no direct interest in the football, I was interested in the activities of Birmingham's Zulu Warrior hooligan element and their links to crime in the city centre.

At about 4.45 p.m. that day, groups of youths started to converge on New Street railway station. Efforts were made to disperse them by uniform BTP officers but with great difficulty. By 5.10 p.m., numbers of Birmingham City fans had swelled considerably on the station. Originally escorted from the ground by West Midlands Police officers, they managed to break out of their containment on arrival and made their way in small groups onto the concourse.

PC Mel Harris, a retired BTP dog handler, was on duty that day with his police dog Sabre and recalls,

After the match, I went to the front of the station approach road and saw groups of Birmingham fans converging on the station. I worked Sabre on both sides of the glass doors to try to prevent them from congregating, but then a group of up to 250 black and white youths appeared. As I tried to break them up, they charged across the station car park, chanting, and got inside the station. Women and children were pushed to the side and knocked to the floor, leaving some people visibly shocked.

DC Ian Mabbett was on the concourse in plain clothes, with a female officer, when he saw a black youth strike out at a football supporter. The officer got hold of him, and immediately a cry went up of, 'Zulu – Zulu,' and people were shouting, 'Get the Coppers', as some 200 crowded around. Acting Sergeant Murtagh and PC Heath went to their assistance, and truncheons were drawn and used to protect DC Mabbett and DC Sharon Duffy, who at that time were being punched and kicked while on the floor, struggling with their prisoner.

I managed to disperse the crowd with Sabre so that the officers could get their prisoner away from the scene, but it took me more than an hour working the dog continuously to clear the youths, who seemed to be intent on trying to attack other officers. We also had information that some of this group were carrying knives. It would be fair to say that football violence in general was escalating at that time, and the routine was always the same on a match day. We would move them on from the station, and they would inevitably appear again five minutes later from another entrance, constantly on the lookout for opposing fans.

Had it not been for the presence of Sabre, there is no doubt that the heavily outnumbered BTP officers would have faced serious problems. Ian Mabbett recalls the incident well:

I have had a few kickings over the years, but it went with the job. Once, I remember having to chase someone who was waving a carving knife around. You just never knew when it was coming. On this particular occasion, I was on the concourse with Sharon. The Blues fans had obviously pre-arranged things, as half of them came down the escalators from the shopping centre, while two other groups came in through both sets of glass doors at the same time onto the concourse. Quite a few scuffles broke out, and I arrested one of them for punching someone in the face. He tried to run off and, as I rugby-tackled him to the floor, the Blues fans started to put the boot in. I was underneath him, holding him, so he got most of the kicks. Sharon came to help but, even though she was a woman, they still lashed out at her. I suffered a few cuts and bruises. Just a normal Saturday really.

The prisoner arrested by the CID, an eighteen-year-old from Chelmsley Wood, was later charged with causing an affray. Later that evening, a group of black youths attacked a lone Newcastle supporter in the station buffet bar and robbed him of a gold chain.

It was not unusual for BTP officers to find themselves facing overwhelming odds, and the increased use of weapons in football-related violence became almost routine. PC Jim Rentell highlights another incident during the same period:

I was on my own at Aston railway station just outside Birmingham city centre, waiting for fans to return from a match at the Aston Villa ground. After the final whistle at 5.00 p.m., a group of more than 200 Villa fans came onto the station, chanting, and went through the tunnel to get to the Birmingham New Street-bound platform.

I followed them through to the bottom of the stairs leading up to the platform, at which point I was suddenly aware that a group of Arsenal fans had also come through the tunnel, and I was the only thing between them and the Villa supporters, who began coming back down the steps to confront them. At this point, an Arsenal fan pulled out a knife. I could see it clearly in his hand and, without thinking, I pulled out my truncheon and hit him on the wrist as hard as I could, while at the same time shouting for assistance. I heard something snap, and it wasn't my truncheon, as he merged back into the crowd screaming. Other officers arrived but it was a truly frightening moment.

On 15 October, I was engaged with enquiries into offences of robbery on elderly and vulnerable victims. I hated this type of offence, and felt nothing but revulsion for people who thought nothing of dragging an elderly person to the ground in the course of stealing from them. Victims of this age rarely recovered from the psychological effects and, in some cases, where brittle bones were broken they took months to recover. In extreme cases, secondary illnesses such as pneumonia set in, with sometimes fatal consequences, especially where hip bones were broken. It was all pointless and mindless.

Newtown Precinct was again the focus of our attention and, after further enquiries in Baldwin House, we managed to get descriptions of some of the persons responsible and to compile a Photofit at Lloyd House. In one of the cases, a near-blind eighty-year-old Asian man, who walked with a white stick, was frogmarched to a derelict school in Burlington Street, after collecting money from a post office in the precinct to pay for a final trip to India. He was attacked and robbed of £460, which a well-wisher from the business community later reimbursed him with so that he could make what might have been his final visit to see family. I was not a great fan of Photofits, but we had to go with what we had. Three days later, we arrested an eighteen-year-old for one of the robberies, and he was charged and kept in custody.

On Tuesday 23 October, I met George and I finished up with thirteen names and information on offences ranging from burglary, assaulting the police, affray and firearms offences. There was some really good stuff, and it confirmed the link even then of these organised gangs with the emergence of the Zulu Warriors. He was well aware of events on the railway station ten days previously, and confirmed the names of some of those present. Days later, he put another two jobs in that had occurred in Evesham and Oldham, confirming that the 'crew' were still operating on a nationwide basis.

On Tuesday 30 October, we started doing static observations in New John Street West regarding our suspect metal dealer. We continued with them the next day and, while other officers remained covertly outside, I paid a visit and signed the registers to confirm that he was not declaring everything correctly. We maintained a running log and continued the following week.

Despite the effects of policing the miners' strike, where large numbers of uniform staff were drafted to other duties, we were holding our own on the section, with no less than 253 persons being processed through the small Bridge Street West cell block in a ten-month period. In addition, not one of them had made a complaint against the police and I was satisfied that we were running a 'tight ship'.

On Wednesday 7 November, we arrested a thirty-five-year-old man from Stechford on suspicion of theft of metal, and lodged him at Steelhouse Lane. Shortly afterwards, we followed up with a second arrest of a sixty-four-year-old from Winson Green. The next day, we visited the scrap-metal dealer and arrested him for receiving stolen property. He couldn't account for gaps in his records, and subsequently admitted his involvement before being charged.

On Wednesday 14 November, I went out with Stuart and one of the beat officers, looking for two juveniles who were wanted for robbery. We found one of them in Burberry Street, suffering from the effects of glue-sniffing, and returned him to the care home in Hospital Street to be seen at a later date. Glue-sniffing was a problem in those days. They simply purchased a tube of glue and squeezed the contents into a plastic bag, which they then held over their nose and mouth and breathed in the fumes.

It spaced them out completely and, in the most extreme cases, gave them brain damage. They couldn't speak properly and lost co-ordination of movements. They were just kids in the main, heading towards disaster. The second youth was detained by Stuart later in the day.

On Thursday 15 November, I again saw George and, this time, he updated me on an armed robbery in the Handsworth area where a firearm was used. On 21 November 1984, my informant on the David Harris murder made contact again and was seen by me in the afternoon of that day. On this occasion, a different full name was given, although the nickname 'Jakey' remained the same. I was also provided with information in relation to the sequence of events that had taken place after the murder.

It was also clear that a number of people were aware of the identity of the killer and Nottingham became a feature of the enquiry in terms of associates. I spent an hour going through everything with the detective inspector the following day. This was thought-provoking information and clearly for some people, with one person already charged and awaiting trial, this was already a closed case.

On Friday 23 November, I went with one of my team to Canning Circus police station in Nottingham after tracking down a potential witness. Another very long day followed, but we were edging forward and the DI was briefed at each step.

On Saturday 24 November, I went to Glen Parva Borstal in Leicestershire with Alan to liaise with prison officers regarding another potential witness, who was serving a sentence for unrelated matters. From there, I went to Aston to try and track another individual down.

The momentum was gathering.

On Sunday 25 November, after an hour searching records held within the Central Information Unit, and other intelligence records, I identified a possible match for the suspect, which tied in with the background I had been given. It was a moment in time where I reflected on all of the hours I had spent in that department over the years, going back to when I was an 'attached man'. It was basic detective work, but the place was a 'goldmine' of information, providing that you had the patience to go through the box files in detail.

The following day, I confirmed with the informant that we had the right man and spent the rest of the day in the Wednesbury, West Bromwich, and Hockley areas, liaising with the DHSS and trying to find another new witness to the murder. I was trying deliberately to keep everything low key. This had to be done right and, by now, I was pretty sure that the man I was looking for would know about it.

Another day of fruitless searching and then, on Wednesday 28 November, with the support of the detective superintendent, we ramped things up using some covert options. By the end of the day, we had found two potential new witnesses, who were not happy to see us but added more pieces to the puzzle with direct information about the murder.

By close of play on Thursday 29 November, we had finalised three key-witness statements and obtained evidence that confirmed that 'Jakey' had been seen running in the area immediately following the murder, with blood on his clothing, which was later allegedly burnt. Certain critical admissions were made and people were warned to keep quiet. It had all apparently gone very wrong.

More briefings with the detective superintendent and, on Friday 30 November, I went to Winson Green Prison to see another potential witness, and then went to Smethwick Magistrates' Court to follow up the enquiry regarding the knife recovered on 18 April 1984.

On Saturday 1 December, we tracked a further witness down and took another statement. There was no doubt that murder focused the minds of people who ordinarily might try to protect friends or associates. Within two days, I had a description of the knife found and obtained a similar one as a sample for identification purposes from one of the gun dealers in the city centre, who also sold 'survival' knives. It was described as being a lock knife with a teak handle, which had gold edges.

More witness statements from the court staff who had found the knife followed. Continuity in such cases was critical and, just to achieve this, we needed to take ten witness statements as the knife passed from the person who found it, a court secretary, a court usher, three police officers who handled it, two property officers, a driver, and finally the force armourer, who destroyed it.

I was doing daily briefings now with the detective superintendent, and there was a sense of rising anticipation. George was still maintaining contact, but there were only so many hours in the day and the murder had to take priority.

On Monday 10 December, I liaised with a pathologist at Wolverhampton Royal Hospital to discuss the nature of the knife wounds inflicted on Mr Harris compared to the type of knife that we believed may have been used as the murder weapon. It was frustrating that the knife we were interested in had been destroyed, but we had to go with what we had.

We continued taking witness statements to make sure that we had all the continuity of evidence right, but we were getting there. On Wednesday 12 December, two more witness statements followed. It was clear that, after the murder, despite the warnings, people had been talking to each other. One uncorroborated statement might prove nothing, but a number taken independently and demonstrating a consistent theme could be crucial.

On Friday 14 December 1984, at 5.25 p.m., I met up with the detective superintendent in Hockley and we went back to Steelhouse Lane to discuss tactics. He was a short guy, with a background in fraud, but he was also a thoroughly decent person, who was prepared to listen and didn't profess to have all of the answers. This was to be a crucial meeting, as I now knew how to get hold of our man and felt that we had as much evidence as we were likely to get. I wanted to strike while the 'iron was hot'. I wanted to go for him straight away – that moment – that day.

At 8.40 p.m., together with the detective superintendent, and another detective sergeant called John, we went to Radford police station in

Nottingham and, at midnight, formally arrested a twenty-year-old man on suspicion of the murder of Mr Harris.

It took us a couple of hours to get back to Steelhouse Lane police station, with the prisoner handcuffed in the rear of the car. He spent most of the time staring out of the window into the darkness that he knew was about to embrace him.

Shortly after he was booked into custody, John and I interviewed him by way of contemporaneous record, and he admitted to being the person seen by witnesses to be attacking Mr Harris. He was charged in the early hours of the morning with the murder of David Harris, and kept in custody in the central lock-up for court.

It had been a long night, but a compelling experience that I have never forgotten.

I drove home in the early light of dawn; shattered but reflective; alone in my thoughts; oblivious and thankfully detached from the myriad of phone calls that I knew would start at 8.00 a.m. I went to bed and slept well. In one month, I had worked nearly ninety hours in excess of my normal working hours, but it was all worth it.

There were no connections between the two individuals charged with murder and no evidence that more than one person had been involved. Interesting times were to follow.

The first person charged with murder was released from custody shortly afterwards and my prisoner was committed to the Crown Court to stand trial for murder. He had already indicated during the course of those proceedings that he intended to plead 'not guilty'.

While he was in custody on remand awaiting trial, there was another twist in the case when, as a result of some further information, we visited a former girlfriend of his. He had written a letter while in prison to her. When we arrived at her flat, she informed me that she had received the letter, but that she had ripped it up and thrown it into her rubbish bin. I went through the contents of the bin and took out all of the pieces, which were covered in pieces of salad and waste food. I pieced the scraps of paper together and within the contents was an important piece of evidence – a confession to the murder. This was to form an important piece of evidence in the trial.

10

ROBBERIES, MORE RIOTS AND A VERDICT

On Tuesday 18 December 1984, I was back in the office at Bridge Street West, trying to catch up, and met a new potential informant in the afternoon. We still had a lot of work to get through on the murder enquiry, but I also needed to engage with my team to make sure that we were fit for purpose in the run-up to Christmas. It was always a difficult time of year for us, and you never quite knew how workloads were going to pan out, as the unexpected was always expected to happen.

I spent a few hours that week investigating an allegation that the Animal Liberation Front had used a poison on turkeys on sale for Christmas that was harmful to humans.

On Saturday 22 December, I saw George for a pre-Christmas meeting and yet again he gave a wealth of information on five suspects, one of whom had smashed up an unattended police vehicle. George and I never became friends – that would have been entirely inappropriate. We did, however, have a unique relationship and he trusted me implicitly. I dropped him back home and booked off duty, but almost immediately booked back on duty to attend a suspected arson attack on an upholstery shop in Newtown shopping precinct. My efforts at an early finish went out of the window and I got home after midnight.

In 1984, reported crimes in the West Midlands rose to 227,566 offences, with forty-five murders investigated, all of which were detected. Nearly 7,500 offences of wounding were reported, and robberies shot up by 29 per cent on the previous year to 2,455 offences. Analysis showed that juveniles were involved in a third of the offences detected. A staggering 43,679 offences of burglary of dwelling houses were recorded and the cash value of property stolen during the course of these offences amounted to £27 million, with just £500,000 worth of property recovered.

January 1985 started off with the usual round of street robberies and burglaries. We were interested in a little robbery team and, on Thursday 10 January, we booked on at 7.00 a.m. and went to Parliament Street, Aston, in an effort to arrest a suspect for robbery. He wasn't there, but we went straight to Gerrard Street in Newtown; Stuart and I arrested a seventeen-year-old, who was taken to Steelhouse Lane, where he was interviewed and admitted offences of robbery. Later that afternoon, we responded to an assistance call from Malcolm Halliday, who had come across a stolen motor car containing two other members of the team in Gee Street.

Malcolm managed to detain a nineteen-year-old at the scene but the second, a relative, made good his escape at that point. We went straight back to Parliament Street where the third offender, a sixteen-year-old, climbed onto the roof of his house as we entered. We called the fire brigade and contained the area with uniform officers. He wasn't going anywhere and, after an hour, we got him off the roof and arrested him. Three in the bag and another good day. While all this was going on, George also provided me with the location of an escapee from prison but we just missed him.

On Monday 28 January, I went to see the detective inspector in charge of the Force Surveillance Unit to have a chat about opportunities. They were advertising for people to go on surveillance courses and were desperate for sergeants. I cannot say I was immediately drawn to the DI, but I was interested and I thought that it would give me other skills.

On Thursday 31 January, I went with Stuart to Hodgson Tower to see a suspect regarding a burglary at the flat next door. He had his answers straight at that stage and we left him. At 9.25 a.m., we arrested a nineteen-year-old who lived on the ninth floor of the same tower block. He was obviously in, but refused to open the door to us. He had nowhere to go and we eventually smashed the front door down in the presence of the caretaker and found some of the burglary proceeds in his flat.

We lodged him and went back to our first suspect, a thirty-nine-year-old. This time he was arrested, and further property was recovered, which was identified by the victim. We spent the day unravelling what had happened, and saw an informant who indicated that other people had also been involved. The next day, we arrested an eighteen-year-old female from Alum Rock, who admitted her part in the burglary. Another three arrests followed over the next couple of days. It had been something of a group affair.

On Tuesday 5 February 1985, I was interviewed as a witness by a chief superintendent from the C11 Metropolitan Police complaints department, who were conducting enquiries on behalf of the force in relation to the Harris murder. On Wednesday 6 February, I was tied up during the day with a serious robbery on a Securicor van in Newtown shopping precinct. A security guard was hit with a club several times by a robber, who attacked him outside Lloyds Bank in Newtown Row. Mr Allen Dagnan, the Securicor employee, suffered head, neck and arm injuries, as he tried to hang onto a cash container with thousands of pounds inside, but eventually had to release his grip. The robber ran with the container to a waiting getaway car, a stolen Ford Cortina, driven by a second person.

The vehicle was later found abandoned in Greenfield Road, Handsworth. Both robbers were described as West Indians and the driver was slim, of average build, clean shaven and wearing a woollen hat. Mr Dagnan was treated at the Birmingham Accident Hospital for his injuries and discharged.

The next day, I assisted John and Stuart following the arrest of a twenty-one-year-old from Aston on suspicion of the robbery. Offences were disclosed and we got a 'Superintendent's Authority' to keep him in overnight while we did a search for a second suspect. He was charged the next day and kept in custody. I loved operational police work, but I was now about to enter a period of different priorities, which were somewhat alien to me.

After a period of annual leave, I started a course with the Force Surveillance Unit on Monday 25 February 1985, which lasted for three weeks. Even after all these years, it would still not be appropriate to comment much on the course, which was a mixture of training to do static, foot, and mobile surveillance. I had great admiration for the skills of some of the trainers, who showed a very high level of expertise in their specialist field.

While I could do the static and foot surveillance with all the other trainees, my police driving grade did not allow me to drive the surveillance vehicles and I was constantly employed as the front-seat observer, reading maps and completing logs while we flew around the West Midlands and elsewhere, frequently at some speed. We found ourselves spending hours waiting for a 'target' to move and, in between the silences, you would hear a lone voice giving a code-numbered signal that would indicate that there was no change in the situation. At times it was mind-numbing.

We would eat as we travelled, and it was not unusual to find someone carrying ten packets of fish and chips, having just done the food run, only to find yourself mobile and on the move again. The food would be cold by the time we stopped again – all designed to test our commitment and mental agility.

Debrief sessions were the most combative situations I have ever witnessed, where no quarter was given, and students in training were encouraged to criticise each other for making mistakes. They were invariably lengthy sessions that you came out of exhausted.

I knew that I was not as good as I wanted to be during the course of the training, but I refused to be consumed by the process and kept my counsel. At the end of the course, I was offered a three-month attachment to the unit. The problem was that I knew that my division would not hold my post open for that long; if I accepted the offer, I would lose my current post. I had to make a difficult decision and consulted my chief superintendent at the time, Barry Kirton, who was very clear: 'Don't go – it's the wrong move. If you do go, there is no guarantee of a job here for you if it doesn't work out.' It was time to reflect.

Dave 'J' recalls a murder case on Saturday 23 March 1985, made all the more tragic because the victim was just twenty-two months old:

> I was working with a DI called Dave Harris at the time, and a DS by the name of Fred Halsey, both very experienced officers. I remember it was a Saturday match-day, with Birmingham City playing at home. This couple reported that their child, Gemma Hartwell, had gone missing in the Bull Ring shopping centre as they were walking round the shops at about 12.45 p.m. They said that she had run off into the crowds. Despite a search by up to 100 officers, we could find no trace of her.
>
> Their home was in Waterworks Road, Ladywood, and we soon discovered that there was a history of violent abuse in the family. The child's father, Phillip Hartwell, aged thirty years, already had convictions for violence towards children; later in the day, we interviewed a close friend, Eugene Wright, aged twenty-eight years. That evening, he led us to a shallow grave in Clent Hills, just outside Birmingham, where the body of Gemma was found buried in a cardboard box. It was a very tragic case.

Following a post-mortem and further enquiries, it was established that the child had been suffocated by Hartwell, who had thrust a ball of wool into the child's mouth and then gagged her with a scarf. Emma also had bruises to her head, face, arms, legs, and buttocks where she had been beaten with a stick.

During questioning, Hartwell sought to blame the child's mother. At the time of the murder, Gemma had been released back into the custody of her parents on a trial basis after originally having been taken into care by social services.

Phillip Hartwell was subsequently charged with murder, although a jury of six men and six women at Crown Court later found him guilty of manslaughter, and he was sentenced by Mr Justice Tudor Evans to ten years' imprisonment. Gemma's mother was sent to prison for six months for child neglect, and Wright got four months in prison for obstructing a coroner in relation to assisting in the concealment of the child's body.

In the spring of 1985, Steve Jordan recalls his final memories of the miners' strike and his views on how policing changed as a result of this, and other significant events:

> By now, I was an inspector and I was sent to County Durham for two weeks. The strike had dragged on for nearly a year. Tempers were on a hair-trigger, with many strikers and families on the breadline – starving, even. We stayed at Chester-le-Street and were deployed to Easington on fourteen hour-days. We were fed like foie gras geese with a huge breakfast, a massive dinner on our return, and two large 'doggy bags' for each day.
>
> In Easington, which was 'Billy Elliot country', the pit gates were on the edge of the village, but the head itself was on the coast, probably a mile away along a private road, with frequent and sharp speed bumps. It was quiet, so we posted a small party at the gates, and everyone else was put on foot patrol in pairs to provide a visible presence.
>
> We were initially shocked by what we found. We had followed a large urban force, who had also gone out on patrol, thanking the community for their financial good fortune and even in some cases showing their pay slips. The folk to whom they were showing these documents were starving. Many wanted to go back to work, but were too afraid of the backlash in such a tight community.
>
> Emotions ran high, but we encouraged our own officers to engage with the public and, if they had too much food, to give some away. Soon we were drinking tea in strikers' homes, and recognising mutual humanity.

It is humbling when someone on the breadline provides for you. It was a powerful experience for many of us.

A week passed and we then had word that there was going to be a push the next morning, because a prominent and vociferous striker was returning to work. We doubled the gate cordon and had a couple of vans with long shields ready at the pithead. The moment came; a push and a shove, and we scrambled to support the gate, getting our kit on as we went, but it was all over in minutes.

These memories are purely personal. It is easy to forget the similarities between mining and policing. Both are hazardous and stressful. In both, one has to rely on colleagues for safety. Both are defined by their own cultures, and are a way of life. The police role, often inaccurately and sensationally portrayed as anti-strikers, was nothing like that. We were neither there to judge, nor to take sides between strikers and strike-breakers.

The striking miners were humans deserving human dignity. Families were drawn in, whatever their own position. Miners I spoke to were reluctant to strike, but found it hard to stand up against militants, who enjoyed significant informal power bases in local communities.

This strike was not a typical industrial dispute. It was about profound life experiences and values.

The police had just emerged from recent public-disorder experiences with race riots and football hooliganism, and had significant expertise, but the nature of the miner's strike was different; Orgreave, significantly so. My experience was that those forces that truly believed in community policing managed far better than those who might have been efficient at public-order policing but were incompetent outside the 'stockade'. Indeed, extrapolating our experiences from Brixton, St Paul's and Toxteth was probably as unhelpful as the use of American Civil War tactics by both British and German military staff colleges at the outbreak of the First World War. This is not a criticism of policing, nor of police leadership, but is a reflection of the enormous and rapid changes in society in the 1970s and '80s.

On Wednesday 3 April, I went to see the DI again at the Force Surveillance Unit – I had come to a decision. The next day, and despite my better judgement, I informed my detective superintendent that I wanted to take up the option of the three-month attachment. Everyone told me I was making a mistake, but I was stubborn and wouldn't change my mind.

The same day I was posted to a murder enquiry, following the death of twenty-five-year-old Carmetta Stewart, and reported to Thornhill Road police station. She was found dead on a settee in her Handsworth home in Whitehall Road the day before, having been subjected to what was described as a frenzied knife attack. She had been stabbed more than twenty times with a 6-inch stiletto-style knife, which had not been recovered.

Described as a shy individual, it was believed that she could have been dead for some days, with no signs of a break-in at her home, and the television set and gas fire still on. Carmetta was an ex-nurse and was also attending a part-time catering course at Sutton Coldfield college. She had attended a christening the previous weekend so, although she was something of a loner, there were a lot of people to trace to confirm her movements.

I spent five days interviewing witnesses and tracing potential suspects and, on Tuesday 9 April 1985, I transferred to the Force Surveillance Unit.

I probably realised within the first week that I had made a mistake, but I needed to give it my best shot. Although I was an experienced sergeant, this counted for nothing on this unit, which had a very strict pecking order. A number of us from the course started doing more training with some newer members of the team, with a dedicated trainer. He was basically a decent person, who had been on the unit a long time but was still grounded in reality. I continued to 'survive rather to excel' and it was not a feeling that I liked.

We continued training, and eventually were deployed on a live operation for the first time on Wednesday 24 April. We then spent another five days on another operation and then switched back to training mode. As before, the debrief sessions were highly charged affairs and prone to get extremely personal. I wasn't prepared to struggle within such an environment, and made my views known. I told them that I wanted to leave at the earliest opportunity.

While I was existing in something of a 'cocoon', back out in the real world major events were occurring. On Saturday 11 May 1985, Birmingham City played at home at St Andrew's with Leeds United. It was a date that was to become infamous in the history of the 'Zulu Warriors'. Birmingham City had already won promotion to the First Division for the next season and Leeds United had a slight chance of promotion, provided they won the match and other games being played by other clubs went their way.

Leeds fans arrived early in Birmingham city centre, occupying a number of pubs. Even before kick-off, skirmishes took place involving Zulu Warriors, and an organised attack took place on thirty Leeds fans, who were drinking in the Australian Bar in Hill Street. During the course of the disturbances, up to 200 Zulus smashed every window in the pub while their 'official photographer' took action shots of the scene of destruction.

At the ground, about 6,000 Leeds fans were fenced in at the Tilton Road end while, at the other end, Birmingham City's hooligan element gathered in large numbers at the Railway End. During the course of the game, there was a pitch invasion at half-time, followed by a full-scale assault by Birmingham City hooligans as they launched themselves across the pitch at the final whistle. Police officers battled to restore order, and it is widely felt that the sheer bravery of a number of mounted police officers saved the day.

Tragically, during the course of the disturbances, Ian Hanbridge, a totally innocent supporter aged fifteen years, lost his life when a wall collapsed on him at the away end of the ground. More than 500 people were injured, and ultimately well over 100 arrests were made, and further arrests made retrospectively.

In his annual report of that year, Chief Constable Geoffrey Dear highlighted the comments of a consultant, who treated many of the casualties, both police and civilian, at the East Birmingham Hospital that day and said,

> One of the things that impressed me most was the stoicism and the calmness of the injured policemen. Their behaviour was remarkable. They were less concerned with their damaged heads, crushed feet and other injuries than with trying to help other people and, if this is the typical 'British Bobby', we have every reason to be proud.

Mike Cresswell recalls,

> I was working with Uniform Bravo serial of the Operations Support Unit on this date and, to start with, we were deployed to a National Front event in the city centre. We started to hear radio transmissions with shouts for assistance and fights occurring and, for a while, it was a bit frustrating for some officers because we were not allowed to redeploy to assist. In any event, the NF event passed off peacefully and we were deployed to St Andrew's football ground.

We were deployed to the end where the Leeds fans were situated behind fences. We had normal helmets on to start with, and then I remember running across the side of the pitch to pick up some NATO-style helmets, which had been put on the touchline. We put them on, and every now and then you could hear a 'clink' on your helmet as coins thrown by supporters bounced off them. One astute officer collected about £20 that day.

If anyone tried to get over the fencing, we drove them back with our truncheons. At one point, Blues fans surged onto the pitch, and we started to get missiles thrown at us from behind. There is no doubt the mounted officers saved the day as, in places, we were just one 'thin blue line' and in danger of being swamped.

During another pitch invasion by Birmingham City fans, one of the inspectors led a charge by officers, but was hit by a brick and carried away. The officers rallied and pushed them back again, eventually onto the terraces. One of the OSU serials from Tipton got a terrible battering, with officers being pulled to the floor and their sergeant attacked with bricks. All the time, you could hear the constant chants of 'Zulu', just like in the film about Rorke's Drift.

At one point, we had to get onto the terraces occupied by the Leeds fans, and I remember one fan throwing punches at me, but I just hit him with my truncheon. At some stage, the wall collapsed and the young lad was killed. It deeply affected me and, as a regular churchgoer, I went the next day to pray and tried to find some peace from my thoughts about what had happened. The level of violence and sheer animosity is something I never encountered again and it took me some time to get over the shock of it.

Dave Cross was on duty at the game and recalls,

I was posted to the touchline at the Railway End, near to the big clock. With me was a young policewoman, who had only been back from the training centre two weeks. It was to be her first, and last, football match duty. The crowd became increasingly rowdy, particularly the Birmingham fans at the Railway End.

At some point, a decision was made to withdraw officers on the touchline, at which point we were standing by the corner flag furthest away from the safety of the players' tunnel. Someone scored a goal, and it seemed to us that the referee had blown his whistle early for half-time, as Blues fans came onto the pitch with constant chants of 'Zulu'.

I drew my truncheon, which was a pretty useless gesture at this stage due to the numbers, grabbed the female officer's hand, and ran diagonally across the pitch to the tunnel. It felt like there were a thousand Birmingham City fans all running behind me.

In the players' tunnel, a sergeant grouped a number of us together and said that we should try to clear the pitch. We marched out in a sort of line, with no protective clothing whatsoever and attempted to push them back. We drew our truncheons and charged towards the marauding mob, but it was impossible to break them up, and we finished up back in the tunnel. At some point the mounted officers assembled and rode their horses onto the pitch, displaying great bravery.

I remember at one point a mounted officer was displaced from his horse, which was running around on the pitch. To my absolute horror, my female probationer constable ran over to the horse, grabbed its reins and pulled its head down. She told me later that she had blown into the horse's nose, which quietened it down sufficiently for it to be led from the pitch. She was recognised for her bravery but handed her notice in on the following Monday, which was a loss to the force.

It was a terrible day for football and the tragic loss of a young life, which we were unaware of at the time, made it so much worse. Among all this chaos, one of my abiding memories of the day was at one stage seeing one of the groundsman trying to remove horse manure in a bucket from one of the goalmouths.

The newspaper headlines for this day, however, also focused on another event as, up in West Yorkshire, more than fifty people died, and over 100 were seriously injured, when the main stand caught fire at Bradford City's Valley Parade stadium. Mr Justice Popplewell, who later headed an inquiry into both major incidents, described the Birmingham–Leeds game as 'something more like the Battle of Agincourt than a football match'.

On 29 May 1985, the world of football marked another day of tragedy and mindless violence at the Heysel Stadium in Brussels, Belgium, at the European Cup final between Liverpool FC and Juventus of Italy. Following disturbances between opposing fans, a number of people trying to escape from the fighting found themselves pressed against a wall and barriers, resulting in thirty-nine people losing their lives, and more than 600 injured.

On Monday 3 June, I was back out operationally with the unit and, after a couple of days, got selected for a job in a static observations point on the roof of a tower block. I didn't like heights much, but had to get over it. We could see for miles, but our focus of attention was simply a door in the distance. For sixteen hours a day, for eight days, that door was all that we looked at as we waited for someone to open it. We had a well-secured tent for some cover as we rotated the observations between three of us, but we were still exposed to the elements and it was a pretty thankless task.

On Monday 1 July, I had a further meeting with Chief Superintendent Kirton. I received a bit more of a 'tongue-lashing', but I knew that he was trying to help me, so I took it. There were no detective sergeant's vacancies on the division at that point, so he offered me a uniform sergeant's post on the basis that I could have the next CID vacancy when one became available. For a minute, I asked him if I could have time to think about it but, as I sensed the blood starting to rise in his neck, I made a snap decision and accepted. I wasn't in a position to negotiate.

I went back to the unit for a couple of weeks and supported some of the training and another operation while I waited for a transfer date. In the meantime, fate took another twist and a detective sergeant's vacancy unexpectantly came up at Bradford Street – it had my name on it.

On Monday 15 July 1985, I transferred back to the F Division and was posted to Bradford Street, where I had been an attached CID officer some nine years previously. The DCI in post was a guy called Bill. He was a real gentleman, who was an expert on major-incident-room procedures and computers, and was very easy to get on with. Nothing much had changed and it was still seen as the 'poor cousin' to Digbeth and Steelhouse Lane sub-divisions.

On Wednesday 31 July, I made contact with George again after our enforced break and he promised some information regarding some till snatches. Within twenty-four hours, he was back in touch and he gave me the names of two people involved in assaulting a police officer, as well as a market trader who was receiving stolen property.

On Wednesday 7 August, I went to Farm Road, where my grandparents had previously lived, and got involved in the forensic examination of the scene of an attempted arson at a house. A vehicle had been seen acting suspiciously in the area at the time; we found the vehicle in Roderick Road and seized it. Two hours later, we arrested a twenty-four-year-old, who lived in the road, on suspicion of attempted arson. He was interviewed back at Bradford Street, where he admitted the offence and was charged and kept in custody.

I spent my thirty-third birthday investigating a group of 'bikers', who had created a base in one of the pubs in Golden Hillock Road. There were fears that they were keeping weapons on the premises and that the pub was becoming a 'no-go' area for the police. We started to do regular observations in the area, building up details of motorbike registrations and detail of the owners. I also got the Force Drug Squad involved as we started to build up the intelligence picture, and tried to get some interest from the Force Surveillance Unit, as well as the Force Intelligence Department.

On Wednesday 14 August, I was out in the evening with the DCI and an attached officer, when we saw a vehicle in Lawden Road, Small Heath, which attracted my attention. The vehicle drove off, but I recognised the two occupants, one of whom, a thirty-two-year-old from Wheeler Street, had been dealt with by me for theft previously. The next morning, we did a check of factory premises in the road and, lo and behold, one of them had been broken into. We went straight over to Newtown to try and trace the two suspects, but they had made themselves scarce.

We visited Wheeler Street again in the afternoon, and then got a phone call from a firm of solicitors in Corporation Street, where the two of them were waiting for us. We arrested them in the presence of their solicitor, recovered their vehicle in Clifford Street and, after interview, charged them both with burglary. We identified a third suspect, who was arrested a few days later in Northfield.

The observations continued in Golden Hillock Road and, on Monday 19 August, I saw George again. I had tasked him with going into the pub frequented by the bikers and he confirmed that drugs were being used on the premises.

On Wednesday 28 August, we went to Henley Street in Sparkbrook, and arrested a seventeen-year-old for burglary of a dwelling house. The prisoner decided to cooperate, and we went out and identified the address to which the stolen property had been taken. Later that day, we went to some shop premises in Alcester Road and arrested a twenty-five-year-old. From his home address, we recovered a stolen video recorder and hi-fi system. Both individuals were charged.

On Thursday 29 August, just as I was going home for a split-duty, I received a call regarding the murder of a security officer, who worked at Victoria Law Courts and had been stabbed to death after apparently trying to take a knife from a man who had entered the courts. John Reilly, who had been quite well-known in the courts, had collapsed in a pool of blood after witnesses saw him stagger to a bench seat and then slump to the ground. He was pronounced dead on arrival at the General Hospital.

Witnesses had seen Mr Reilly search a man at the main entrance to the court, who had been allowed entry but then produced a knife and threatened him with it. Despite being asked by the security officer to put the weapon down, the man lunged at Mr Reilly, who had only recently returned to work after being in hospital, and stabbed him in the back. The incident took place in full view of solicitors, police officers, members of the public, and staff, some of whom went into shock after the incident.

Glenville Benjamin, aged twenty-seven years, from Camden Street in Ladywood, was arrested and subsequently charged with murder. Like many such offences, it was just an absolutely futile crime and a waste of the life of an innocent man who was just trying to do his job. I had been through the security checks many times at court and found all of the security staff to be extremely courteous and tolerant. They managed abuse with a professional dignity and I had every respect for them.

Unfortunately, violence was not uncommon in the courts, as Dave 'J' recalls,

> I think it was around the time of the murder of the security officer when myself and DS Rex Langford were assaulted in the courts. We had just finished the trial of a fifteen-year-old, who had been convicted of the rape of a woman whom he had attacked in the street near to the city centre. After the verdict was announced, we were mobbed by his family inside the court, and men and women alike started to attack us. The fighting spilt out into the main area outside and police officers came rushing over to us from all directions, making several arrests. I got a cut on the face from a ring on someone's finger – otherwise, I was lucky. In those days, we expected to suffer a few knocks and didn't make too much of it.

We assisted the staff at Steelhouse Lane in taking witness statements and, in the evening, I put George into the pub in Golden Hillock Road to monitor the movements of a drugs dealer. I picked him up again a couple of hours later and he was a bit the worse for wear. He had clearly consumed a few drinks for a bit of 'Dutch courage', and I dropped him off near to his home so that he didn't get in harm's way. I had known him a long time and I could sense that he wasn't his usual self – it was not a good sign.

Unfortunately, he didn't stay home and got arrested a few hours later, trying to do a burglary. As the saying went – 'don't do the crime, if you can't do the time'. George knew this and took his punishment at court – those were the rules.

During the course of 1985, the West Midlands Police recognised the scale of the drugs problems they were facing by increasing the strength of the Force Drugs Squad to fifty-five officers, the largest of its type in the country at that time.

On Monday 9 September 1985, a riot situation developed in Handsworth, reportedly sparked by the arrest of a man near to the Acapulco Cafe in Lozells, and a police raid on the Villa Cross pub in the same area. Hundreds of people were involved in the disturbances, with police officers being attacked, shops looted, and cars and property set on fire. Two brothers, Kassamali and Amirali Moledina, died in a fire at the post office, which they ran. 122 people were injured, including seventy-nine police officers.

At its height, over 1,500 police officers were deployed to the area and, in the aftermath, it was found that more than forty-five shops had been looted and burnt, with indications that some of the rioting had been planned to draw police into a confrontation in which petrol bombs were used from the outset.

Property valued at more than £15 million was destroyed.

In such situations, the priority is to put uniforms on the street, in order to restore normality at the earliest opportunity. The role of the CID was to provide support in terms of post-incident investigation, where the emphasis was on trying to arrest offenders. That said, Handsworth was a ten-minute drive from Birmingham city centre. Clearly, the police also had to have a plan to protect the commercial heart of the city and additional resources were deployed to prevent the disorder spreading.

Dave 'J' recalls his own experiences:

I was at Bradford Street at the time on the CID. A couple of the lads had been to Belfast for a prison escort and, after they got back at about 6.00 p.m., we went round to a pub, which we all called 'Murphy's' although it was actually the Moseley Arms, for a drink. While we were in there, the uniform inspector on duty came in and told us all to book back on duty, as Handsworth was going up in flames. We thought he was joking to start with but, when we went outside, we could see a red glow in the sky. Five of us went back to the office and went out in two plain cars, looking for looters coming back through the side streets from Lozells. I personally had nearly a dozen prisoners and, between the five of us, we made twenty-six arrests and lodged them all at Steelhouse Lane, which rapidly got full. We spent the next day interviewing them all.

This is Liam's recollection of events:

I had four years' service and was twenty-two years old. I started work that day on a plain-clothes team in Aston, where I was based. I started the shift at 8.00 a.m. During the afternoon, we were made aware by the radio controller that there had been an incident in Handsworth and that no officers were allowed to stand down from duty. I was feeling a little apprehensive and excited at the same time as, being a young officer, I had never been involved in any real serious disorder. I had only been to Handsworth in the course of making arrests and carrying out criminal investigations. I was totally unfamiliar with the area and the residents.

At about 6.00 p.m., I was instructed to make my way, in uniform, to a van, where I was joined by a sergeant and nine other constables from the division. Long shields were placed in the rear of the van, which was cramped due to the number of people sitting in it. I can't remember who they all were but, like me, they were feeling nervous and apprehensive about what was going to happen. The next eighteen hours were then just totally chaotic.

What I can tell you is that over that period the van travelled to various incidents of looting at shops, stores, and garages, all over the Handsworth area. It was difficult to know where you were going in the back of the van, but all praise to the driver who was being dragged from pillar to post. Every incident to which we went, there were people of all ages and nationalities looting these premises.

I arrested seven people for burglary and public-order offences in Handsworth, and took my prisoners to custody blocks all over Birmingham, as they all progressively became full to the brim. Every time you visited a custody block, a photograph was taken of you with the prisoner and brief details of the offence given. During the night, we had missiles thrown at our van, as well as when we got out of the van. We also had petrol bombs thrown at us, which was quite terrifying, as we were totally inexperienced in this sort of disorder. In the dark, they were all masked-up.

As daylight came, it seemed to calm down a bit and I then remembered that I had to go back to all those police stations to deal with my prisoners, most of which I had never visited before, or even knew existed. I managed to finish my duty shortly after midday, after one of the most frightening and exhilarating nights of my young service.

The next few nights, there were only small pockets of disorder and we spent several hours standing behind long shields on the Soho Road in a stand-off with large groups confronting us. At one stage, there were eight senior officers standing in a group about 30 yards in front of us. People were passing comments and joking about perhaps how they would start making decisions if the rioters threw a few stones at them.

Steve Burrows was a PC at Acocks Green at the time and recalls,

I was on a course on the first day and got a call at 2.00 a.m. the following morning to be on duty for 5.00 a.m. I met up with a bunch of 'old sweats' somewhere on the E Division, and piled into a van, before making our way to Handsworth. We were put on standby in the back yard of Thornhill Road police station. There was a row of public-order and dog vans lined up, and we sat in groups behind the vans, waiting to deploy. The local superintendent came into the back yard to do a television interview but, every time he started to speak, someone kicked one of the dog vans and the dogs inside went ballistic and started barking. The superintendent couldn't work out was going on, but he was furious because he kept having to start again.

Douglas Hurd was home secretary at the time, and came to Handsworth to visit the scene. Lozells Road looked like a scene from the Blitz. While he was out, he was pelted with missiles, and we were deployed to support the cordons put in place to protect him from rioters. The majority of the local residents were decent people, and I recall at one point we were standing outside a newsagent's. The owner had just given us some crisps to eat when, during a lull, an elderly Afro-Caribbean man appeared with a tray, a silver tea-pot and proper cups with saucers, and gave us all a cup of tea. He was a real gentleman.

I finished the day standing with officers with long riot shields, stretched out across Heathfield Road and having petrol bombs thrown at us.

In the following days, I was deployed in normal uniform on patrol in Handsworth, trying to restore public confidence in the police. On one occasion, I was out with John Cudd and we had our photographs taken by the press with some local children wearing our helmets. A lot of the residents were upset with what had happened, as a lot of outsiders came into Handsworth just to get involved in looting.

On Tuesday 10 September 1985, we were put on standby for further serious public disorder in the Handsworth area and, in the afternoon, we were moved into the city centre to carry out patrols as further trouble was anticipated.

Dave Faulkner recalls his experiences after the initial riots had taken place:

I was a beat officer at the time, waiting to get transferred to the CID. We were deployed to Handsworth and I did some patrols in the Villa Road area. There were reports of crowds here and there, but most of the problems we had were in the vicinity of the Black Café on the Lozells Road, near to the Villa Cross. It was a focal point for agitators, and something of a place of refuge for them – almost a bit of a no-go area.

Five of us were outside the café at one point, and started to get the usual abuse with words like 'Bloodclot' and 'Babylon' being hurled at us. We called a van in and went inside to tell the owner to control his customers, otherwise we would close the place. As we went out, the abuse started again as we walked through a cloud of 'ganja' – otherwise known as cannabis.

We had to make a decision as to whether to start making arrests but decided against it, although we left officers working short on foot to show a presence while we did a van patrol. Twenty minutes later, they called us on the radio to pick them up outside the café, which by this time was empty apart from two or three Rastafarians standing at the door, shouting something about guns. It transpired that someone had let a load of fireworks off and the occupants of the café had left, after convincing themselves that the police were shooting at people in the streets.

Mike Cresswell has his own memories of events:

I was still on Uniform Bravo serial of the Operations Support Unit. In the weeks prior to the riots taking place, I was involved in a couple of drugs raids; one on the Villa Cross pub and the other a place called The Nightspot. Both places were on the Lozells Road, and cannabis was placed out on tables and being sold on a wholesale basis. The tactic used was to put us into normal delivery vans with roller shutters, near to the premises to be raided. At a given signal, the shutters would go up and we would surge out of the back and run into the premises.

On the Monday, when the riots started, I had been on duty until 6.00 p.m., and then went home and went for a run. Just as I got back, the phone went and an officer appeared at my door at the same time. I was told to report for duty – I literally said some prayers before leaving home. We had all of our public-order kit stored at some premises in Newton Street, and had to spend time breaking a door open to get at it before we could deploy. By this time, we had some long shields and a few short shields for supervisors.

There must have been more than 100 OSU officers deployed to Handsworth and, at one point, we went down Lozells Road in single file, with buildings on fire close by. You could feel the heat – it was like being in a corridor of fire. We eventually formed a line abreast and moved forward. An inspector walked in front of us in the midst of it all – he was a very brave man, with bricks coming at us from everywhere.

We continually deployed and redeployed from one location to another until about 4.00 a.m., when we were stood down. We were exhausted, and I went home and got some sleep, until getting another phone call at 2.00 p.m. to report in again for duty.

I drove back into work past the Birchfield Flyover and could already see groups starting to gather again. We kitted up again in public-order gear and went out into Handsworth on mobile patrol. One guy came alongside the passenger side of the van and tried to throw a brick at the inspector sat in the front seat. Fortunately, the brick deflected off the panel of the door, otherwise he would have been seriously injured.

Three of us jumped out of the van and chased this guy, who went into a back garden and down some alleyways. We thought that we were going to lose him but, suddenly, the footsteps went quiet. He had run into a locked gate and couldn't get over it – we had him and, although he struggled, we had no intention of losing him.

During another disturbance, we chased a guy into his own back garden who had been throwing bricks at us. The whole of his family came out and started remonstrating with us, in particular his father, but we stood our ground and arrested him. During another patrol, I did a stop-search and arrested someone in possession of a flick knife. Eventually things calmed down, but they were frightening times.

We remained on standby that following day, and George updated me on trouble that was occurring in the Stechford and Bordesley Green areas, and gave me details relating to a suspect for a petrol bombing. The next day, we carried on doing patrols and, at midnight, dealt with a person who had been arrested for burglary at a shop.

We continued patrolling the city centre and Newtown areas over the next two days and assisted regarding the arrest of five people for robbery in Constitution Hill. It was a tense time, and three more days followed before things went back to relative normality.

On one of these patrols I went out with Dave 'J', who was a DC at this time. He was a really friendly character, but prone to falling asleep if he had a drink. He was a non-driver and travelled home to Wolverhampton regularly on the train. The problem was that he would often get on the train at New Street station, fall asleep and then wake up at Stafford. He would then get back on a train to go back, fall asleep again, miss his stop at Wolverhampton, and finish up back at New Street.

Liam reflected afterwards, 'we spent a couple of weeks afterwards walking around Handsworth and talking to local people. The residents were very genuine people who disagreed with the violence.'

Chief Constable Geoffrey Dear adopted a very high profile with operational officers during this time, and 'Alex' commented,

> He came out on patrol with me on nights, and we had a walk around the city centre. I had been on the DSU, so my hair was still long and collar-length. All went well as we strolled around and he behaved totally normally. Then, on the Wednesday, I had a summons to see the chief superintendent when I arrived for a 2.00 p.m.–10.00 p.m. shift, and he suggested quite strongly that I might like to get my hair cut.

On Wednesday 18 September 1985, I sat down with my detective superintendent to discuss the David Harris murder case, as the trial date was looming. On Wednesday 2 October 1985, I attended Birmingham Crown Court Number 5 regarding the murder trial. As I was a witness, I was not allowed inside the court once proceedings had started, but I needed to be available at short notice and checked in on a daily basis while trying to do other things. This was a big case and it was difficult to concentrate on anything else.

On Wednesday 9 October, it was getting closer to me giving evidence, and I spent the next three days at court, with plenty of time to pace up and down and to lose shoe leather. When I eventually gave evidence, I was subjected to the usual grilling by the defence as to when my notes had been made up, just small things to try to find differences in officer's accounts, but my evidence stood the test and it would soon be a matter for the jury to decide.

On Wednesday 16 October, the jury reached a verdict – the defendant was found guilty of murder and sentenced to life imprisonment. I went with the detective superintendent to the Woodman LH and informed the family, and staff, of the result. Small comfort for the loss of a life and a loved one, but justice had been done. I did not feel any sense of elation. We just knew that the right thing had been done and that the right result had been achieved.

While we weren't seeking any form of recognition, the reality was that none of the officers that were involved in the second arrest ever received any formal acknowledgement for their efforts. On Thursday 17 October 1985, the newspaper headline read, 'Life sentence for killer of publican', and went on,

A community centre supervisor was found guilty yesterday of the brutal murder of Birmingham publican Mr David Harris and was sentenced to youth custody for life. The twenty-year-old fainted in the dock at Birmingham Crown Court as Mr Justice McNeill told him that the sentence for this offence was fixed by law and he would go to custody for life. Three prison officers and a police officer carried him down the steps to the cells. The verdict was by a majority of 11–1 of the jury of six men and six women, who took six hours and forty-two minutes to reach their decision. He was the second man to be arrested and charged with murdering Mr Harris, aged 36, who collapsed and died with 23 stab wounds while taking one thousand five hundred pounds from the Woodman public house in Well Street, Hockley, Birmingham, to a nearby branch of Barclays Bank in March last year. In January another man was found not guilty in the same courtroom of the same charge when the prosecution offered no evidence against him. He had been due to stand trial on December 3rd last year but his case was put back after the arrest of the second man. In a taped interview with police officers the convicted man admitted stabbing Mr Harris after bumping into him in the street, although he never admitted killing him. In the witness box he claimed to have been with his mother elsewhere when Mr Harris, a married man with a six-year-old daughter, was attacked. He said he went along with the police because he knew that the first person was in custody and he thought that he would be allowed to go. After the case detectives said that an informant had told them in the middle of last year that the man who had really done the murder was a man called 'Jakey', the nickname used by the convicted person.

Another media headline read, 'Police probe murder reward', and went on,

> Police have launched a full enquiry into how a two thousand five
> hundred pounds reward was paid to an informer who named the
> wrong man in a murder hunt. The informer named the individual who
> was arrested in April 1984 and held in custody until December, when
> he was bailed. Yesterday at Birmingham Crown Court a twenty-year-old
> man was sentenced to youth custody for life for murder. The cash was
> half the reward put up by the Midlands brewers Mitchells and Butlers
> after the murder of one of their publicans. Now a police report on the
> investigation into the wrong man being charged and the payment of the
> reward money is expected to be sent to the Director of Public Prosecutions.
> In addition his lawyers are likely to press ahead with a compensation
> claim. Detectives have revealed that the informer who was paid the reward
> has since disappeared. The man was originally said to have admitted
> stabbing Mr Harris once. On January 14th 1985 he was acquitted after
> Mr Brian Escott Cox QC prosecuting offered no evidence. Defence
> Counsel Mr Anthony Palmer QC described the confessions as complete
> fabrications. In January Tom Meffen the Assistant Chief Constable of
> Crime of West Midlands Police said a review of the case had been carried
> out by other officers and a complaint file had been received from his
> solicitors.

On Friday 18 October 1985, one of the media outlets had the headline,
'Forced into Murderous Lie', and went on,

> A man, who spent eight months in jail charged with a murder he did not
> commit, yesterday demanded a full inquiry into police handling of the
> case ... A twenty-four-year-old from Hockley spoke out after another twenty-
> year-old man from West Bromwich was given a life sentence for the savage
> murder of Birmingham Publican David Harris. He claimed police evidence
> against him, given on oath in a written statement in court, included an officer
> saying he was overheard in his cell praying to Jesus for forgiveness for the
> crime he didn't do. The man who had been waiting for trial was freed in
> January after another twenty-year-old from West Bromwich was arrested and
> charged with the killing outside the Woodman pub in Hockley. Yesterday he
> talked for the first time about his prison ordeal and claimed police made no
> attempt to establish he had a cast-iron alibi; used psychological pressure to
> force him into a confession; based their case entirely on their own evidence;

submitted wildly inaccurate statements. Last night his solicitor Graham McGrath said that his client takes the view that justice will only be served if there is a full judicial enquiry and that it had been a disgrace the way the police had acted. An official complaint with West Midlands Police had been lodged and a claim for compensation was being pursued.

On the same day, another headline read, 'Cleared man's inquiry plea' and went on,

The solicitor representing the man wrongly accused of murdering Birmingham Publican Mr David Harris has demanded a judicial investigation into the police handling of the case. Speaking after a twenty-year-old was sentenced to youth custody for life for the killing, Mr Graham McGrath said that he was talking about a very substantial miscarriage of justice. Had his client been convicted, it would have been on the basis of police evidence. His client had been arrested in April last year and held in custody until December 17, when he was bailed following the arrest of the second man. In January 1985 he was acquitted when the prosecution offered no evidence. Mr Justice Bristow said that at that time that he could not order an inquiry into the case, but that it was plain that something had gone badly wrong. Mr McGrath, his solicitor, said that while the trial of the second man was ongoing that his client would not have wished to do anything that might have interfered with him having a fair trial and that they were now looking for a totally independent judicial inquiry. It is understood that a detective from Scotland Yard examined the case and a report is to be submitted to the Director of Public Prosecutions.

As a postscript to the story, the first man arrested did eventually receive £20,000 in a cash payout from West Midlands Police for the nine months he spent in custody awaiting trial before his release. Aged twenty-five years, unemployed, and living in Hockley, he said in a statement to the press in August 1987, 'I am now living with the woman who stood by me during my ordeal and we have two children.' At the same time, a senior West Midlands Police officer confirmed that, following an investigation, the Director of Public Prosecutions had decided not to prosecute any police officers.

I carried on at Bradford Street throughout October, dealing with a serious wounding and the biker group, who were still active. On Thursday 24 October 1985 I went to Ladywood to swap notes with the local CID regarding an affray involving another biker faction. Senior uniform officers were becoming increasingly concerned that these groups were operating beyond the reach of the law, and fears were subsequently raised about a potential public-order situation developing in Castle Bromwich involving the group.

As I suspected he would, George dropped out of the scene for a while. He had not been in a good frame of mind last time I had seen him and I left him to his own devices – I was not his keeper. I strongly suspected that he had crossed over to the 'dark side' again, and was directly involved in criminality. I also felt that I was treading water and needed a new challenge. I wanted to get back into the city centre, but I needed to be careful given my last move.

I spent three days at Birmingham Crown Court regarding the arsonist we had dealt with on 7 August 1985. He was found guilty on 18 December 1985, and was sentenced to two years' imprisonment. After court, I was summoned to see the chief superintendent and given some news – I was on the move. Later that day, I went to meet the inspector in charge of the divisional Shoplifting Squad to talk about my new posting.

The run up to Christmas was fairly quiet, and I worked both Christmas Day and Boxing Day. New Year's Eve likewise came and went, and we were into 1986. 'Nick' had a slightly different memory of Boxing Day in 1985 and recalls,

> I had been to a match at St Andrew's with a mate called Mark and, at the time, we both had some nice things to wear. I had on some suede shoes and was wearing a ski jacket. After the game as usual, we were standing just outside New Street station, when a black lad and a skinny white lad came up to us. The black lad punched me in the face and unzipped my jacket. It was called 'draping' in those days, as he demanded my shoes and coat, while they demanded Mark's trousers, which were 'Nike Wimbledon'. We both ran and managed to get away. The stupid thing was that they were both 'Blues' fans as well. Mark saw the black lad later, who scolded him and told him that we needed to learn how to defend ourselves.
>
> There were always stories about shoplifting to be told. In one instance about this time, a lad called Keith, who was a 'Blues' fan, went into Olympus Sport, which was in New Street by the Old Odeon, and hid in a cupboard until after closing time. When the staff had gone, he got the doors open and his mates turned up in a van to take a load of ski jackets.

He recalls the nature of how football violence changed during this period:

We used to hang around Cagney's and Le Pub in Birmingham city centre, as well as the Dome and Pagoda Park. There was always somebody trying to sell something stolen, and some of the 'Blues' fans started to get involved in smash and grabs, where shop windows were smashed and shop fronts looted of clothing. The violence got worse and the Zulus started to get a bit like the mafia. I know a lad who once had a row with one of the younger Zulus, and someone else came along and slashed his face from his ear to his chin. I have seen him recently, and he still has the scar to this day. Another lad I know who was a Zulu had an argument with his girlfriend and finished up hitting her with a billiard cue.

I was in a group of 236 Blues fans in London the day that we were playing West Ham. There were lots of Zulus, including 'Cuddles' there, but he managed to avoid the police, who stopped and searched everyone, and found a dozen knives on the floor. No one owned up, so we all got detained until after the match, which we lost 4–0. Violence was never far away and I once saw one of the Zulus, who was also a known shoplifter, get stabbed in the eye with a screwdriver, following a fight with the door staff at Boogies nightclub.

In 1985, recorded crime in the West Midlands rose to 231,606 offences, which included thirty-eight cases of murder, with just one unresolved investigation by the end of the year. Offences of wounding rose to 7,644 offences, with 2,349 robberies, 39,833 burglary dwelling houses, and 131 cases of rape.

Behind each of these serious crimes was a victim, and the lives of some would never quite be the same again. In terms of financial loss, the cash value of property stolen amounted to £15 million.

11

SHOPLIFTING, INTELLIGENCE, AND THE ZULUS GO TOO FAR

On Monday 6 January 1986, I was transferred to Steelhouse Lane police station as the officer in charge of the Shoplifting Squad. Nothing is ever easy in the police service and, while the previous postholder had been an inspector, I was to perform the role in my current rank of detective sergeant and supervise a team of uniform and CID officers, which included a uniform sergeant. He was none too pleased at the thought of being told what to do by someone of the same rank, but I knew a little bit about him and felt that it was unlikely that he would want to be confrontative.

The Shoplifting Squad was made up of two sergeants, two detective constables and ten uniform constables, and had its own administrative system. It dealt with an average of fifty-one arrests per week.

At that time, the Shoplifting Squad dealt with all arrests relating to shop theft in the city centre, the vast majority of which were initially detained by store detectives. They were a good bunch of people, for whom I developed a great deal of personal respect, and they had a very good relationship with the police, which I was determined to maintain.

The Shoplifting Squad consisted of a mix of experience but, in the main, they were committed to their job and worked hard as a team. In many ways, it was like a 'conveyor belt' in terms of numbers, and you had to crack on with things to keep up to date. The team was, however, very reactive and did no proactive work whatsoever. I was determined to change that as soon as I could, and I also had a secret weapon – George, who would need to 'shape up' and get back into the swing of things.

On my first day I assisted with the arrest of thirteen prisoners. On Wednesday 8 January, I took the uniform sergeant out for a walk in Birmingham shopping centre. He was a decent person, and I was not looking for conflict with him. He did, however, need to understand that there could only be one 'alpha male' in the pack, and it was going to be me. We also attended a sub-committee meeting of Sutton Coldfield and Birmingham Crime Prevention Panel and, by the end of the afternoon, we had developed some form of understanding.

On Thursday 9 January, I held an office meeting to discuss the way ahead and the sub-divisional Superintendent Bob Jones, who was a 'real gentleman', sat in on the proceedings. I was clearly under scrutiny, but that was fine by me. That afternoon I managed to track George down and arranged to meet him.

On Friday 10 January, I met George in one of our regular pubs. He was back on form and gave me details about three stalls on the open market who were receiving stolen property, as well as another receiver in Bordesley Green, and the usual suspects operating still in the city centre. On Monday 13 January, I started to research George's information and identified an Indian restaurant in Bordesley Green that was taking stolen property from local criminals.

The following day, I attended an anti-theft group meeting, which was attended by Barry Kirton, the chief superintendent. They were a very influential collective of 350 stores in the city centre, prone to expressing their views in a forceful manner. Quite rightly, they wanted a city centre that was safe to shop in, free of both the perception, and the reality, of crime. Lost trade meant lost income and that would not do.

On Thursday 16 January, I was pleased to assist with the arrest of three of the Bordesley crew, who were well known to me. They were none too pleased to renew the acquaintance. On Friday 17 January, I saw George again twice and he put more city-centre shoplifters in. I also showed him a security video with a suspect for theft on and he was able to put a name to the face – we were back in business.

On Monday 20 January, I introduced the concept of proactive patrols to the team and met one of the constables whom I rated highly in the city centre. Within an hour, we had arrested three females from Stechford for theft 'shops and stalls' in New Street, as a result of following them. They were an active team but, on that day, they got a bit of a shock when they were detained.

The following day, I attended a store detectives meeting with a CID officer and the anti-theft coordinator, and outlined our new approach, which went down well. I then took one of the PCs to a local pub to meet a new informant, and now we had two people giving information. The officer had never been exposed to this type of activity before and loved it. Word was going round that the Shoplifting Squad was a good place to work.

On Saturday 25 January, George identified another four people for thefts from Rackhams and, the day before, our other source put two suspects in for shoplifting in the city centre. Six days later, George put another two females in, and I spent as much time as I could briefing the stores regarding our new approach. I took different members of the team out with me so that I could get to know them, and got involved with as many arrests as I could. The Shoplifting Squad generated huge amounts of paperwork, much of which I was required to read and sign, so I needed to balance my time. That said, I knew from experience that the key to success was the people not the processes.

Some people regard shoplifting as a victimless crime, but the reality is that the public pay when stores pass on the costs of their losses through increased prices. It also drives a lot of other criminality, such as drug addiction, where users need to find easy money to pay for daily fixes. Equally, it acts as a precursor to other criminality, as people learn their trade in this business before moving on to other types of crime.

Shoplifters ranged from under-aged juveniles, groups of schoolchildren, gangs of females, or organised crime groups from all walks of life and all ethnic backgrounds. It was a complex social issue, and one which I wanted to understand fully.

On 5 March 1986, my DI commented in my annual review, 'He supervises with quiet confidence, insisting from junior officers the same levels of competence that he sets for himself. Something of a perfectionist, he is not always as tolerant as he might be with others less capable than himself ...'

On 24 April 1986, I attended a meeting of the youth-crime sub-group of the Inner-City Working Party of the Birmingham and Sutton Coldfield Crime Prevention Panel. I presented the findings of a survey we had completed in respect of 200 juveniles dealt with in the city centre in December 1985 and January 1986. Two-thirds of those dealt with were classed as white, and a third black or Asian.

A third of all property stolen related to clothing, and nearly 10 per cent of cases involved records and tapes, with property valued at less than £30 being stolen in 80 per cent of the cases. Two-thirds of those caught were classified as 'first offenders', not to be confused with the phrase 'caught first time'. At the end of April 1986, I commissioned further research regarding the extent of juvenile involvement in shoplifting offences in the city centre between 1 January 1986 and 31 March 1986.

In three months, we processed a total of 635 persons for such offences, of which more than half, namely 334, were juveniles under seventeen years of age. During that period of time, 889 arrests of other persons took place at Steelhouse Lane, meaning that my relatively small team was dealing with over 40 per cent of the prisoner throughput.

We did some research on days of the week, which showed that juvenile shoplifters were most active on a Saturday, with almost a quarter of arrests taking place. The other days showed an even spread, but they also started to point towards levels of truancy from schools, which we started mapping. If we could keep them in school, then we could reduce offending.

Midday to 4.00 p.m. showed up as the major times for offences to be committed, which again seemed to indicate that, in some cases, juveniles were registering at school in the mornings, and then playing truant in the afternoon, often without the knowledge of their parents. As predicted, two-thirds of the juvenile shoplifters were male, and a third female.

The youngest juvenile that we dealt with was only seven years of age, and 77 per cent were in the fourteen-to-sixteen-years age category. Some 60 per cent of the offenders committed crimes as truants, or during school hours.

Not surprisingly, the E Division led the league table in terms of where offenders lived – in other words, Stechford and Bordesley Green areas, the home territory of my city-centre crew. This statistic clearly showed that older generations were bringing the youngsters through and teaching them their trade. This was compounded by the final statistic, which showed that only a quarter of the juveniles were found to be committing crime on their own. The remainder were found to be working with others and, in 6 per cent of the cases, it was with four or more persons. Shoplifting often entailed either direct intimidation of shop staff, or distraction methods, and the figures supported our theory that a large number of gangs were operating.

It was fascinating data, which for the first time was starting to provide a comprehensive picture of both the scale of the problem – and some potential remedies, which we could work on together with other agencies. While it might seem an obvious thing to do now, it was seen as groundbreaking then, with very little intelligence analysis taking place at that time.

Further meetings took place with the Crime Prevention Panel on 25 and 26 June 1986, where I also presented details of more than 100 schools that juvenile offenders were attending, as well as details of the numbers of offenders involved in committing offences at forty-five particular stores in the city centre. It allowed the panel to start thinking about how to apply prevention tactics and was well received. Following the meeting, we received a letter of appreciation on behalf of the chairman of the Birmingham Anti-Theft Group, thanking my team for their efforts and commenting on the high level of arrests in May, including a male and female who had been caught carrying an empty Pampers box with the flap opened, in which to conceal stolen property. They had been operating throughout the north of England, targeting one particular well-known outlet.

Between 1 January 1986 and 31 August 1986, the Shoplifting Squad dealt with a total of 1,637 prisoners. During my tenure, we recovered stolen property valued in excess of £20,000 and, in conjunction with the Crown Prosecution Service, charged three organised teams with criminal conspiracy charges.

Jon Lighton, who retired as an inspector with the West Midlands Police, describes the unpredictability of working in plain clothes in the city centre:

I had been on the Shoplifting Squad for about a month, working for Mike Layton. On 4 July 1986, I was out on plain-clothes observations with Dave Rischmiller, when a store detective from Marks & Spencer, who knew us, approached us and told us that he had just observed two men stealing from the store. He pointed the two out in Union Street. They were both in their twenties and from Wolverhampton. We stopped them and searched their bags, which contained some stolen meat pies.

At this point, one of them decided to run off, and I chased and caught him in Carrs Lane, where he was handcuffed. During the chase, I dropped my police radio and, although I managed to recover it, I didn't realise that it was damaged. I got back to Dave, who had the other prisoner handcuffed, and stood there trying to get through on the radio for transport, but without much success. As I was distracted, my prisoner suddenly lunged forward and head-butted me in the face. After a violent struggle, we got him under control again and restrained him until the arrival of a police car.

I am 6 feet, 4 inches tall and I could look after myself, but he took me completely by surprise. I had a check-up at the General Hospital and an X-ray revealed a fractured cheekbone, which just had to heal by itself. For a while, I could actually click the bone in my face. The guy who attacked me later got sentenced to six months in prison for 'wounding with intent' – all for the sake of a meat pie.

In July 1986, objectives and action plans were formally drawn up for the education services and colleagues on the E Division to seek to reduce juvenile offending by 20 per cent in the coming year, and to increase arrests of adults by 15 per cent in the area of our priority risk stores. This was a ground-breaking approach and had not gone unnoticed.

At this time, I had the support of another sergeant by the name of Barry, a very serious and thoughtful individual, who could be relied upon to make considered assessments and come up with realistic outcomes. In later years, he was to become an expert in the field of counter-terrorism and worked with me in a key role in the British Transport Police. This was a constant feature of police work and, as you moved from posting to posting, you built up a range of contacts, most of which remained purely professional and, on the odd occasion, developed into friendship.

Barry's reflection on life in the police service at the time covers a variety of issues:

> There was a drinking culture within the service at the time, which was not short of characters. I was a custody officer at Steelhouse Lane for a while, and one of the first to work under the new Police and Criminal Evidence Act procedures. Just after it was introduced, the CID came down from their office and asked me to book the prisoner out to them, so that they could take him upstairs for interview. I refused to let them take him out of the custody block, in accordance with the new procedures. The detective chief inspector came down, and started ranting and raving at me, but I still refused and the superintendent had to get involved. I got my way but from then on the DCI did everything to make my life difficult.
>
> PACE changed everything, with tape-recorded interviews, proper reviews and everything recorded, and more use of police surgeons to examine prisoners. The prisoners used to get marmalade sandwiches, but

they then had to be fed properly. It was not unusual for people in the police service to 'borrow other people's ideas and work with pride', and I will always remember an inspector using all the data Mike and I collated for the research paper on shoplifters for his university degree thesis.

On Monday 4 August 1986, I was posted again and this time it was to the newly created post of detective sergeant (local intelligence officer) at Steelhouse Lane police station. One such post had been created on each of the divisions, and most of the post-holders were qualified for promotion. Our remit was to create a policing environment that was 'intelligence-led', and we were clearly under the microscope to do well. It would not have been my first choice for a new job, but I could not turn it down, and set about trying to make a difference.

The initiative was launched in conjunction with the setting up of divisional observations teams, which were described by the news media as follows:

'Crime War in old Bangers'. West Midlands Police today unveiled plans for a huge war against crime in a bid to combat the rocketing numbers of robberies, street muggings, burglaries, woundings, and murders. Top secret surveillance operations are to be mounted on the streets by specially selected police teams in unmarked old 'bangers' and second-hand vans. The force has bought twenty-two second-hand vehicles – mostly vans and estate cars – from dealers for major surveillance operations. Each division would have two vehicles manned by a sergeant and five constables. They were being made as comfortable as possible, and observation equipment including cameras and binoculars were being installed. Mr Tom Meffen, Assistant Chief Constable (Crime), said, 'There is nothing glamorous about this work. It means sitting for eight hours at a time in cramped conditions. A pilot has been an amazing success. The first vehicle was on the streets for no more than ten minutes before three young men were spotted going round the back of a house after knocking on a front door. They were caught. There would also be a computer crackdown with a squad of sergeants analysing crime patterns on each of the divisions.

This was a difficult time politically for the police in general, with rising crime and limited funding issues and, as such, senior police managers in the West Midlands Police were very keen to promote any new initiatives.

On Friday 3 October 1986, a *Birmingham Evening Mail* reporter was granted unique access to the F Division DOT team and observed an operation set up to deal with robberies in the city centre:

> It is 8.30 a.m. at Steelhouse Lane police station, and Operation Marple begins with a briefing. Eight officers in casual clothes and boiler suits squeeze into a cramped first-floor office, their fingers cupped around cigarettes and morning coffee. Sergeant 'Dundee' stands in front of a plan of the operation on a blackboard and addresses them ... The eyeballs are two tower blocks and a roving van will be covering the blind spots.
>
> At 09.25 hours, Dundee arrives at Eyeball One ... Security dictates that only the caretaker knows about the police operation. On the roof, 'Fozzie' and 'Mike', only nicknames are used, are scanning the streets through binoculars. They have put cardboard against the glass parapet to hide their silhouettes, with squares cut out in order to take photographs. They have an excellent view of the banks about 300 yards away ...
>
> At 14.30 hours, on top of Eyeball Two, 'Bazzer's' radio crackles and they are alerted to an armed robbery that has just happened ... All the DOT team can do is keep their eyes open for the getaway vehicle.
>
> A man wearing a red crash helmet ... threatened a security guard with a fake automatic pistol, moments after he had collected cash from a Bank in Newhall Street. He stole a bag containing £10,000 and ran to an accomplice waiting on a motor bike nearby. The robbers sped off ... they threw the imitation firearm away, which was recovered in Cornwall Street, loaded with blanks.

Although the DOTS, as they quickly became known, were not strictly speaking my staff, I invariably had first 'port of call' on their use and we quickly developed a close, and very successful, working relationship as autumn came. It was a winning formula and, just by putting dedicated resources in the right place at the right time, we were able to take the fight to the streets, with many a criminal receiving a nasty shock as police officers appeared from nowhere guided in by the observations team.

In a sign of the times, on Saturday 4 October 1986, the media announced that the government was launching a £300 million campaign to drive crime out of run-down inner-city areas in Britain. The environment secretary, Mr Nicholas Ridley, authorised local authorities to spend the extra money in a move that he said could lead to 2,000 more officers on the beat in the UK, and which amounted to a rise of more than

11 per cent in police budgets. The move was announced on the eve of the Conservative Party conference and was widely seen as an effort to silence critics, who were worried about increasing crime trends.

The local media put this issue very clearly into the public domain the following week with some detailed data released by West Midlands Police, who had set two objectives for 1986: to cut crime and improve detection rates, and were currently failing on both, although part-way through the reporting year, there had been an 11 per cent increase in crime, which amounted to more than 17,000 extra crimes in an eight-month period.

A senior detective said at the time,

> We have not got any real gang-warfare here and a very successful 'super-grass' operation wiped out a lot of organised heavy crime. Birmingham is still a safer place than, say, Glasgow or Liverpool. There is no doubt that we would have a lot more murders to deal with but for the skill of the surgeons in our hospitals. Many woundings are associated with drunkenness and, if someone is alone, they would be advised not to use subways after midnight. I would not dream of doing so and, to my mind, it is a matter of common sense.

The statistics continued to make depressing reading, with nearly 1,700 recorded victims of robbery, or assault with intent to rob, of which 134 victims were aged over sixty and represented a rise of 9 per cent in recorded offences. Thefts from the person and pickpocketing had increased by 21 per cent, and it had been calculated that one home in the West Midlands was broken into every twenty minutes.

Of the 124 robberies that had occurred where firearms had been carried, in three cases shots were fired: one at two security guards and, on the other two occasions, at bandit screens in post-office raids. Thankfully, the use of firearms still remained a comparative rarity, but their impact on victims was often underestimated and, in 1986, the decision was taken by West Midlands Police to form a dedicated Firearms Unit – the first of its kind outside London.

In one such robbery on my division, three months previously, a gunman staged a robbery at a bank in Newtown, together with a hooded accomplice armed with a knife. They held three little children at gunpoint, ordering the frightened toddlers and their mothers to put their hands on their heads, and demanded cash from the cashier, who was behind a screen. When she refused, one tried to smash the screen with his gun and, fearing that someone would get hurt, she handed over more than £200. Unbeknown to the two robbers, the entire sequence of events was captured on CCTV within the bank, and later released to the press.

In the period between January and August of 1986, a total of 533 police officers were the subject of attack, and many other officers were injured policing football matches and public demonstrations. The detection rate for the force stood at just over 27 per cent and was falling.

On a more positive note, the chief constable of the West Midlands Police, Geoffrey Dear, confirmed that the force had made 2,000 more arrests than in 1985, and that the Force Drug Squad had seized cocaine and heroin worth over £1 million in a seven-day period. In a message no doubt aimed at the politicians, he said,

> The problem is that we have got ourselves in a hell of a mess with an under-equipped, under-staffed force. Manchester is smaller in area, population and crime – and yet they have more men, and better buildings and equipment. They have got them through constantly adding in – whereas we for ten years have just economised by running round and round chasing our tail, and are now having to buy ourselves back out of problems. It's like having a house and not bothering to paint the window frames; you suddenly have to put new frames in. The county council saw us as an easy economy option. They have left us in a hell of a pickle. The 999 system could blow up at any time. Today it is okay, but the technology has a finite life. Ideally, we should have been down the road of a replacement eighteen months earlier than we are. We can just about get through by the skin of our teeth.

In a frank statement, he said that he needed 1,000 more officers to add to the existing establishment of 6,700, and was critical of a judicial system that did not always appreciate the tremendous dangers of knives and Stanley knives, which were being used more and more, and required a severe sentencing policy. In an equally rare move, some of the officers on my division were invited to have their say, and responses were printed along with the article by the chief constable.

Chief Superintendent Clive Roche, aged forty-two years and my divisional commander, said,

> When I joined the job twenty-three years ago, I thought that the job was difficult enough then. It is certainly more difficult for young PCs today.

The stress factor has increased – not only from violence, but also from complaints and changes to working methods. But they seem to be able to accommodate it.

Detective Sergeant Dick Leary, who went on to become an expert in forensic science and is sadly no longer with us, was then aged thirty years. He said,

The police force can only act with the backing of the community. We are doing quite well on community relations. The problem is that the people who knock relations between the police and the public do so for their own political or selfish reasons.

Police Constable Julie Edkins, then aged twenty-two years, who used to work for me on the F Division Shoplifting Squad, said,

Sometimes I do feel sorry for the people I arrest. The majority are older women, who are doing it as a cry for help or because of unemployment. I don't take a personal view about the offence itself, but emotionally I do get involved. I think what a shame, it could be my grandmother.

PC Derek Bradbury, aged thirty-nine years, was a well-known local beat officer for a quarter-of-a-square-mile area around the Bull Ring, and also a next-door neighbour when I lived in a police house, said,

The courts never seem to think about the victims of crime. They are the forgotten people. If magistrates and judges knew more about what went on at street level, it would frighten the pants off them. Until victims of crime get some form of recompense through the courts, all we are doing is keeping the lid on.

Geoffrey Dear concluded that, 'There are ways of beating the problem. If we are inventive enough and if people are prepared to give support.' I was well up for the idea of change and innovation – covert policing was now well on the agenda, and I was attracted to its potential.

On an entirely different political front, on Thursday 16 October 1986, Councillor Dick Knowles, leader of Birmingham City Council, lit an Olympic torch on the balcony of the Council House to symbolise the city's hopes of hosting the 1992 Olympic Games. The following day, those hopes were dashed when the city came fifth in the voting in Lausanne, and was eliminated in the second of three ballots, with the final winner being Barcelona. Had they have won, the policing implications for the West Midlands and the UK as a whole would have been enormous.

On Monday 20 October 1986, a twenty-three-year-old man from Wiggin Tower in Newtown went on trial for the murder of Carmetta Stewart at Birmingham Crown Court, after pleading not guilty. It was alleged that a video recorder that had been stolen from the home of the former nurse was found when police raided his flat after his current girlfriend was arrested for shoplifting six months after the murder. They also seized an alarm clock similar to the one stolen from the murder victim's flat and, on the strength of this, interviewed him. After initially saying that he had purchased the video recorder from an unknown friend, he was alleged to have said, with tears in his eyes, 'You know I did it. Why are you asking all these questions ...'

On Tuesday 11 November, a hunt was launched by city-centre detectives for two men who fired a shotgun at a bandit screen in the Bristol Street sub-post office, spraying the fifty-four-year-old sub-postmaster with pellets in the face, neck and chest from a sawn-off shotgun. As the two robbers, described as one white, and one black, burst in at closing time, the sub-postmaster slammed his anti-bandit screen down and collapsed on the floor. His two female assistants managed to drop to the floor behind the counter and activate the panic alarm button, as well as dragging a phone down to them so that they could call the police and ambulance services.

The robbers ran out of the post office to a waiting maroon-coloured Austin Maxi motor car, which was found abandoned half a mile away. Police used the Regional Criminal Intelligence office computer to link the two suspects to four other recent raids on post offices and, in an appeal to the public, said, 'These men must be caught before they strike again. They may kill next time.' It was a sign of the times and just another illustration of the lengths that people would go to steal money. Every one of these robberies with weapons involved was a potential murder in the making.

On Saturday 15 November, a thirty-one-year-old man from Ward End Park Road in Washwood Heath appeared at Birmingham Magistrates' Court, charged with three offences of robbery and one of attempted robbery. One of the charges related to the Bristol Street incident. He also faced charges of wounding with intent to cause grievous bodily harm in relation to the shotgun attack, as well as burglary offences, criminal damage, assault with intent to resist arrest, and failing to surrender to bail. He was remanded in custody to police cells for two days for further enquiries to be made.

On Sunday 16 November, our eyewitness from the GPO robbery in Revesby Walk, who was now in his early twenties, was stabbed at least twice in an Indian restaurant in Newtown, with what was described as a double-sided dagger with a narrow blade. Following an alleged argument with an Asian man over music in the Sky Blue restaurant, the twenty-two-year-old was stabbed in the chest in front of members of his family, who gave evidence that it was an unprovoked attack.

He suffered massive internal bleeding and was found to be dead on arrival at the hospital from his injuries. His attacker was later jailed for life, and released after sixteen years in prison. There was no connection whatsoever between the two incidents, but it served to show the frailties of human life. The senior investigating officer was Detective Superintendent Michael Murphy, whom I had worked for on the David Harris murder.

As Christmas 1986 approached, the time had come to take on another challenge, only this time the focus was to be organised football violence, and the activities of Birmingham City's infamous Zulu Warriors. Mike Cresswell has his own memories of the Zulu Warriors in 1986:

At this time, I was working on Uniform Bravo serial of the Operations Support Unit as a PC. On one particular Saturday evening, we were out on a public-order van patrol in the city centre, finishing at 2.00 a.m. There would have been a sergeant and about eight PCs on the van.

During the afternoon, Birmingham City had been playing Aston Villa, and there were large numbers of Zulus in town. At about 9.00 p.m., we were sent to Cannon Street, where an Aston Villa-sponsored Mini Metro car was turned over onto its side. As we got there, we heard on the radio that the group responsible had made their way down towards John Bright Street and attacked a police officer, who was patrolling on his own. He shouted for assistance and we dashed there.

On arrival, we saw a group running off but, as we were facing them, I suddenly heard a huge roar of 'Zulu – Zulu' behind me. We turned around to see another group of at least 100 stretched out across the road, chanting. We charged at them, and I remember drawing my truncheon. Initially, they stood their ground but, as we ran into them and arrested five of the ringleaders, they began to disperse as more officers arrived. Officers and prisoners were everywhere struggling on the floor – it was mayhem. We piled the prisoners in the van, which put about fifteen of us inside as we made our way to custody. None of them were handcuffed and, when we searched the van after we had deposited them in the cells, we found a number of knives hidden under the seats in the back. The level of violence they displayed really bothered me at the time.

I had already dealt with some of them as individuals, but this was to be about dismantling a whole criminal structure where violence and intimidation was the norm. I was about to embark on one of the most fascinating and demanding periods of my service – Operation Red Card. This operation was set to occupy me on a full-time basis until October 1987, and has been the subject of a separate book called *Hunting the Hooligans*. It was time to be inventive and to come up with some new tactics.

Steve Burrows also has his own memories of the Zulus during this period:

It was a Saturday afternoon, and I remember we were really short of staff. I was a sergeant on a shift at Steelhouse Lane police station, and I was having my break with three female officers in the station when we got a call to say that there was a big problem with Birmingham City supporters, who had come up through Digbeth and turned a police panda car over. We rushed out, and the four of us drove to Stephenson Place, by the ramp up onto the shopping centre, just in time to see up to 200 supporters advancing towards us, chanting 'Zulu – Zulu'.

There was a crowd of shoppers watching with interest on the balcony above, as the four of us fronted the group and forced them to stop. One of the ringleaders, a white lad, who really fancied himself, tried to attack me. I put him into a 'half Nelson' and held him on the ground, as a sea of boots surrounded me. I was absolutely livid with him, and there was no way I was going to let him go, as I yelled as loud as I could for the others to clear off.

After what seemed an age, a large number of officers arrived and dispersed the group, while I secured my prisoner, who was dealt with for threatening behaviour. From the balcony, we received a round of applause from the shoppers. Afterwards, one of the female officers smiled at me and said, 'I've never seen you angry before. I could see the vein throbbing in your temple!'

At the end of 1986, the force faced a 10.3 per cent increase in reported crime over the previous twelve months, which for the first time in its history exceeded 250,000 offences in the year.

On Saturday 10 January 1987, off-duty PC Harry Doyle went into Boogies nightclub in John Bright Street, Birmingham city centre, for a late-night drink. I knew Harry, who was a well-built individual and not easily intimidated. This was, however, the preserve of Birmingham City football fans, as well as some of the hard-core Zulu Warriors. He was eventually confronted by a number of individuals, including two prominent Zulus. Harry was punched and knocked to the floor, and one of his attackers then pushed a glass into his face, causing injuries that required thirty-two stitches and left scars from his left eye down to his jaw.

Some said at the time that Harry was working undercover, but I can categorically state that this was not the case. The incident did, however, act as one of the catalysts for police action – the Zulu Warriors had simply gone too far and I was tasked with leading a team that included a number of undercover officers, who would be used to infiltrate their activities.

In January 1987, the force announced that it was providing funding for a professor from Aston University to come up with a new formula for monitoring tension within the community, so that the police could be better prepared for further outbreaks of violence. The announcement came on the same day that the force also announced that it was purchasing two bulletproof vehicles and that the ambulance service was going to provide flame-resistant clothing to wear during riots.

At the same time, customs officers declared that the price of heroin on the streets of Birmingham had rocketed, following a crackdown, and was higher than in any other city in the UK, barring Edinburgh. We still lived in very challenging times and, during this period, the work of the fifty-five-strong West Midlands Police Drugs Squad, the largest team operating outside London, came into sharp focus as seizures and arrests increased.

Dave Faulkner eventually spent some time working on the Drugs Squad towards the end of the eighties and recalls,

> First it was cannabis, skunk and then mostly resin, LSD micro-dots with heroin, and crack cocaine right on the periphery. Within a year, heroin and crack cocaine took over and I had informants who would specialise in giving information about specific drugs, which had a devastating effect on inner-cities. You could see kids totally wrapped up in a culture of addiction and, even if they were not addicted themselves, their lives were affected by the people around them who were. I worked with lots of informants. One of them actually introduced me to his family as being a social worker, and I used to get Christmas cards and chocolates from the kids.

While I was immersed in my own priorities within the job, life was still dealing out its fair share of tragedies within the world at large. Shortly after 7.00 p.m. on Friday 6 March 1987, the British ferry, the MS *Herald of Free Enterprise*, turned on its side after leaving the Belgian port of Zeebrugge. According to the captain, who was rescued, it went down within a minute, without time for an SOS message to go out.

More than 400 people were rescued, but 193 passengers and crew lost their lives. Prime Minister Margaret Thatcher asked the question, 'How could it have happened?' It didn't take long to establish that the ferry had left port with its bow door still open, and that the sea had flooded decks very quickly. Such disasters served to keep you firmly anchored in reality.

On 20 March, the veteran television presenter Shaw Taylor announced his retirement from the *Police 5* programme after twenty-five years, as a result of the success of its rival *Crimewatch UK*. He had a vast network of contacts, many of which were in the police service, and there is no doubt that his skills as a presenter led to valuable information on serious crime cases being routinely uncovered in the West Midlands area and elsewhere.

The public were, and still are, fascinated by police investigations, particularly the forensic angles, and it is not surprising that CSI-type programmes remain popular today. The role that the media play in detecting crimes should never be underestimated, and they form a unique bridge between the public and the police. Shrewd police officers maintain positive relationships to get their messages across.

One such example appeared in the *Birmingham Evening Mail* on Friday 27 March 1987, which was headlined 'Shop the Brutes', and contained a plea from Assistant Chief Constable (Crime) Tom Meffen, following what was perceived to be a four-fold increase in crimes of robbery and violence against the elderly over a ten-year period.

In a direct plea to the criminal fraternity, following a knife attack on an eighty-seven-year-old woman, he asked them to help bring to justice those who attacked the elderly. A front-page picture showed a photograph of another weeping seventy-six-year-old woman, who was robbed of just £2 by three white men who threatened to kill her in her own home.

The robbers did not always get their own way and, later that year, one thirty-five-year-old man was sentenced by Judge Toyn to five-and-a-half years in prison for an offence of robbery at the Derbyshire Building Society, in Colmore Row, Birmingham city centre. At the time of the offence, he was wearing a balaclava and carrying a piece of plastic piping in a carrier bag to make it look like a firearm. He was tackled by four members of the public, one of whom had a pacemaker fitted, and held by them until the arrival of the police.

Dave Rischmiller remembers another case where the offender came off worse:

I was attached to the CID at Digbeth in 1987, and we dealt with an allegation where a black male had been going around fast-food outlets, demanding money from the tills. He tried it on with the owner of a fish-and-chip shop in John Bright Street, who rejected his demands. The offender jumped over to attack him, whereupon the owner threw the contents of an entire pan of hot fat over him. He ran off, and we later traced him through a hospital where he had gone for treatment to his burns.

Dave also remembers the culture of the CID at Digbeth well:

There was a difference between the CID at Digbeth, who often dressed down and used backstreet pubs, and the CID at Steelhouse Lane, who always wore suits and ties, and frequented the nightclubs. One common factor, however, was the constant banter that took place among the staff. For instance, one of the detective sergeants, who was of rather large build, managed to get an old director's chair from the wholesale markets, in which he occasionally used to doze off during the afternoons.

Someone got hold of a pig's tail from a butcher and pinned it underneath the chair. After about a week, the sergeant started contacting the estates department to complain about the number of flies that were appearing in the office. He was also perturbed by a strange smell that prevailed. Eventually, he was put out of his misery and someone told him it was there. He went ballistic and tried to complain to the chief inspector, who took no notice of him.

They were not the best of friends and I recall, on another occasion, the sergeant was given a warning about not attending the matches at Birmingham City in duty time on threat of being removed from the CID. He was a big 'Bluenose' and, despite this, he carried on going. Then, one Sunday, the *Mercury* newspaper published an article about the match, together with a photo of one of the goalmouths. Firmly positioned in the photo next to the goalposts was the detective sergeant, plain for all to see. Numerous copies were made and posted around the station and, as fast as the sergeant removed them, other photocopies were put up.

The chief inspector was determined to bring him into line and, because of his weight, threatened to remove him from the CID as being unfit for duty. He actually ordered him to go to the weighbridge in the wholesale markets and to stand on it to record his weight with a ticket so that he could monitor him.

Stories within the police service sometimes became legendary and I recall three in particular, which I am sure are all true.

On one occasion, a man entered the front office of a police station and asked to see an officer from the firearms department. The wily office man went off and found the officer, but told him that his visitor was deaf and that he would need to shout to be heard. He then went back to the visitor and told him that, because the firearms officer had been routinely exposed to weapons being fired, he was deaf, and that the visitor would need to shout. He then sat back and watched two grown men both shouting at each other.

On another occasion, rumour had it that a dog handler, renowned for liking a pint, had lost his Alsatian police dog when it ran off after a road accident. Despite a lengthy search, he couldn't find it, so the following night he took his own Jack Russell terrier out in the back of the van, which constantly barked. The dog man told his colleagues that the dog had a sore throat and couldn't work, and so refused to take it out. Four days later, the Alsatian returned.

Finally, a certain superintendent had his own toilet attached to the rear of his office. Someone placed a notice on the ladies' toilets saying 'out of order', and directing staff to use the superintendent's toilet instead. The senior officer spent the day wondering why there were a stream of women coming in and out of his toilet.

In October 1987, a series of planned and co-ordinated arrests took place of people linked to the Zulu Warriors. In all, during the course of the operation, sixty-seven persons were dealt with for a variety of offences and their veil of anonymity was lifted. They were no longer seen as untouchable and, while there was a realisation that we had not eradicated them completely, we had nevertheless inflicted some serious damage on a very violent group.

12

ANOTHER SAVAGE MURDER

Following on from the successful conclusion of Operation Red Card, I continued working as a detective sergeant at Steelhouse Lane in the role of local intelligence officer. I had a thirst for setting up large-scale operations and was determined to carry on, stretching the limits of the resources I had access to, which included the divisional observation team, who had developed a high level of expertise in surveillance. Each division had access to a team and, collectively around the force, they had made a big impact.

One example of their work was that undertaken following a series of nineteen serious sexual offences, which took place on women in the Newtown, Aston, and Ladywood areas between September 1985 and June 1987. The attacks in the main occurred in multi-storey blocks of flats; the attacker generally assaulted his victims in the lift, before forcing them to the top floor and roof areas where further serious offences were committed. A major incident room was set up, and forty officers, mainly drawn from DOT teams across the force area, were deployed. After three weeks, a man was arrested and charged with fourteen of the offences recorded.

In another instance, DOT officers maintained lengthy observations in the early part of 1987, looking for a person committing robberies on elderly victims in the Lee Bank and Highgate areas. The amounts of property stolen were relatively small, but the violence used was gratuitous and caused major concern in the community. No arrests were made in this case but the offences eventually stopped.

John Swain spent a period of time as a DOT officer, and recalls that, as well as being hugely rewarding work, it could also be tedious, and innovative ways were sometimes found to relieve the boredom of long hours in static observations:

> Three of us each bought a harmonica for £5 each and, when we were in locations where no one could hear us, we started to learn how to play. We learnt three tunes, which included 'Happy Birthday' and 'John Brown's Body'; at one point, I created a tape of them. When people rang the DOT office, I used to put them on hold and play the tape to them. They must have thought that we were mad!

At the end of 1987, the West Midlands Police reported an increase of just 1.5 per cent in reported crime overall, which was a significant decrease on the previous year, and the detection rate rose to 36.1 per cent. More than 6,000 fewer dwelling house burglaries were recorded.

More locally on the F Division, our collective efforts at trying to reduce car crime in an area that boasted a daily population of more than 200,000 led to offences reducing from 6,359 in 1986 to 5,891 in 1987. In 1988, the force planned to introduce the tape recording of interviews with suspects.

On Friday 5 February, I met with the DOTS team to discuss offences of robbery in the city centre. We planned and executed Operation Phoenix over a five-day period between Tuesday 16 February 1988 and Saturday 20 February 1988. I hadn't got football out of my system, so we combined the operation on the last day with some observations in respect of the Birmingham FC home game against Nottingham Forest. We never failed to get results with these static and foot surveillance operations and, after debriefing the results on Wednesday 24 February, we moved onto the next one.

That month, an article appeared in *The Sunday Times*, outlining what was described as a 'brutal new street crime sweeping Britain, namely "Steaming"', where large groups of individuals were engaged in offences of mass robbery, on the public transport network in particular. The Metropolitan Police had set up Operation Trident, which even to this day is seen as one of the force's responses to serious and organised criminality.

In London, robberies were up by 13 per cent, with 400 offences a week, and on the London Underground there had been a 100 per cent increase in such offences. Traditionally, buses in particular had been a 'police-free zone' and therefore left potential victims more vulnerable. It was a crime that had its origins in the deprived urban areas of Los

Angeles and New York in the early 1980s, and had featured in the previous year's Notting Hill Carnival. I needed to be alive to these new trends and to try to address them before they got a foothold on my area, but there was evidence that we were starting to make a difference.

On 4 March, one of the detective chief inspectors on the division announced in the press that undercover officers had hit back at shoplifters and car thieves who had blighted shops in Birmingham city centre. Thefts from cars had been slashed by nearly a quarter on last year's figures, and extra vigilance by shops had reduced the level of recorded shoplifting offences, with the launch of a 'Stop It' campaign.

This was coupled with a big increase in the number of crimes detected in the area. Figures showed that in January the previous year, at the height of the sales rush, only fifteen thefts from cars were detected out of a total of 347 offences recorded. This contrasted sharply with the figures in January 1988, which showed eighty-seven thefts from cars detected and that the number of offences had dropped to 280.

He attributed this success to the work of the DOT team, linked with my intelligence role and the use of hot-spot crime analysis. At a force level, the overall detection rate had improved from 27 per cent to 36.5 per cent on the previous year, with a 9 per cent reduction in offences of dwelling house burglary. In some areas of policing, the West Midlands Police was starting to turn a corner, and it was good to be part of the intelligence-led approach.

In something of a twist, the same detective chief inspector hit the headlines again just the following day, with a somewhat different headline – 'CID chief drank and drove' – after he appeared at a magistrates' court, charged with a number of offences relating to an accident. He had pleaded 'not guilty' to driving with excess alcohol, but was fined and made the subject of a driving ban, both of which were suspended subject to an appeal. Following an earlier incident, the off-duty officer was breath-tested at his home by officers and found to have an alcohol level of 80, with a legal limit of 35.

His solicitor detailed the level of his alcohol consumption between attending a police retirement party and his arrival at home, but raised issues as to the level he had consumed after he had finished driving. Even in those days such a conviction exposed a police officer to internal discipline proceedings, which could lead to a range of punishments from a reprimand to dismissal from the force. He was not the first police officer to be dealt with for such matters and would certainly not be the last.

Times were, however, changing and, while in the past some officers simply took their punishment at court and carried on in the job, the ethical pendulum was swinging towards the ultimate sanction of dismissal. The public would not tolerate the thought that the police themselves were applying double standards and senior officers on discipline panels were mindful of this.

Days later, a circular was sent out from the office of the chief constable to every police station in the West Midlands, highlighting the fact that research conducted eighteen months previously had indicated that some police officers were resorting to drink to deal with the stress of police work. The five-page circular detailed the policy of the force and listed potential symptoms of behaviour to look out for, such as a falling-off in work performance, reluctance to accept responsibility, moodiness and becoming a loner, as well as trembling hands, and a deterioration in handwriting.

Superintendent Martin Burton said, 'Drink problems have been identified but are not disproportionate to those in other professions involving a high degree of stress. We are taking positive action.' While welfare support was stressed, it was made clear that, for those who did not seek help, sanctions might well apply.

Between 14 March 1988 and 27 March 1988, Operation Half Century was mounted using a number of joint resources and aimed at combatting vehicle crime in Birmingham city centre. A similar operation twelve months previously had netted a total of eighty-four people in a four-week period, so we were confident of getting good results.

At the same time, I got involved in detailed discussions with the British Transport Police and West Midlands Travel, based in Summer Lane. It had become apparent that large numbers of stolen and forged travel cards were being used on the bus network throughout Birmingham. Many of the cards were from burglaries, or thefts at railway booking offices, and a number had been stolen by means of street robberies. It was simple in that the robbers just removed the photograph of the victim and replaced it with their own. You needed a keen eye to spot the alterations and, having decided to set up an operation to combat this, we made full use of the revenue inspectors.

We coordinated two operations in March 1988, using resources separate from Half Century, and set up road checks on the outskirts of the city centre covering the Handsworth, Castle Vale, and Wolverhampton routes. In the first Operation Buzz, we detected eighteen offenders for a variety of offences including theft, forgery, deception and possession of cannabis, and they all appeared in court on the same date.

The second operation, conducted over a three-day period a few weeks later, was a much bigger affair. West Midlands Travel Revenue Protection Squad inspectors, working with the West Midlands Police Operations Support Unit and the British Transport Police, stopped more than 3,000 buses carrying a total of 20,320 passengers.

A total of 7,113 tickets, 7,663 travel cards and 5,544 passes were checked. The operation was concentrated on the Old Snow Hill and Summer Lane area. During the three days, 165 fare discrepancies were recorded, and some 92 pre-paid travel cards and tickets were withdrawn because they were stolen, forged or altered.

Police officers made fifty arrests for fraud, deception, theft, robbery, possession of offensive weapons, and possession of controlled drugs. We literally had queues of prisoners waiting to be booked in at Steelhouse Lane and, while I had pre-warned the custody staff, I was none too popular with them for some hours as I declined to slow the pace of the operation down. It was great fun and I wasn't about to lose the potential for more prisoners. It also had the knock-on effect of reducing overall crime in the city centre, as people's behaviour was moderated before they got to their destination, or they had simply been arrested.

Despite success stories, there were constant reminders of the violence and serious criminality that pervaded at that time. On Thursday April 21 1988, a businessman foiled two armed bank raiders in Birmingham city centre by forcing them to drop their stolen haul of cash. He was driving along Smallbrook Queensway, when he saw two black men armed with iron bars attacking two security guards outside Barclays Bank in the Horsefair. Despite the fact that he had his wife and two children with him, he drove onto the pavement, colliding with them and forcing them to drop two cash bags they had stolen onto a nearby carriageway. They then fled into a nearby block of flats, and the money was recovered intact.

Following on from this operation, I started to focus on the high-street area of the city centre between the hours of 10.00 a.m. and 6.00 p.m. I wanted to try and maximise on the potential for arrests, as well as reducing offending by diversion tactics. Thus Operation Sweeper was formulated, using a number of resources over a two-week period between 9 May 1988 and 20 May 1988. We focused on plain-clothes patrols to address vehicle-related crime, static observations using the divisional observations team to address shop theft, and uniform staff to address thefts of travel cards. In addition, we identified additional uniform staff to target juveniles playing truant from school specifically, and to remove them from the streets and put them back into the care of responsible adults.

All persons arrested would appear at special court hearings, when maximum publicity would be sought. I had used this successful formula time and time again, and knew that the mix of overlapping circles of activity would work well. In all, more than forty officers were deployed to different elements of the operation at any one time.

During the period of the operation, only one offence of vehicle crime was recorded in Masshouse multi-storey car park and no offences of robbery or theft from the person occurred. Nearly forty persons were arrested and charged with a variety of offences, including thirty for receiving stolen property, a prison escapee, a disqualified driver, and five persons involved in a number of burglary dwelling houses in the Wolverhampton area.

We recovered forty-two car radios, and a car phone, which we believed to be stolen, as well as other property with a total value of £10,600. In some cases, the car radio systems were more expensive than the vehicle that they were found in. In all, we interviewed sixty-five persons, and removed 105 school truants from the city-centre streets.

The subsequent media headline read, 'Car Radios Police Blitz is Success', and went on to describe how forty officers scoured Birmingham city centre, seeking out old cars carrying expensive modern radios and cassette players. Drivers unable to explain how they got the set were arrested.

The operation used experience gained from a similar operation run in the Liverpool area twelve months previously, codenamed 'Waveband' and co-ordinated by Inspector Paul Baines, which led to a significant drop in vehicle crime. I read an article about the initiative that he wrote in *Police Review* and, after contacting him, knew that he had a formula worth adopting.

As 30 per cent of our crime was vehicle-related, we expected to see similar reductions as the market for stolen goods dried up. People liked the idea of a cheap bargain 'bought from an unknown man in a pub', but this tactic was designed to kill that market and they were not too keen on getting caught and being charged with receiving stolen property. A similar operation run in Kings Heath the previous year had resulted in the recovery of stolen property valued at £6,000 and ten people being charged.

Figures published later in the year revealed that, in the first seven months of 1988, there were 4,000 fewer vehicle-related crimes across the force compared to the same period in 1987. Between May and June 1988, thirty-three offences of robbery and theft from the person were reported in Birmingham city centre, whereas in the previous two months that figure had been eighty-one offences recorded.

In June 1988, I was transferred back to the sub-divisional CID at Steelhouse Lane to effectively fine tune the implementation of a number of new force policies and procedures on the division prior to promotion. In addition, I was nominated to become part of a planning team to implement the reorganisation of the F division, which was to be completed in July 1988 and encompass an area known as the Middle Ring Road.

The development of a city-centre strategy by the local authority gave a clear steer that significant investment was required to promote commerce and entertainment. In practical terms, this could be seen in the redevelopment of the Jewellery Quarter, the Markets, the Shopping Centres, the proposed Convention Centre, and the Broad Street area, in terms of the 'night-time economy'. There was also a defined Chinese quarter, which presented unique policing challenges within a fairly closed society.

The city centre was a compact area with complex issues; for example, in the Jewellery Quarter alone, there were 2,000 alarmed premises and it was home to the Birmingham Assay building, with narrow streets originally designed for horsedrawn traffic. At its peak in the 1900s, more than 30,000 people were employed in the area but it declined in the twentieth century due to competition and lack of demand.

Some of the outer residential areas were classified as socially deprived, with 19 per cent of the population coming from Commonwealth countries, and unemployment in parts was put at 27 per cent, which was three times the national average. The police needed to respond to change and, although I was not in my 'comfort zone', the experience of being involved in these changes was to stand me in good stead in later years. The division was to be split into nine zones, with twenty-eight dedicated beats, and thirty-five permanent beat officers. Additionally, there would be shift officers who would provide a 24/7 response, with up to forty officers on each of five teams, and a number of specialised squads. All of this would be managed by one central control room.

Brutal reminders were never far away and figures released in August 1988 clearly illustrated that, while overall crime was down by

10 per cent, and the detection rate had risen further to 42.4 per cent, violent crime was one area where we were not doing so well, with the number of woundings and attacks up by a fifth – much of it fuelled by alcohol and the carrying of weapons. Only three months earlier, in one initiative to reduce the availability of such weapons, the force had concluded a month-long amnesty, which had resulted in an array of potentially lethal articles being handed in by the public. This included 319 knives, forty-three Rambo knives, 156 flick knives, seventeen swords, twenty-nine bayonets, forty-two machetes, thirteen flails, eight catapults, and forty-two weapons described as homemade. Seated in front of the haul, displayed at force headquarters, which also included 112 firearms and 6,000 rounds of ammunition, Assistant Chief Constable Paul Leopold showed the press a stick with nails embedded in it, and a glove with blades protruding from its fingers, which he said could only have been for use in crime, describing them as 'horrific and awful'.

Not all of these attacks were on members of the public and, during the course of the year, concern was raised by senior officers in relation to the increase in assaults on female officers, with serious attacks occurring at the rate of one a week. Using language which would most definitely not be replicated in today's society, a force spokesman said, 'There are no social barriers or common courtesies extended to policewomen now, as there might have been in days gone by … No matter how much you talk about equality, we can foresee situations where they will become a liability because their male colleagues will try to look after them.' Chief Constable Geoffrey Dear described the rise in attacks on police in general as a 'slow riot'.

Notwithstanding this, in June 1988, Geoffrey Dear proudly announced, 'We're winning war on crime', as he reflected on the year's annual report, with success stories in many crime categories based on comparisons with crime figures for 1986 and 1987. A cocktail of practical measures, such as the implementation of the DOT teams, as well as freeing officers' time up with further civilianisation projects such as administrative support units were all highlighted.

There was praise for the new Midlands Air Operations Support Unit, which had a helicopter and fixed-wing plane and was based at Birmingham Airport. Meanwhile, the introduction of new identification parade suites and better interviewing facilities painted a picture of a 'force on the move', with the highest detection rate since West Midlands Police had been set up some fourteen years previously.

One of the issues highlighted by the media was that the force was attracting 'brighter bobbies', revealing that 8 per cent of recruits to the force had university degrees, with 10 per cent having two or more GCE A Levels, and a further 30 per cent possessing five or more GCE O Levels.

As someone who had left school at the age of sixteen years in 1968 and had no further education, I would have just scraped into the third category; but this emphasis on education, on both the initial entrance to the police service and, increasingly, in relation to promotion prospects, was a sign of things to come. Promotion on pure merit in the future was to become much harder; there had been calls the previous year from one Midlands MP, John Stokes, for an elitist class of senior officers to be created, such as those turned out from Sandhurst Military Academy.

Just prior to my departure from the F Division, there was a graphic illustration of the impact of violent crime on the community. On Wednesday 10 August 1988 at 9.45 a.m., a security guard was stabbed to death in Birmingham city centre as he fought off robbers, who had attacked him as he was delivering cash to a bank. A window cleaner, twenty-six-year-old Gerald Hall, who went to his aid suffered life-threatening injuries after being stabbed in the stomach and spleen, and was treated at Birmingham Accident Hospital. The attacks happened outside Barclays Bank in the High Street, which was packed with shoppers at the time.

The security guard, forty-four-year-old John Worwood, staggered back to his van after the attack and placed the cash he was carrying, which was believed to be less than £5,000, into a secure safe before collapsing in a pool of blood in the driver's seat. An eyewitness described how two men jumped on him as he was about to enter the bank, but he refused to let go of the steel briefcase in which he was carrying the cash, and was stabbed in the chest in the struggle. This wound severed a major artery, and he was also stabbed twice all the way though an upper arm. He was rushed to hospital in an unmarked police vehicle but doctors were unable to save him.

The two attackers, both described as black, and armed with a 10-inch bladed knife, ran off through the crowds in the direction of the Bull Ring shopping centre, chased by other members of the public, but made good their escape. Securicor offered a reward of £25,000 for information leading to the arrest and conviction of the two robbers. It was a senseless crime, which shocked the public and highlighted how fragile human life was. 100 officers were posted to the investigation in the search for the two men, and artist's impressions were made of both, who were described as being in their mid-twenties.

Gerald Hall spent two hours in major surgery and, while recovering in hospital from wounds to his liver, lung and diaphragm, he said:

> The only way murderers should be sentenced is a 'life for a life', and that means they should be hanged. My first reaction was to drop what I was doing and get in there and help the security guard. I grabbed the man who was doing most of the damage and he turned and knifed me sidewards.

Chief Constable Geoffrey Dear visited him in hospital and praised his heroism, and the *Birmingham Evening Mail* published 3,000 posters appealing for help from the public to find the killers. A group of housewives in Birmingham also created a fund to raise money for the 'have-a-go' hero.

The enquiry was headed by Detective Superintendent Michael Jenkins, who later in his career went on to become the head of the force CID. He made a specific plea for help from leaders from within the black community to help in identifying the attackers, one of whom had significant blood stains on his clothing.

A HOLMES (Home Office Large Major Enquiry System) incident room was set up at Nechells Green police station, and 160 police officers and twenty police staff were allocated to the enquiry. Two men were arrested on 2 September 1988.

Dave Rischmiller was a member of the enquiry team:

> I do remember that two black guys were convicted of the job. I believe that someone tried to manually pump the security guard's heart to keep him going on the way to the hospital, but all to no avail. At one stage, the suspects actually burnt their clothing in a back garden before they were arrested, I think by the Regional Crime Squad.

While Gerald Hall's plea on capital punishment ignited the debate again on hanging, it was to be short lived. Conservative MP for Selly Oak, Mr Anthony Beaumont-Dark, said, 'I think it is absolutely horrific that someone can be knifed to death and another man who comes to his aid also stabbed in the centre of a civilised city. It does point out the need for those who perpetrate such horrendous crimes to suffer the supreme penalty of death ...'

History confirms that society and the government were not for turning.

John Worwood was described as a quiet, friendly man, who had lived with his seventy-one-year-old frail mother all of his life, and looked after her following a heart attack. He had a passion for fishing and had worked for Securicor for fifteen years, who described him as a loyal and trusted employee.

An innocent man who paid the ultimate price for doing his job.

EPILOGUE

On 18 August 1988, Chief Superintendent Clive Roche, who had been a great supporter on Operation Red Card, commented in my annual review, 'He will be posted as a uniform inspector at the end of the month. I have every confidence that he will give excellent service in that rank, but I feel that it will not be long before his particular skills are required once again in the CID.'

That same day I saw my new superintendent, who advised me that I would be taking over an under-performing shift and that I would be expected to turn it around. I had heard such things said before, and found that normally the officers were fine and just needed proper leadership and direction.

On the national stage violence in the form of terrorism was equally not far away. Some two months previously, the Belfast Brigade of the IRA claimed responsibility for the murder of six British soldiers killed in a bomb attack after a charity fun run in Lisburn, County Antrim. A bomb made up of 7 lb of high explosives was used to blow up their unmarked Transit van taking them back to their barracks in Londonderry. It served as a reminder that the police were not the only ones involved in planning and executing intelligence-driven operations. This in a part of the UK that was just one hour's flying time from Birmingham.

On Saturday 20 August 1988, seven soldiers were killed and twenty-nine injured from the Light Infantry, when a massive landmine explosion wrecked an unmarked army bus in Ulster as it was returning soldiers to barracks who had been on leave in England. The bus was blown up as it rounded a corner on the Ballygawley–Omagh Road in County Tyrone, just 9 miles from the barracks at Omagh. The bomb blew a crater 12 feet in diameter and 6 feet deep in the road; the dead and injured were catapulted into nearby fields over a radius of 50 to 100 yards, as the bus careered off and finally came to rest straddling a hedge.

A further thirteen soldiers had already previously been killed in terrorist attacks in Northern Ireland in 1988. The MP for Fermanagh and South Tyrone, an ex-UDR Major Mr Ken Maginnis, himself the target of an unsuccessful parcel bomb in the same week, called for the introduction of selective internment. While at the scene helping the injured, he described seeing the last moments of one of those fatally injured: 'Four of us went in through the side of a shed. There was a young man gasping his last. He had crawled into the most available cover and died over a bale of hay.'

The Reverend Ian Paisley, leader of the Democrat and Unionist Party, demanded the reintroduction of capital punishment, as it was noted that, so far in 1988, a total of sixty-one soldiers, police officers, UDR men, and civilians had been killed in Northern Ireland through acts of terrorism.

On 30 August 1988, I was promoted to the rank of inspector in uniform on the D Division at Sutton Coldfield Police Station, covering both a wealthy suburb of Birmingham, and a deprived inner-city area.

I no longer felt young, nor did the label stick any more. It seemed that I had come of age; after all, I was now thirty-six years of age. While the country was celebrating the birth in August of a new princess, to be known as Her Royal Highness Princess Beatrice of York, with two forty-one gun salutes in London, mine was a more sedate affair the day after, with a couple of pints after work.

The cycle of violence in Birmingham city centre continued and, within three weeks of my departure, Dave Rischmiller was investigating a serious assault on a police officer outside the Crown pub in Hill Street. The officer, known as 'Moley', who has since risen to a very high rank in the service, was attacked, and three men, two of whom were brothers, were later charged with wounding offences.

Operation Mistletoe was mounted in Birmingham city centre at Christmas, which led to the arrest of eighty-seven offenders, some of whom were operating in organised gangs.

At the end of 1988, the West Midlands Police recorded a staggering 11 per cent reduction in overall recorded crime, which equated to 28,000 fewer offences, with an overall detection rate of 42.4 per cent. All forty-one murders committed in the force area for the year were detected, and a number of key crime areas continued to show reductions.

In line with national trends, however, violent crimes against the person continued to rise, with most offences committed on, and by, males aged between sixteen and twenty-three years.

Locally, it was again stressed that, while the F Division covered the smallest geographical area in the force with just 30,300 local residents, it was the daily focus by now of some 225,000 people.

The city centre attracted a large number of marches, rallies, and demonstrations, which required policing and, during the course of 1988, more than 100 were planned for. Chamberlain Square, a public square named after the statesman and mayor of Birmingham, Joseph Chamberlain, was a favourite meeting point, as it has a natural amphitheatre setting that lends itself to gatherings.

During the course of this year, the city of Birmingham celebrated its 100th anniversary, with plans to build an international convention centre in the city centre that could accommodate 9,000 people, as well as a national indoor arena capable of seating 12,000 spectators.

Police work for me remained unpredictable, at times exciting, routinely challenging and often frustrating, but I personally was never bored. We lived, and still do, in a democratic society that was often tilted far more towards the rights of those accused of crimes rather than those of the victims, who frequently never truly recovered from the experience. It might be said that it is the price we pay for being civilised.

I met my former colleague 'Liam' some months ago, who worked with me on Operation Red Card, and listened to him as he recounted his last day as a serving police officer in the West Midlands Police after thirty years' service.

His comments captured for me just exactly how policing gets into your bloodstream and provides you with principles in life that are hard to let go of.

It was a Saturday and I remember that there had been an armed robbery at an off-licence. It was a nasty offence and I went with a colleague to have a look at the CCTV images of the offender, which had been captured in the shop.

I had been doing offender management for a while and I knew all of the local criminals well. We had a look at the video, and I immediately recognised who it was. My sergeant said, 'Just leave it, it's your last day; we will pick him up on Monday'. I refused point blank and, after a few phone calls, we went to an address to try to arrest the robber. We got in with no problems but, when we searched the place, including the loft, and couldn't find him, my sergeant said, 'That's it – we're leaving.'

I knew for sure that he was in the house somewhere, and sent an officer back up into the loft, telling him with a bit of banter to do a proper job this time. A couple of minutes later, I heard shouting from the loft. The suspect had been rolled up in the fibre glass loft insulation and was going crazy scratching himself. It was a good result. Even though it was my last day, he had to come in – it was my job.

Every police officer has a story to tell about their experiences of front-line policing in Birmingham, and they are often recounted in a very matter-of-fact way. In 2015, I sat in the living room of a retired BTP colleague, Alan Morecock, as he described one such incident as if it had happened just the week before. In fact, it took place on Wednesday 13 March 1974, the year before I started my CID career:

I was on duty at New Street station when we got a call to the NCP car park regarding suspects breaking into vehicles. I went there with PC Keith Fleetwood. We were both well built; I was more than fifteen stone at the time and frightened of nobody. Keith was even bigger than me.

We approached a car on the ground floor and, suddenly, all the doors flew open and four people, including a female, started to run off. I got to the driver's door and a black male, in his twenties, started to unfold himself out of the vehicle. He was at least 6 feet, 3 inches tall and huge. Before I could open my mouth, he simply punched me in the face, and then turned round and punched Keith in the chest, who fell to the floor with his eyes and mouth wide open.

We had no way of shouting for assistance, because the car park was constructed of concrete and we couldn't get a radio signal. After 'seeing stars', I jumped onto his back and tried to pin him onto the bonnet of the car. At the same time, I grabbed his testicles and pulled as hard as I could, ripping his trousers in the process. It was strange, because I vividly remember him shouting 'Mum' as we struggled. I shouted to Keith to hit him with his truncheon. He had one go, which seemed to just bounce off him and then Keith hit him again and the truncheon broke in half. Eventually, he left us both lying on the floor and ran off, and I was left holding his overcoat belt.

We went back up to the office, and all the sergeant was interested in was why we were covered in dust and dirt and not dressed properly. When the CID searched the car, they found a doctor's appointment card for the female so we quickly found out who we were looking for.

I had a bad week that week because, on the Saturday, I was on duty for a football match between Birmingham City, at home, and Manchester United. After the match, I was in the shopping centre above the station, directing fans down the escalators, when another black male came up behind me, hit me over the back of the head and I collapsed.

Retired BTP officer Mel Harris concludes the story:

On Monday 18 March 1974, I was off duty in plain clothes, making my way up the ramp towards the Birmingham shopping centre and New Street station, when I saw a Jamaican male run past me, being chased by two BTP officers. I immediately joined in and managed to rugby-tackle him to the floor at the bottom of the ramp where, after a violent struggle, we managed to handcuff and arrest him. He was wanted for assaulting two BTP officers in the NCP car park the week before.

These two events were described with a great sense of humility, and with some humour, by retired officers who felt that they were simply doing their duty in a job that they loved – they were, however, certainly not routine nor boring!

Michael Layton, QPM (2015)

PERSONAL BIOGRAPHY
OF THE AUTHOR

Michael Layton QPM joined the British Transport Police as a cadet on 1 September 1968 and, after three years, was appointed as a police constable in 1971, serving at Birmingham New Street station. In 1972, he transferred to Birmingham City Police, which amalgamated in 1974 to become the West Midlands Police, where he eventually reached the rank of chief superintendent in 1997. On retirement from that force in 2003, he went on to see service with the Sovereign Bases Police in Cyprus. He then returned to the British Transport Police in 2004, initially as a detective superintendent (director of intelligence), and then, in his last two years, as the operations superintendent at Birmingham, where he continued with his passion for combatting football violence. He finally retired again in 2011. In the January 2003 New Year's Honours list, he was awarded the Queen's Police Medal for distinguished police service.

He is the co-author of a book entitled *Hunting the Hooligans – the True Story of Operation Red Card*, which was published in July 2015 by Milo Books, and the author of *Violence in the Sun – a History of Football Violence in Cyprus*, which was published as an eBook, also by Milo, in May 2015. More recently he has co-authored books titled *Tracking the Hooligans: The History of Football Violence on the UK Rail Network* and *Police Dog Heroes* – both by Amberley Publishing.

Michael is a self-employed consultant engaged predominantly with crime and community safety issues.

DEDICATION

To all of the colleagues and friends I worked with in the West Midlands Police and British Transport Police during the period covered by this book. To my wife Andry, for her constant support and encouragement, and to our families, children, and grandchildren.

ACKNOWLEDGEMENTS

Birmingham Evening Mail and *Sunday Mercury* newspapers

Andy Murcott – Retired Inspector (West Midlands Police)

'Alex' – Retired Covert Officer (West Midlands Police)

Jon Lighton – Retired Inspector (West Midlands Police)

'Nick' – a dedicated 'Bluenose' and ardent Birmingham City FC supporter

'Liam' – Retired Detective Constable (West Midlands Police)

'Cheryl' – Retired Detective Constable (West Midlands Police)

Paul Majster – Retired Detective Constable (British Transport Police)

Mel Harris – Retired Dog Handler (British Transport Police)

Jim Rentell – Police Constable (British Transport Police)

Steve Burrows – Retired Chief Superintendent (Warwickshire Police)

'Barry' – Retired Detective Inspector (West Midlands Police and BTP)

'Ada' Howles – Ex-Police Constable (West Midlands Police)

Ian Mabbett – Retired Detective Constable (British Transport Police)

Alan Morecock – Retired Police Dog Handler (British Transport Police)

David Rischmiller – Retired Inspector (West Midlands Police)

Malcolm 'Doc' Halliday – Retired Detective Sergeant (West Midlands Police)

Andy 'B' – Retired Sergeant (West Midlands Police)

Joe Tildesley – Retired Inspector (West Midlands Police)

Robert Endeacott – Writer

Paul Rainey – Retired Police Constable (West Midlands Police)

Peter Keys – Retired Officer (West Midlands Police)

David Faulkner – Retired Detective Constable MIR (West Midlands Police)

Mike Cresswell – Retired Police Sergeant (West Midlands Police)
Steven Jordan – Retired Chief Superintendent (West Midlands Police)
Richard Bryant – Retired Superintendent (West Midlands Police)
Dave Cross – Retired Constable (West Midlands Police) and Keeper of
    WMP Museum
Bill Rogerson MBE – Retired Sergeant (British Transport Police – Bangor)
Bryan Davis – Retired Sergeant (West Midlands Police)
Tony 'Bunny' Everett – Retired Police Constable (West Midlands Police)
Paul Newbold – Retired Police Constable (West Midlands Police)
John Swain – Retired Police Constable (West Midlands Police)
Dave 'J' – Retired Detective Sergeant (West Midlands Police)

With special thanks to Debbie Menzel from the West Midlands Police Museum Group, and a former Detective Constable, for her efforts in assisting in the compilation of some of the photographic material.

Every effort has been made to seek permission for copyright material used in this book. However, if I have inadvertently used copyright material without permission/acknowledgement, I apologise and will make the necessary correction at the first available opportunity.